DIFFICULT PEOPLE MADE EASY

Your Guide to Solving
People Problems at Work

ELEANOR SHAKIBA

First published in 2016 by New Holland Publishers Pty Ltd
London · Sydney · Auckland

The Chandlery, Unit 704, 50 Westminster Bridge Road, London SE1 7QY,
United Kingdom
1/66 Gibbes Street, Chatswood, NSW 2067, Australia
5/39 Woodside Ave Northcote, Auckland 0627, New Zealand

www.newhollandpublishers.com

A record of this book is held at the British Library and the National Library of Australia.

ISBN 978 1 74257 832 3

Managing Director: Fiona Schultz
Publisher: Alan Whiticker
Project Editor: Holly Willsher
Cover design: Andrew Quinlan
Internal design: Thomas Casey
Production Director: Olga Dementiev
Printer: Toppan Leefung Printing Limited

10 9 8 7 6 5 4 3 2 1

Keep up with New Holland Publishers
www.facebook.com/NewHollandPublishers

CONTENTS

ACKNOWLEDGEMENTS

▶ Writing this book involved collaborating with many talented, supportive people. I am grateful the following people for their feedback, creativity and guidance.

Humphrey Armstrong has coached me through many stages of my career. His wisdom and encouragement once again kept me on track during this 'book project'. Editor Susie Stevens also provided valuable coaching on the structure of the book. Thank you both for many wonderful conversations and suggestions.

I am deeply appreciative of the team at New Holland, who turned my manuscript into a book to be proud of. Special thanks to Alan Whitaker, Holly Willsher and Thomas Casey for your guidance and the professional skills you brought to this book.

For the vibrant illustrations in both the book and its supporting videos, I thank Josey Thomas Malayil from Krepesh Virtual Artistries. For author photographs, my thanks go to Fiora Sacco. Thanks are also due to the team who helped me put the Difficult People Made Easy website resources together: actors Kai Raisbeck and Shelley Booth; studio director Mike Tuelon; web content writer Kirsty Racher and web designer Casey Lightbody.

My personal support team kept me on track and healthy during the writing process. Emma Wilson deserves a special mention for her ability to keep me – and my dreaded diary - organized. Thanks also go to James Elliott, Simon Watson and Florence Biancardi for keeping my 'computer muscles' working despite long hours at my desk.

And finally, thanks to my husband Mark Shakiba for his tolerance, inspiration and love – even when the task of writing turned me into a 'difficult person'.

INTRODUCTION

▶ Are people problems causing you grief? This book will help you turn that situation around. It will give you tools for handling 'difficult people' confidently and resourcefully. Right now you might feel like some people in your life are controlling, exploiting or frustrating you. The good news is that YOU can decide the terms of your relationships from now on.

Yes. You can choose whether or not another person's behavior brings you down, fires you up or has no impact on you at all. All you need are some new mental 'programs' for managing difficult conversations. This book contains the software for these programs. *Difficult People Made Easy* is your guide to repairing broken relationships and handling tough conversations.

How is this book different?

Most books on dealing with people problems focus on labeling or describing difficult behaviors. They tell you why people become 'difficult' but they don't tell you how to handle their behaviors. That's where this book is different. My aim in writing it is to give you step-by-step instructions for responding to the tactics 'difficult people' use.

Why read this book?

When you apply the tools covered in *Difficult People Made Easy*, you'll be able to stop 'difficult people' controlling conversations, situations and YOU. Imagine how in control of your life you'll feel then. You'll be able to maintain your personal power no matter what other people do. That sounds good, doesn't it? As you read, you'll see how easy it can be to prevent conflict eroding your relationships. You'll learn to build positive relationships and connect deeply with others. Imagine how satisfying that will feel. And, if you're someone who wants to be a truly masterful communicator, this book will build your skills and abilities. You'll learn how to avoid wishy-washy interactions and build a reputation as a great communicator.

That 'difficult person' could be anyone you come across at work. As you read this book, you'll discover how easy it is to create and keep your personal power – even when others resort to toxic behavior. Do you want to feel confident and in control of tough situations? Would you like to hear yourself saying exactly the right thing when someone else shouts or whines? Do you wish you looked calm and assertive even when other people behave badly? This book will give you the skills you need for achieving results like these.

What's in this book?

Difficult People Made Easy is an introduction to dealing with challenging behavior in practical ways. It is not a psychology text, but it will give you an understanding of the psychology that drives difficult behavior. More importantly, it offers you tips and techniques for taking action when other people behave in challenging ways. Whether you're dealing with outright hostility, passive-aggression or psychological game-playing, reading this book will set you up to handle 'problem people' confidently and assertively.

The first chapter explains the mental programs that cause people to use difficult behavior. You need to understand these so you don't get caught up in psychological game-playing. My argument is this: giving a 'difficult person' the reaction they expect reinforces their negative program. You need to respond from a resourceful 'alright' position. This puts you in control and prevents the other person pushing your buttons. It lets you build healthy relationships even when toxic dynamics exist. And it sets you up as a mature, emotionally intelligent communicator who can handle 'difficult people' with ease.

Chapter Two covers the topic of 'relationship dynamics'. It explains how difficult behavior leads to 'boundary violations'. Then it outlines the six toxic communication patterns that 'difficult people' use to push your boundaries. Once you can detect these patterns you can counteract them. That's why Chapter Two is a must-read chapter.

In Chapter Three you'll learn how to turn toxic conversations around. You'll discover how to resist baiting and game-playing – so you can focus on sorting out the issue driving the other person's difficult behavior.

Chapter Four builds on the skills covered in Chapter Three. It explains how you can maintain your boundaries even when 'difficult people' try to violate them. The tool for doing this is called an ACE statement. This is a three-part statement which helps you speak assertively by acknowledging the other person's intent, challenging their behavior and explaining what you want them to do in future. It's simple to remember and easy to use – no matter what tactics other people resort to.

Chapter Five covers six language patterns you can use to counteract the toxic communication patterns used by 'difficult people'. This is the 'toolkit' chapter of *Difficult People Made Easy*. If you're in a hurry to find solutions to a specific problem, you may want to dip into this chapter first. But remember this: in order to use language patterns artfully you need to understand the principles they're based on. So reading Chapters One through to Four will ensure you get the best possible results from your toolkit.

Once you've mastered your toolkit you're ready to apply it. This means learning to use each tool in a range of ways. Chapters Six through to Nine explain how to do this. In Chapter Six, you'll learn a core process for handling difficult behavior. Then, in Chapter Seven, you'll hear how to use that process to handle aggressive people. In Chapter Eight, you'll see how to modify the core process when you're dealing with passive behavior. And, in Chapter Nine, you'll come to grips with using the core process to counter passive-aggressive tactics.

Finally, in Chapter Ten, I answer the question, 'What should you do when the problem keeps occurring?' I explain that there is a big difference between dealing with reactive, one-off difficult behavior and handling chronic, long-term patterns of problematic behavior. This chapter will be of interest to you if you're dealing with a situation in which nothing seems to work. Sadly, you may never be able to change the other person. But reading this chapter will help you remain psychologically 'safe' around them. It will also help you make robust decisions about the long-term viability of maintaining the relationship.

▸ Throughout this book you'll find links to videos and tip sheets on my website: http://difficultpeoplemadeeasy.com. Some skills are easier to learn when you see them in practice. That's what the video links are for.

The techniques you'll read about in *Difficult People Made Easy* can be used in all walks of life. You can use them at home, at work and in social situations. Each technique is based on principles of applied psychology. This means that what you read here isn't just theory – it is tried and tested. Every technique is underpinned by a psychological model. This book teaches you step-by-step methods for using each technique in your real-life situations. That's what makes it different to other books on dealing with 'difficult people'.

Right now, you might think that some of the people you deal with are just too hard-to-handle. But once you've learned some basic skills, you will be able to prevent these people from impacting on you emotionally. Even if you've found it hard to be assertive in the past, you can take comfort in the fact that assertiveness can be learned. Today you're taking your first step towards becoming more assertive, flexible and resourceful. Other people have learned to manage 'difficult people' and so can you.

WHAT IS A 'DIFFICULT PERSON'? ▸

CHAPTER ONE

WHAT MAKES 'DIFFICULT PEOPLE' TICK?

What is a 'difficult person'?

A 'difficult person' is someone who breaks the unspoken rules of socially-acceptable communication. Their behavior sends a subliminal message about their need to control and have power when communicating with others. It doesn't feel good to be at the receiving end of such power games, which is why you react to them.

The 'difficult person' could be a client, a colleague, your boss or someone who reports to you. For some reason, this person pushes your buttons and makes you feel stressed. To stop this happening, you need to understand that 'difficult people' use a very specific set of behaviors. I call these 'toxic communication patterns'. The good news is that there are antidotes for every toxic habit.

To stop someone else pushing your buttons, you need to do two things.
1. Know the power mode they're operating from.
2. Understand the tactics they're using.

This chapter explains what a power mode is and outlines the three power modes that are the source of difficult behavior. The following chapter walks you through the tactics you're likely to come across when people are using toxic communication patterns.

What is a power mode?

A power mode expresses the power position someone is taking during communication. Are they trying to have power over you? Do they see you as more powerful than them? Or are they sabotaging the relationship so that no-one has power? If you can identify any of these agendas, a toxic communication dynamic is happening.

Three main power modes lead to toxic communication. These are fight mode, flight mode and spite mode (you may have heard them referred to elsewhere as aggressive, passive and passive-aggressive behavior). There is also one power mode that results in open, productive and safe communication. I call this the 'alright mode'.

Non-assertive modes are used when people sense their needs are not being met. As a result, they exhibit behaviors that are intended to satisfy those needs.

Of course, no-one communicates in a single power mode all the time. Most of us, however, develop a dominant style over our lifetime. The majority of people learn how to communicate from a balanced power position, the 'alright mode', which results in collaborative, assertive and effective communication.

Unfortunately, some people don't understand that power can and should be shared. These people act as though communication is a battlefield. They try to win at all costs (fight mode). They run away from uncomfortable topics of conversation (flight mode). Or they use sneaky tactics to kill off the relationship (spite mode). These are the people we come to recognize as 'difficult'.

▸ To work out what style of behavior you're dealing with, take the free Behavior Analyser questionnaire on my website: http://difficultpeoplemadeeasy.com

---

Why do people use power modes?

Fight, flight and spite reactions are natural. They help people survive in critical situations and everyone experiences them. For example, if you're crossing the road and see a car hurtling towards you, you'll jump out of the way. You won't stop and think about it. Your **flight** reaction will kick in and you'll live to tell the tale of your near miss.

An example of the **fight** reaction occurs when one driver cuts in front of another in heavy traffic. In this situation, it's likely the second driver will either shout out loud or mutter nasty comments. The instinct to fight for survival is being expressed through this aggressive language.

If the second driver went into **spite** mode rather than fight mode, they would follow the first driver. They'd wait for the driver to park and leave and then scratch the car. Vengeance without accountability – a typical spite-driven behavior.

In a communication context, the survival reaction is triggered by psychological threats rather than physical danger. These threats trigger exactly the same part of the brain that responds to physical hazards – the amygdala.

Your amygdala is the survival hub of your brain. It doesn't critically assess signs of danger nor does it evaluate whether a threat is real or imagined. It merely reacts to any image, sound or feeling that *seems* to be threatening. Your amygdala simply switches you into survival mode. When communicating, this means adopting a fight, flight or spite way of talking.

▶ To find out more about how the amygdala triggers fight, flight and spite reactions, watch, *What is emotional intelligence?* It's on my video page at http://difficultpeoplemadeeasy.com

---

Fight-based behaviors include shouting, demanding, finger pointing and tantrum throwing. Common flight-based behaviors include staying silent, talking very quietly or failing to express disagreement. Spite-based communication behaviors include being sarcastic, sulking, making smart comments or refusing to discuss problems.

Usually, stress triggers difficult behavior. First, someone becomes fearful or encounters a stressor. Next, their amygdala reacts and sends their body into self-protective mode. Finally, the person speaks from fight, flight or spite mode. Of course, not all stress is a reaction to what has just happened. You'll come across many people who are chronically stressed. You might think of these people as having 'difficult personalities' because they habitually operate in fight, flight or spite mode.

This means it isn't always possible to tell *why* someone else is behaving in a challenging way. For example, imagine you're dealing with a co-worker who reacts defensively to any form of feedback at work. You don't know it, but her amygdala reaction was primed during childhood because she was criticized and abused on a regular basis. Her amygdala hears feedback as an attack.

Or consider the boss who comes across as a control freak. You hear him demanding that you follow his instructions to the letter. You might think his desire for control stems from a fear of looking bad in front of his own manager. But you can't know that for sure. There could be any number of reasons for his controlling behavior. You need to focus on handling the situation professionally rather than trying to understand his motivations.

So how do you do this? You need to take three steps. First, you assess what power mode your boss is operating from. Next, you calm him down and get him into an alright mode of communication. Finally, you address whatever problem triggered his seemingly difficult behavior. You'll hear more about this process later. For now, let's quickly explore what fight, flight and spite modes look like in real life.

Fight mode

You may recognize some of these behavior patterns.

▸ Clients screaming abuse down the phone.
▸ Co-workers throwing temper tantrums.
▸ A boss micro-managing and controlling every step you take.
▸ The staff member who argues with every instruction you give.
▸ A manager who never gives you fair feedback then says, 'I don't know what made me hire you. I should have known you'd be hopeless.'
▸ A co-worker who blames you for something you haven't done and shouts about your 'problems' loudly in a public space.
▸ The team leader who bangs files on your desk and says, 'Stop what you're doing right away and start working on these files. And I mean *now*.'

These are all examples of people operating in fight mode. The intent behind their aggressive tactics is to gain power over you. Their hostility is expressed verbally, physically and tonally. For example, many 'difficult people' will hurl insults and threats until they get what they want. Some will use physical tactics, such as slamming doors, using threatening gestures or invading your personal space. Others will express their aggression vocally, by speaking in a hostile, demeaning or abrasive tone.

People functioning from fight mode are ready to do battle and fight their way to safety. After all, fight-based behaviors happen when people are trying to stand up for themselves but don't know how to do this assertively.

For example, Jenni is being abused by an angry customer who is obviously in fight mode. The customer's words trigger a stress reaction in Jenni, who then tries to protect herself by arguing with the customer. This is a classic example of a fight reaction being triggered by another person's behavior. Jenni's reaction creates a problem because she is now operating defensively rather than focussing on resolving the customer's complaint.

Benefits experienced by people in fight mode

Often, people in fight mode experience *benefits* from their behavior. For example, I was once running a course on conflict resolution. One of the participants walked in and announced that she didn't really need to be there. The problem, she said, was that her colleague had 'baited' her into a fight at work. It was her colleague's fault, she claimed. And her boss had sided with the colleague. It was all a big conspiracy.

That afternoon, the same woman was participating in a listening exercise. She was supposed to listen to a partner describe a real-life problem and then she was meant to respond empathically. When her partner outlined his problem, the woman laughed at him. This triggered a fight mode reaction from her partner who shouted, 'Don't laugh, it's serious.'

The woman replied, 'No it's not. It's ridiculous.' She then made a number of barbed jokes about the problem. Because her partner was getting visibly upset, I intervened. The woman then shouted at her partner, 'See, now you've got me into trouble.'

This woman was blaming everyone else for the consequences of her own actions. People in fight mode often do this. They blame others for their behavior rather than sorting out their problems. Doing this gives them the sense that they are superior to other people. This feeling can be a very attractive reward for aggressive behavior. Understanding this helps you grasp the psychology of difficult behavior. **People resort to difficult behaviors because those behaviors benefit them in some way.**

The bottom line is this: fight, flight and spite behaviors reap benefits. That's why people use them. Aggression, for example, can give someone a sense of power. A second benefit of using fight mode communication is that the person feels in control. Controlling people are those who interfere with your decisions, tell you what to do and micro-manage everything you do. Because control matters so much to them, they thrive on getting their own way. Their real intention is to stop things going wrong because they're scared of dealing with uncontrolled situations. But they don't realize this. Instead they fervently try to gain compliance from everyone around them.

A third upside people experience from aggressive behavior is speedy communication. Some people seem stuck in fight mode. This is because they are highly stressed. They want to get things done quickly. They believe problems should be dealt with promptly and efficiently. They don't want to waste time on talking things through. So they speak abruptly, with inappropriate honesty and sometimes, perhaps, with hostility. Many of these people have no intention of being rude – they just want to get their message across efficiently.

For other hard-to-handle people, a huge payoff for aggressive behavior is attention and what they perceive as respect. Fight mode behavior comes to the fore when people with low self-awareness feel they are not being taken seriously. To gain respect, they throw their weight around or act as though they are superior to you. Aggression becomes a way to assert their right to be heard.

Signs you're dealing with someone in fight mode

▶ See an example of someone in fight mode on my video page: http://difficultpeoplemadeeasy.com

---

Think of someone you believe operates in fight mode under pressure. Recall a specific situation when they were stressed. Tick the characteristics you observed them displaying.

Body language and behavior
☐ Finger pointing.
☐ Standing with hands on hips.
☐ Standing over others.
☐ Glaring at others.
☐ Invading another's space.
☐ Moving rapidly and/or erratically.
☐ Throwing objects.

☐ Slamming doors.
☐ Breathing very quickly.
☐ Having a tense facial expression.
☐ Jabbing, staccato hand gestures.
☐ Finger drumming.
☐ Clenching fists.

Communication patterns
☐ Blaming others rather than taking personal responsibility.
☐ Criticizing unfairly.
☐ Seeking flaws in others and raising them over and over again.
☐ Talking over others.
☐ Threatening violence.
☐ Swearing.
☐ Insulting others.
☐ Using a lot of put downs.
☐ Speaking rapidly.
☐ Using loud, dramatic sighing.
☐ Making overly direct and challenging statements.

Words and phrases
☐ This is your fault.
☐ You'd better/you have to/you should/you must.
☐ Do it my way.
☐ You're wrong.
☐ I said to …
☐ Don't you dare …

Voice tone
☐ Loud.
☐ Angry.
☐ Demanding.
☐ Hostile.
☐ Controlling.

Write your total number of ticks here: _ _ _ _ _ _
  A score of nine or more indicates you're dealing with someone in fight mode.

Flight mode

Here are some behaviors you may recognize.

▸ Team members who know problems are brewing, but tell no-one about them.
▸ Bosses who can't make decisions.
▸ Co-workers who cry whenever you give them feedback.
▸ Clients who play victim in order to get what they want.
▸ People who can't solve problems for themselves.
▸ Co-workers who never contribute to team meetings because they're too shy.
▸ Service providers who pass the buck and never take action to solve problems.
▸ Staff who don't leave a smoke-filled building until their supervisor tells them to.

These are all examples of people who operate from the flight power mode. Theirs is a passive style of communication. They are fearful of making mistakes or being the focus of attention. They hesitate to think for themselves and instead wait for instructions from other people.

Although at first glance their behavior might not seem difficult, it can create havoc in the workplace. After all, most team members need to make decisions and operate independently. But passive people hesitate to do so.

Many people who operate in flight mode are scared of confrontation and don't feel they have a right to make their desires and wishes known. They react to stress or fear by retreating to a safe space. Without being aware of it, they try to make themselves look smaller. This leads to hunched, self-protective postures. It also causes hesitant

I'M NOT HUNGRY. YOU HAVE IT.

speech patterns and a tendency to back down in conflict situations. The psychological aim of flight-based behavior is self-protection.

Flight behavior is designed to protect the user by helping them stay hidden and thus avoid being attacked. When people use flight behavior, they are attempting to protect themselves by withdrawing from a threat. They avoid being in situations that feel threatening. This means they avoid taking risks, taking the initiative or being independent.

Some people appear to get 'stuck' in flight mode. At work, these are the people who hold back on presenting ideas or fail to volunteer for additional assignments. Many are frightened of failing and will therefore avoid learning new skills or taking on new tasks.

Benefits experienced by people in flight mode

From a psychological perspective, people learn to operate in flight power mode because they have been encouraged to hold back (suppress) their emotions. It is often in early life that a child learns not to express their needs or feelings. Slowly and gradually their self-esteem drops so that when they reach adulthood they feel scared to speak up for themselves. What they want, above all else, is to be liked and accepted by others. So they avoid disagreeing with others' opinions or asserting their needs. Over time, people in this position develop unhelpful self-talk, which undermines their ability to say 'no' or to make requests.

As an example, Tara's internal dialogue says, 'I am already really busy with work that I need to complete by tomorrow. But I can't say "no" to my boss. I'll just have to fit in this extra job I've been asked to do.' This results in Tara working unpaid overtime while her more assertive colleagues pack up and go home.

Dan is another example. His internal dialogue runs along the lines of, 'I don't like the way Rita snapped at me just now. But that's just her personality. There's nothing I can do about it.' This means he accepts Rita's verbal abuse even though it verges on bullying.

To someone whose dominant power mode is the alright mode, Tara and Dan may seem foolish. But their flight-based behavior actually reaps many psychological rewards. For example, Tara feels important and valuable because she works so hard. By working long hours, she may also be avoiding going home to a toxic relationship. Dan spends hours in the pub telling stories about Rita's obnoxious behavior. His behavior gains him attention and gives him a sense of belonging.

If you're dealing with someone who is operating in flight mode, remember that they're probably gaining something from taking the 'one-down position'. This is a psychological stance in which someone thinks of themselves as being powerless and others as being powerful. For example, many passive people won't even try to solve their own problems. Instead, they take a one-down position and wait until someone else steps in to rescue them. This takes the pressure off the person; they have learned that being in flight mode reaps results. They can avoid stress while others sort out problems for them.

Similarly, people operating in flight mode rarely need to make their own decisions. Their colleagues, bosses and friends do all the thinking for them. This means they don't run the risk of making mistakes. And even when something goes wrong, the person who has been passive can blame someone else. This prevents them from feeling anxious about being 'to blame' for any negative consequences that may arise from a decision.

Taking a passive stance can also make relationships seem more harmonious. People operating in flight mode don't address conflict openly; they can pretend it doesn't exist. This makes them feel safe and secure. By being passive, they avoid unpleasant situations and tough conversations.

Operating in flight mode also has emotional benefits. Many passive people focus more on others' feelings than their own. This means they can avoid being aware of their own painful emotions. They keep themselves busy pleasing other people so they can numb their own feelings. Their seemingly altruistic behavior also gives them the tag of being 'nice' and this makes them feel validated.

Signs someone is in flight mode

▸ See an example of someone in flight mode on my videos page: http://difficultpeoplemadeeasy.com

Think of someone you believe operates in flight mode under pressure. Recall a specific situation when they were stressed. Tick the characteristics you observed them displaying.

Body language and behavior

☐ Avoiding eye contact.
☐ Hugging themselves or folding their arms a lot.
☐ Waiting for instructions rather than taking independent action.
☐ Staying silent in group situations.
☐ Avoiding dealing with conflict.
☐ Asking others to do difficult tasks for them.
☐ Avoiding demanding assignments.
☐ Opting out of situations in which they'll have to present.
☐ Trying very hard to be nice and to be liked.
☐ Rarely expressing their own thoughts, opinions, feelings or needs.
☐ Using email when telephone or face-to-face communication would be better.
☐ Waiting for other people to solve problems.
☐ Allowing others to invade their physical or psychological boundaries.
☐ Failing to speak up about bullying or abusive treatment.

Communication patterns

☐ Complaining without acting to sort out the problem.
☐ Telling a lot of 'poor me' stories.
☐ Using vague and non-specific language.
☐ Changing the subject when you ask about them.
☐ Avoiding giving their opinion.
☐ Not speaking up when something bothers them.
☐ Saying 'yes' when they need to say 'no'.
☐ Apologizing unnecessarily.
☐ Using tentative, unassertive language.

Words and phrases

☐ Sorry.
☐ What do you think?
☐ I can't do this.
☐ Yes, but …
☐ I couldn't say that …
☐ There's no point …
☐ Nobody cares about me.
☐ What should I do?

Voice tone

☐ Quiet.

☐ Submissive.

☐ Whining.

☐ Child-like.

☐ Hesitant.

Write your total number of ticks here:_____

A score of nine or more indicates you're dealing with someone in flight mode.

Spite mode

You may recognize some of the following behaviors.

▸ Co-workers who are sniping and sarcastic.

▸ Customers who cut you down to size with churlish remarks.

▸ Sulking team members who play mind games.

▸ Bosses who put you down in a 'joking' way.

▸ Clients who tell you the cheque's in the mail.

▸ People who say they'll do something, then back out at the last minute.

These are all examples of people operating from spite mode. Their behavior is commonly called 'passive-aggressive'.

Spite-based behavior is a way of communicating hostility covertly. It is a uniquely human form of behavior, which taps into our ability to assign meanings to words and patterns of behavior. For example, a dog can't bark sarcastically, but a human can speak sarcastically.

Spite mode is an unhealthy way of expressing anger. Typical tactics employed by passive-aggressive people include sarcasm, nasty jokes, sulking, taking ages to complete a simple task, deliberately making mistakes or breaking things 'accidently'.

Most people operating from spite mode want to look innocent and docile while in the process of attacking you. They intend to be mean or to hurt you, but they won't admit this. They can generate a lot of emotional confusion because their tactics are so covert. Sometimes you may wonder if you're being too sensitive or totally misinterpreting what's happening, because a passive-aggressive person sets you up to feel disoriented.

The aim of spite-based behavior is to do maximum damage with minimum accountability. People who communicate in this mode are often angry and hostile – but they refuse to admit this openly. Instead, they resort to covertly hostile tactics like making sarcastic comments or undermining you in front of people you care about. Someone who operates in spite mode fears the repercussions of openly telling you what they think. So they use roundabout tactics for getting their point across.

The most common spite-based behavior you'll come across at work is sarcasm. Sarcasm allows people to express their anger or resentment by delivering a pleasant message in an attacking tone of voice. For example, a manager says sarcastically to a team member arriving late, 'Nice of you to join us.' The words in this message are polite but, when tonality is taken into account, the meta-message is hostile.

Another tactic often employed by people operating from a spite power position is sabotage. One example of this is the team member who deliberately does a bad job on a task they resent doing. Another example is the person who is sent to a team training session they don't want to attend. They arrive late and immediately take out their phone and send messages to friends about how bad the session is. They contribute minimally to group discussions and try to sabotage activities by pretending not to understand instructions.

The intention of spite-based behavior is to warn off potential aggressors so that the speaker can stay safe. When people resort to spite mode, they are trying to scare away whatever is threatening them. For example, if an employee is anxious about a change, they might use sarcasm to influence their manager to drop the matter.

Benefits experienced by people in spite mode

Like all power modes, the spite mode reaps benefits for the user. Often, people who use this power mode are feeling hard done by. They genuinely believe that you misunderstand them or that you are treating them unfairly. Even if you are being supportive, someone in spite mode will interpret your actions as hostile.

For example, I once ran a workshop for participants in a multinational company's mentoring program. Although these people had been *invited* to apply for the program, one of the attendees was convinced she had been forced to attend. She believed the program was intended to make her toe the company line. Not surprisingly, this participant didn't get on with her mentor and soon dropped out of the program.

The participant wouldn't, however, accept responsibility for any part of the communication breakdown. It was all someone else's fault. Her supervisor shouldn't have 'forced' her to have a mentor. The process for matching mentees and mentors wasn't done well. The mentee training was too long. Her mentor was a control freak. The rationalizations mounted up. Everything the woman said was underpinned by spite-based thinking. So it wasn't surprizing that other people described her as a 'negative person'.

The woman herself, however, was benefitting from her behavior. For example, her disruptive actions probably made her feel powerful. Like her, most people operating from spite mode sabotage, disrupt and antagonize in order to make themselves feel better. They rationalize their own behavior by telling themselves others deserve to be treated badly. They feel like they have 'won' when you react defensively to their tactics. The more defensive you become, the more powerful a spite-based communicator feels.

Another perceived benefit from operating in spite mode is control. Many people who resort to passive-aggressive tactics gain a huge amount of control over their team or family. Everyone tiptoes around them, trying not to set them off. I have been called in to work with many teams in which a passive-aggressive team member had more control over group dynamics than the team leader. Not only does this make the team member feel good about themselves, it reinforces their behavior. So why would they stop taking the spite position?

The third benefit of being in spite mode is that it enables the person to maintain rigid boundaries. This makes them feel psychologically safe. Frequently, people who use passive-aggressive tactics are likely to feel deeply hurt. They strive to protect themselves from possible attacks on their self-esteem by refusing to connect with you. They're establishing a psychological wall to protect their fragile sense of self.

This is why, for example, some employees have difficulty building normal team relationships. Their rigidity prevents them from accommodating others' needs. People who get 'stuck' in spite mode can be prone to intense and illogical outbursts of anger. These outbursts release the pent-up pessimism and negativity they feel. The outbursts make them feel good for a short while.

Unfortunately, the taxing conduct of spite-based communicators often drives other people away. Over time, this makes them more defensive and angry. Their behavior creates a vicious cycle, which destroys their ability to build healthy relationships. Because spite-based communicators are experts at rationalization, they will blame other people for their social isolation. They will say things like, 'He deserves to be cut off' rather than admitting that they have behaved inappropriately and destroyed a friendship.

Signs someone is in spite mode

▸ See an example of someone in spite mode on my videos page: http://difficultpeoplemadeeasy.com

Think of someone you believe operates in spite mode under pressure. Recall a specific situation when they were stressed. Tick the characteristics you observed them displaying.

Body language and behavior
☐ Rolling their eyes.
☐ Glaring at you or giving you the 'evil eye'.
☐ Turning away when others talk to them.
☐ Cutting certain people out of conversations.
☐ Making a show of ignoring someone.
☐ Using contemptuous gestures.
☐ Working very slowly, seemingly to irritate other people.
☐ Setting other people up to look stupid.

☐ Sabotaging others' work.
☐ Agreeing to do something, then claiming to forget their promise.
☐ Sulking.
☐ Deliberately withholding information or resources.
☐ Breaking things 'accidently'.
☐ Deliberately making mistakes.
☐ Arriving late at meetings so that others must wait for them.
☐ Spreading malicious rumors.
☐ 'Playing stupid' or pretending not to understand simple messages.

Communication patterns
☐ Delivering double-edged compliments.
☐ Sending ambiguous messages and then blaming you for 'misinterpreting' them.
☐ Gossiping.
☐ Making nasty, cutting jokes.
☐ Laughing at others.
☐ Refusing to talk about problems or issues.
☐ Making smart remarks to express their anger.
☐ Turning the conversation around to negative topics.
☐ Making sarcastic remarks.
☐ Talking about other people in a stage whisper.
☐ Using silence to make others feel uncomfortable.
☐ Setting others against each other to generate conflict.
☐ Delivering pleasant messages in a sarcastic tone of voice.
☐ Joking about topics that others hold dear.

Words and phrases
☐ You're too sensitive.
☐ Whatever …
☐ Talk to the hand.
☐ All I meant was …
☐ Can't you take a joke?
☐ What's wrong with you?

Voice tone
☐ Sarcastic.
☐ Indirectly attacking.

☐ Sickly sweet.
☐ Provocative.

Write your total number of ticks here: _____

A score of nine or more indicates you're dealing with someone in spite mode.

Alright mode

Imagine being able to hold fair and assertive discussions even when other people resort to difficult behaviors. What would it be like to hold conversations in which everyone feels powerful, without playing power games? This is what it is like to operate from the alright power mode. People communicating from the alright power mode are able to share power and create 'win-win' conversations.

When you're operating from the alright power mode, your body is relaxed and comfortable. You're able to distinguish between sensory data and the meaning you give to it. Your thinking is clear and lucid. Your emotions are stable and resourceful. No matter what other people say and do, *you* feel okay.

When you're speaking from the alright position, you are free from distressing emotions such as anxiety or stress. This means you can access the higher thinking processes of your neo-cortex rather than be driven by your amygdala. The neo-cortex is the part of your brain that drives rational thinking. This is why being in the alright power mode helps you stay calm during tough conversations.

THE SOLUTION IS... BAKE ANOTHER CAKE.

Benefits of operating in alright mode

Being in alright mode allows you to minimize the impact of others' negative behaviors on you. For example, Jocelyn is a customer service officer in a community college. Most of her customers are positive, pleasant people. But, like all service providers, Jocelyn has a few clients who are really difficult to deal with. She's handling an angry customer right now. And that customer is trying to push her buttons.

The conversation starts calmly enough. But when the customer learns he is not eligible for a refund of course fees, he becomes aggressive and abusive. Not content to criticize just the college, he begins hurling personal insults at Jocelyn. Luckily Jocelyn knows how to mentally separate herself from her customers. She focuses on calming her breathing and relaxing her body. This prevents her slipping into fight, flight or spite mode. And she is able to calm the customer and sort out the situation.

This is the main benefit of working from the alright power mode. You're able to mentally separate yourself from others – so you can avoid feeling unhelpful emotions such as stress, hurt, guilt or worry.

Another benefit of adopting the alright power mode is that it supports rational thinking. If you can think straight, you can steer tough conversations towards positive outcomes. You can detect the conversational traps laid by other people, so you can avoid falling into them yourself. Instead of adding fuel to the fire when conflict sparks, you can damp down negative emotions – both in yourself and in other people. And you can prevent conversations petering out before you reach a successful agreement. When you remain rational, you can become a fully successful negotiator.

Signs someone is operating in alright mode

Think of someone you believe operates in alright mode under pressure. Recall a specific situation when they were stressed. Tick the characteristics you observed them displaying.

Body language and behavior
☐ Keeping arms and legs uncrossed.
☐ Holding appropriate, confident eye contact.

☐ Matching your facial expressions and voice tones.
☐ Holding a relaxed posture.
☐ Using gestures to help others understand.

Communication patterns
☐ Collaborative.
☐ Solution focussed.
☐ Power shared equally.
☐ Problems approached calmly.
☐ Others' feelings acknowledged and respected.
☐ Own feelings expressed honestly and appropriately.
☐ Questions used to draw out others' opinions.
☐ 'I' statements used to express own opinions.

Words and phrases
☐ We.
☐ Us.
☐ Together.
☐ We can sort this out.
☐ I'd like to discuss this with you.
☐ Thanks for raising this issue.
☐ How can we solve this problem?

Voice tone
☐ Warm.
☐ Conversational.
☐ Calm.
☐ Appropriately expressive.
☐ Tone matches messages.

Write your total number of ticks here: _ _ _ _ _ .

A score of nine or more indicates you're dealing with someone in alright power mode.

CHAPTER TWO

HOW TOXIC DYNAMICS MAKE CONVERSATIONS 'UNSAFE'

▶ When you talk to someone else, each of you is subliminally monitoring the dynamics of your conversation. Subtle changes in body language and verbal patterns help both of you interpret the tone of the conversation. When that tone is constructive, each person feels secure (or safe) enough to open up.

When the conversational tone is hostile, however, one or both of you feels insecure. The conversational dynamic becomes 'toxic' or psychologically unsafe. And that can cause the situation to spiral out of control. Here's an example of how this happens.

Jared is a high achiever. He works long hours and expects everyone – including himself – to do their work perfectly. Not surprizingly, Jared finds it hard to wind down and relax. He also resents doing anything that he considers to be a diversion from his core tasks. This means he doesn't like spending time in long meetings.

Imagine you're in a meeting with Jared. His body language and verbal patterns are creating a hostile vibe. Your brain's emergency response centre, the amygdala, reacts to that vibe. You begin to feel insecure and stressed. You deal with your feelings by joking with a colleague, in an attempt to lighten the mood of the meeting.

Jared interprets your joking as a time-wasting, diversionary tactic. His amygdala reaction is also triggered. He becomes angry and goes into fight mode. He makes a sarcastic comment. This activates your amygdala reaction again, so you make a smart reply. The meeting is now out of control. And your relationship with Jared is now 'toxic'. It's quite likely that this unhealthy dynamic will be carried out of the meeting room and into future conversations. You'll start to think of Jared as a 'difficult person'.

If someone has a reputation for being difficult, chances are they're resorting to behaviors that undermine psychological safety. Most commonly, they'll be doing or saying things that invade others' boundaries. Knowing this will help you get tough situations under control.

How personal boundaries keep communication 'safe'

Personal boundaries are like a fence around your home. That fence separates your private territory from the street. It keeps intruders out as well as keeping the kids and the cat off the street. It also has a gate, which you can open to let others in or out of your home.

Your personal boundaries perform exactly the same functions as that fence. They keep you safe. They let you manage what (and who) you let in, and they allow you to choose when you want to give out information about yourself. If your boundaries are healthy, you are able to open and close your psychological 'gate' in appropriate ways.

You also have physical boundaries. These keep your body safe. They determine how close someone else can come to you. Your physical boundaries define the point at which a toxic person invades your personal space.

One example of a physical boundary is the limit you place on who touches you and which parts of your body it is okay for each person to touch. Another physical boundary is the point at which you feel uncomfortable when someone stands next to you. A third physical boundary is set by the limits of your workspace. For example, you may consider your desk drawers to be 'private space', which your co-workers should not violate. If your colleague goes through your drawers, they've violated your boundary.

▸ Find out more about what personal boundaries are in my video, *How to set boundaries and limits*. You'll find it on my video page at http://difficultpeoplemadeeasy.com.

How boundary invasions erode healthy communication

All difficult behaviors involve boundary violations. A boundary violation happens when someone else invades your physical or psychological space. Even small actions can have a huge impact on how safe you feel around another person. Personal boundary violations could include:

▸ Standing too close or getting 'in your face'.
▸ Butting in on your conversations.
▸ Giving unwanted advice.
▸ Criticizing you harshly and unfairly.
▸ Staring at you.
▸ Filming or photographing you without your permission.
▸ Rifling through your personal belongings.
▸ Teasing you.
▸ Making jokes at your expense.

Your physical boundaries can be compromised through actions such as unwanted touching, slapping (even in a 'playful' way), pinching or standing too close.

Your psychological boundaries can be invaded by someone intruding on your private persona. For example, someone who reads your personal diary without permission would be invading your emotional space. A colleague asking about areas of your life you'd prefer to keep private would be invading the boundary between your personal and public personas. A highly controlling person who demands that you do something you feel is wrong is violating your psychological boundaries. So is someone who aggressively criticizes you or shames you in front of a group.

When 'difficult people' violate your boundaries, they project their issues onto you and they invade your personal space, either physically or emotionally. This makes you feel unsafe, uncomfortable or outright violated.

Take Denise. She has great leadership potential. But she's struggling to manage a long-term employee, Mike, whose work is not up to standard. Mike is demanding that he be allowed to work overtime (even though it is not required from a business perspective) because he 'needs the money'.

Denise feels guilty saying 'no' to Mike. Although she has told him several times that the overtime is not required, Mike raises the issue in every weekly meeting. He switches between being sarcastic and shouting aggressively in an effort to push his point time after time.

Denise continues to hear Mike out every time he raises the issue. She communicates from the flight position, keeping her voice soft and trying to be nice to Mike. Denise feels worn down and disempowered. She is 'catching' Mike's distress. She needs to separate her own feelings from his. She also needs to set limits on the behaviors she will accept from Mike. In order to do this, she needs to understand how Mike is using words to poison the communication.

How 'difficult people' turn words into poison

At work, most boundary violations involve the use of **words** to poison the relationship. Remember a time when someone made a comment that irritated or annoyed you. Or cast your mind back to a situation in which you felt manipulated. In either of these situations 'toxic communication patterns' would have been used. Toxic communication patterns are sentence structures that are used to invade psychological boundaries.

There are six main toxic communication patterns 'difficult people' use to violate your boundaries. Each of these patterns can manifest in a variety of ways, depending on the power mode the 'difficult person' is operating from. Reading this chapter will help you detect toxic communication patterns. More importantly, it will help you choose communication antidotes to neutralize those patterns.

Verbal intrusions on your personal zone

Verbal intrusions on your personal zone are a type of boundary invasion. They occur when a 'difficult person' says something judgemental or which attacks you at a personal level. For example, Judith's boss, Bradley, says, 'You're too sloppy.' His message is judgemental and Judith will hear it as a personal attack. A more appropriate way of getting his point across would be for Bradley to say, 'I've noticed several errors in the reports you wrote last week.'

Verbal intrusions are possible because communication happens in three different zones. These are shown on the diagram below.

The inner circle of this diagram represents your personal mental space. Your self-talk (or the 'voice in your head') exists within this space. Messages that penetrate this space from the outside world have immense power because you take them personally. If you're not skilled at maintaining your personal boundaries, verbally attacking messages will get through to this level and hurt you emotionally.

The middle circle on the diagram symbolizes the communication space you use when talking to friends or loved ones. If someone's message penetrates to this level at work, you're likely to feel their words were inappropriate. This is because communication that happens within the intimate zone is more personal than communication within the professional zone.

The diagram's outer circle illustrates the communication space you share with co-workers, your manager, customers and suppliers. Message exchanges within this space should be neutral and objective.

When a verbal message penetrates your personal zone, you will take it personally. There are two main reasons why this might happen. First, you might have weak personal boundaries. In this situation,

you'll draw professionally-worded messages into your personal zone. This will cause you to misread appropriate messages and 'take them personally'. The problem is not the words themselves – it is the level at which you interpret them.

The second reason words might penetrate your personal zone, however, is that they were designed to do so. In this case, the person who spoke those words *was* intending to attack you in some way. An intrusion of your personal space has occurred. Here are just a few examples of ways others' attacking words might intrude on your personal space.

Fight mode intrusions on your personal zone

People with ill-defined boundaries who are operating in fight mode need to make you feel bad. Why? So they can feel okay. These people can seem very abusive because their sense of self-esteem comes from destroying your self-esteem. They use aggressive tactics such as shaming you in public, shouting at you or constantly pointing out your flaws.

If any of the following behaviors seem familiar to you, you've encountered a fight-based attack on your personal zone:

▸ Shouting at you or calling you names.
▸ Accusing you of doing something you haven't done.
▸ Constantly criticizing you, but never praising you.
▸ Asking intrusive questions.
▸ Talking over you or refusing to let you speak.

Flight mode intrusions on your personal zone

Some people have such poorly-defined boundaries themselves that they have no concept of where they end and you begin. This means their psychological sense of 'being okay' depends on you. They believe that their happiness depends on you being happy. You might think of someone like this as being a 'people pleaser'. They genuinely don't know what they want.

These people invade your personal space by becoming too intimate. They give you too much information about themselves. They assume they're entitled to hear personal details about your life. They might even relate to you as a member of their 'family' and expect you to help with their personal issues.

You're likely to be dealing with a flight-based intrusion on your personal zone if someone does something like the following.

▸ Discloses too much information about their personal life.
▸ Relies on you to make their decisions for them.
▸ Cries in order to get you to do something for them.
▸ Uses 'emotional blackmail' to influence you.
▸ Constantly wants to be near you.
▸ Is 'needy' and drains your emotional energy.

Spite mode intrusions on your personal zone

When someone intrudes on your personal space from spite mode, they'll use snide remarks and sarcastic comments to cut you down. Their hard-to-handle behavior functions to build their own self-esteem.

Here are some types of behavior you'll notice when someone invades your boundaries from the spite position.

▸ Teasing or shaming you in public.
▸ Making disparaging comments or jokes about your personal characteristics – e.g. your weight, your sexuality or your religious beliefs.
▸ Setting you up to look foolish in front of your boss, colleagues or customers.
▸ Making sarcastic remarks.

Handling intrusions on your personal zone from alright mode

When other people verbally intrude on your personal space, you need to set clear verbal boundaries. Your mode of response is critically important. Keep reminding yourself that the best way to respond to boundary invasions is from the alright position.

It's always wise to give other people the benefit of the doubt, particularly when asserting a boundary for the first time. Don't blame or shame the other person – give them feedback. Avoid demanding that they change. Instead, raise their awareness of the need for change.

Later, you'll learn how to use a language pattern called an 'I frame' to deal with intrusions of your personal space. You'll also find that WISH statements, which are also covered later, are useful for responding to verbal boundary invasions from an alright stance.

Head/heart mismatches

Here's an example of a head/heart mismatch that you may be familiar with.

You're giving a factual account of what was said in a project meeting. Meanwhile, your co-worker is focussing on what people meant by their words. You believe the meeting was successful because an action plan was developed. Your co-worker thinks it was a disaster because so much was going on beneath the surface of team members' conversations. This is what happens when head and heart collide at work. Head-based people focus on facts and realities. Heart-based people concentrate on emotions and relationships. When the two types try to communicate, things can go wrong very quickly.

What is a head/heart mismatch?

Have you ever noticed that some people seem to value logic more than feelings? These people have a preference for analytic 'head-based' decision making. They talk about facts, pros and cons and rational thinking.

The other portion of the population values emotions more than logic. They prefer to use 'heart-based' decision making. They talk about emotions, feelings, gut instincts and the impact of decisions on other people. These are the people who work hard to avoid hurting or offending other people.

Neither style of decision making is better than the other. But when you're talking to someone with the opposite decision-making style to you, conflict can occur. If your natural style is to tackle problems logically, you may be irritated by someone who wants to talk about their feelings. Or, if your preference is to approach problem solving from an emotional angle, you may find logical decision makers to be 'hard-hearted' or 'too impersonal'.

Here are some common problems that happen when head-based people communicate with heart-based people.

▸ The more logic-driven person dismisses the emotionally expressive person as being 'too emotional'.
▸ The emotion-based person accuses the logical thinker of being insensitive.
▸ Statements made by the head-based communicator are taken personally by the heart-based communicator and resentment sets in.
▸ The rational thinker shuts down when the feelings-based person expresses strong emotions.
▸ Both parties try to convince each other that they are right – at the same time, they refuse to listen to each other.
▸ Each person labels the other as 'difficult'.

If the mismatch between head and heart-based communication goes on too long, the fight, flight or spite cycle kicks in. This can create a toxic dynamic in the relationship.

Fight mode head/heart mismatch

When a head-based communicator is in fight mode, they are likely to try and prove they're right. They'll move into 'debate' mode rather than collaborating with you. They'll talk over you, attack the logic of what you've said or criticize you for not being 'sensible'.

A heart-based communicator behaves very differently when they're in fight mode. They'll blame you for the negative feelings they feel you have generated and insist that you need to make things up to them. They'll accuse you of being insensitive or being the cause of their emotional pain. They'll express their feelings loudly and dramatically.

Flight mode head/heart mismatch

If someone with a preference for logical thinking is operating in flight mode, they're likely to shut down when you talk to them using heart-based language. They might not say anything but, internally, they'll dismiss what you're saying because it seems illogical to them. If you value having your feelings respected and acknowledged, this reaction may be very upsetting. Although the head-based decision maker didn't mean to do so, they've accidently sent the message, 'what you feel doesn't matter to me'.

Similarly, someone with a preference for emotional decision making can accidently send a negative message when they communicate from flight mode. Unwilling to hurt someone else's feelings, they won't speak up when you make a logical statement they disagree with. If you value 'battling things out' through a robust debate, this can be infuriating. This is because the feeling-based person has subconsciously sent the message, 'what you think doesn't matter to me'.

Spite mode head/heart mismatch

When someone with head-based decision making is operating in spite mode, they will be dismissive and sarcastic. It's likely they'll make smart comments about your lack of intelligence. They'll try to make you feel stupid and may use pointed jokes or biting comments to do this. Their jokes and comments will suggest that you lack the ability to solve problems logically, or that you are too emotional.

Sarcasm and put-downs are less likely to be used by heart-based decision makers. What they'll do instead is sulk, because they believe you've hurt their feelings. Their pointed silence or pained looks will send a clear message that you're in their bad books. However, the heart-based decision maker will never say this out loud.

Handling head/heart mismatches from alright mode

To handle a head/heart mismatch assertively, start by shifting your language patterns to match the other person's. It helps to focus on using neutral language. You'll learn more about neutral language in the following chapter. For now, here are some examples of how a message can be framed in different ways to match each preference.

	What to say to a head-based communicator	What to say to a heart-based communicator
You want to raise a problem	There is a problem with... What do you think about this?	I've noticed people are uncomfortable about ... How do you feel about this?
You need to give feedback	I have some ideas about how you can improve your efficiency on this task.	I know you're keen to do the best job possible. Would you like some feedback that will help you get even better?
You're making a proposal	I've analysed the problem and found three ways to solve it. I'd like your thoughts on these.	I value your opinion and would like your feedback on this proposal.
You're requesting more staff	To get the best possible results, we need to rethink our staffing levels.	The team is working very hard but they've reached their maximum capacity. We don't want to overload anyone, so I'd like to increase our staffing.
You don't agree with what the other person has said	I have some questions about the viability of that idea.	I see things differently.

In the next section, you'll learn about 'you frame' messages and how they can get your point across without inflaming a situation that involves a head/heart mismatch.

Baiting

Baiting involves setting you up to react. For example:

▶ The colleague who whispers, 'Have you heard what Tim has done now?'
▶ A customer who shouts, 'You're a bureaucratic little stamp-licker.'
▶ That co-worker who asks, 'Do I look fat in this dress?'

All of these people are using baiting behaviors. Once you take the bait, they'll hook you into a toxic or time-wasting conversation.

What is baiting?

Imagine a fisherman getting ready for a weekend fishing trip. He'd pack a fishing rod, hooks and bait. But what sort of bait would he pack? That would depend on the type of fish he wanted to catch. Like that fisherman, a hard-to-handle person will know exactly what bait they need to reel you in.

Baiting is behavior that is used to push your emotional buttons. When someone baits you, they want to trigger a defensive reaction. They want you to lose control so they can satisfy their own needs and get what they want. For example, a hard-to-manage person may want to make you feel bad. Why? Because when *you* feel bad, *they* feel powerful. Or they may want to trigger feelings of guilt so you'll comply with their demands. Or a challenging person perhaps wants you to lose your cool so they can complain that you shouted at them.

Just as a fisherman will choose a specific type of bait to catch a particular species of fish, 'difficult people' will use a range of behaviors to reel you in. They may test several baiting strategies before finding the one that gets you to bite. Here are some behaviors you may come across when dealing with baiting behavior in the three different power modes of communication.

Fight mode baiting

When someone in fight mode uses baiting tactics, they're aiming to gain power over you. They want you to lose your cool, become defensive and fight back. They may resort to some of the following behaviors.

- Deliberately starting an argument.
- Accusing you of something you haven't done.
- Insulting you.
- Telling you what to do when you don't want advice.
- Bringing up the same mistake over and over again even though you've corrected the situation.
- Asking pointed questions that make you feel defensive.

Flight mode baiting

People who bait from flight mode usually want you to step into rescuer mode. Their tactics are designed to manipulate your emotions so that you'll listen to their problems or take on unpleasant tasks for them. Here are some typical behaviors you'll see flight-based people using when they bait.

- Sighing loudly so that you'll ask, 'What's wrong?'
- Putting themselves down in order to win a compliment.
- Complaining that someone has hurt or upset them.
- Telling 'poor me' stories.
- Crying in order to gain sympathy (not because they're genuinely sad).

Spite mode baiting

The aim of spite-based baiting is to make you feel inferior. This helps the baiter feel better about themselves. It's a sad fact that some people can only feel okay when they know you feel unhappy. You might recognize some of the following behaviors used by these people to bait.

- Gossiping about you to someone they know will pass the message back to you.
- Deliberately making mistakes.
- Using 'go-slow' tactics to sabotage the completion of a task.
- Making sarcastic remarks during meetings.
- Joking about things or people you care about.
- Stirring up conflict or playing people off each other.

Handling baiting from alright mode

The best way to handle baiting is to refuse to take the bait. This involves three steps. First, you need to spot the lure that has been thrown your way. Next, you need to manage your emotions. Finally, you need to give an unexpected response. In the next section, you'll learn how to word that response using a four-step process called WISH.

Perceiving problems as personal attacks

Some people take every problem personally. For example:
▸ You give a colleague feedback on a small mistake and she bursts into tears.
▸ You question an instruction your boss has given you and he snaps, 'Don't argue with me. Just do it.'
▸ You forget to clear your dirty cup from the sink before going home. The next morning a sign is taped over the sink. It says, 'I am not your mother.'

All of these situations involve people taking neutral situations personally. If you work with someone who does this a lot, you'll know how exhausting the habit of blowing things out of proportion can be. People who take things personally display exaggerated reactions to small issues. When problems crop up, they don't focus on solving them. Instead, they shout, cry or whine. And no matter what *you* do, *they'll* find a negative way to interpret your actions.

What does perceiving a problem as a personal attack involve?

People who feel attacked when they encounter problems usually have difficulty separating themselves from external events. Rather than seeing issues as separate from themselves, they internalize the issue. They can't 'step back' from a problem and assess it logically. Instead, they experience it as being part of themselves.

When others raise or address issues such people perceive the problems as 'part' of themselves and react defensively. To protect themselves, they switch into fight, flight or spite mode. And that's why they resort to difficult behaviors.

Fight mode reactions to a perceived attack

People with low self-esteem hear criticism – even constructive feedback – as an attack on their identity. This causes them deep internal pain. But they won't admit that. Instead, they will fight tooth and nail in an effort to make you feel pain too.

When someone tries to defend themselves in fight mode, they will try to prove they're right and win what they perceive to be a life or death battle. Instead of assessing the situation rationally and trying to sort it out, they'll respond to problems in various ways. These might include:

▸ Blaming you for a different problem, in order to divert attention away from the issue they're taking personally.
▸ Talking over you.
▸ Insisting that there is only one way – their way – to resolve the situation.
▸ Reacting aggressively to feedback.
▸ Loudly asserting that there is nothing wrong and that you are foolish for thinking there is.

Flight mode reactions to a perceived attack

If someone reacts to a perceived attack in flight mode, they will try to ignore the problem or escape from what they see as a highly threatening situation. This style of reaction leads to behaviors similar to the following examples.

▸ Failing to raise problems, due to a fear of being blamed for causing them.
▸ Crying when an issue is raised or feedback is given.
▸ Claiming that you are attacking them when all you've done is raised an issue assertively.
▸ Asking someone else to stand up for them and protect them from what is perceived to be an unfair attack.
▸ Taking sick leave the day after an issue is raised in order to avoid sorting out the situation.

Spite mode reactions to a perceived attack

Someone experiencing a spite reaction will use dirty tactics to defend themselves when they feel attacked. Their defence strategies may include sulking, passing-the-buck, sabotage, back-stabbing or making snide remarks. The following behaviors suggest you're dealing with someone who is handling a perceived attack from a spite position.

▸ Sulking for days after you raise an issue.
▸ Refusing to discuss the problem with you and claiming that there is nothing wrong.
▸ Suggesting that you're too sensitive or deluded and that no problem exists.
▸ Making a sarcastic remark in response to feedback.
▸ Agreeing to take action to resolve the situation – but then doing nothing at all about it.

Handling reactions to a perceived attack from alright mode

Dealing with someone who takes everything personally can be frustrating. It helps to remember that their behavior stems from emotional immaturity. This person has not learned how to manage their own feelings. Your job is to stay focussed on the issue rather than reacting to the challenging behavior the other person is displaying.

You can use flameproof language and spotlight questions to help turn the conversation around. Both these tools are described in the next section.

Interpreting difference as a threat

Some people automatically see *difference* as dangerous. This leads them to react from fight, flight or spite mode instead of making the most of diversity at work. Here are some examples of people who perceive difference as a threat.

▸ The male professional who loudly claims that a female co-worker is not suited to her role 'because she's a woman'.
▸ The group of team members who make racist remarks to target one of their colleagues.
▸ The bullying boss who flies into a temper when you disagree with her.

All of these challenging behaviors are underpinned by a fear of difference. This fear triggers the fight, flight or spite reaction and trouble brews.

What does interpreting difference as a threat involve?

When two people become aware of differences between them, they can focus on those differences or they can look for what they have in common. They feel threatened by the fact that someone else fails to share their worldview and their feelings trigger a stress reaction, which then leads to fight, flight or spite behavior. They don't realize that exploring differences can be enriching and engaging, as can discovering the things they have in common.

In particular, you are likely to spark a stress reaction in people who are threatened by difference or a difference of opinion in the following circumstances.

▸ You are challenging a core belief they hold.
▸ There is reason to be jealous of you.
▸ Your values clash with theirs.
▸ Your success will show them up.
▸ Something they want might be taken by you.
▸ There's a risk you will show them up in some way.
▸ You belong to a cultural group that they have been taught to fear.
▸ What you're saying or doing threatens their way of life.

Once the stress reaction has set in, people who perceive difference as a threat will try to defend themselves. This will lead to fight, flight or spite behavior.

Fight-based defensive reactions to difference

When someone reacts to difference from fight mode, they'll attempt to beat you down in order to diminish the threat you pose. They'll aim to prove that their worldview is right. And they'll use stand-over tactics to get this point across. You may recognize some of the following behaviors.

▸ Aggressively arguing that their beliefs are superior to yours.
▸ Physically or verbally attacking you.
▸ Shouting or screaming in order to make you back down.
▸ Talking over you when you try to describe your own perspective.
▸ Using threatening words and body language.
▸ Insisting that you shut up and accept what they've said is right.
▸ Ganging up on you.
▸ Loudly criticizing your beliefs, physical characteristics or ideas.

Flight-based defensive reactions to difference

Someone operating in flight mode will react to differences by trying to hide from you. Threatened by the fact that you think, look or behave unfamiliarly, they will retreat. You may recognize some of the following specific behaviors, which can indicate you're dealing with a flight-based defensive reaction to difference.

▸ Avoiding being alone with you.
▸ Asking others to communicate with you on their behalf.
▸ Making requests by email rather than communicating with you face to face.
▸ Being very guarded about what they say and do in front of you.
▸ Keeping a watchful eye on you, in case you do something that might harm them.
▸ Giving minimalist answers when you ask for their ideas or input.

Spite-based defensive reactions to difference

Like fight-based communicators, spite-based communicators will attempt to put you in your place if they feel threatened by you. They will target your vulnerabilities and attempt to shame or humiliate you. They'll aim to silence you, or get rid of you altogether, by taunting and overwhelming you. Here are some behaviors that show a person is reacting defensively from spite mode.

▸ Refusing to communicate with you.
▸ Giving you the cold shoulder.
▸ Joking about your beliefs, physical characteristics or lifestyle choices.
▸ Posting or emailing offensive pictures, cartoons and photos.
▸ Leaving nasty notes on your desk or in your workspace.
▸ Ignoring your comments during team meetings.
▸ Playing humiliating practical jokes that highlight the ways in which you differ from them.

Handling difference as a threat from alright mode

Responding to people who perceive you as a threat can be very challenging. You'll often feel that your boundaries are being invaded by their words or actions. So it's very important that you mentally separate yourself from what these people say and do. Essentially, this means setting and maintaining boundaries that will keep you psychologically safe.

Some specific tools you can use when dealing with people who see you as a threat include accord statements, 'you frame' messages and ACE statements. All of these communication tools are explained in the next section.

Perceptual distortion

You may have heard the saying, 'perception is reality'. What it means is that everyone creates their own version of what any particular event means. And during communication, particularly if a touchy issue is under discussion, this can cause problems. For example, a manager sends a quick email to her team. Because she's in a rush, this email is very to-the-point. The manager thinks she's being efficient. Members of her team believe she's rude. The problem here stems from perceptual distortion, which happens when a message is not received in the way the sender expected it to be.

What is perceptual distortion?

Perceptual distortion happens when someone misinterprets the information they're receiving through their senses. For example, you ask a customer for information about their account details. You're intending to use the information to solve their problem. However, they interpret your questions as a challenge and think that your request is prying, or that you are suggesting that their account is somehow the problem. They react by flooding you with abuse. Their behavior is a direct result of their perceptual distortion.

Actually, distortion is a very natural process. It happens because everyone has their own unique way of filtering experience. Even when two individuals are looking at exactly the same painting, for example, they will see it differently. But when people are in fight, flight or spite mode, they assign negative meanings to sensory data. And this escalates their stress reaction.

There are two main forms of perceptual distortion to be aware of when handling difficult behavior.

Deletion

The first distortion process is called deletion. It involves ignoring or disregarding aspects of the person's experience. For example, you have a colleague with low self-esteem. He only seems to remember critical feedback the boss has given him. Even though you have heard the boss making lots of positive remarks about his work, this colleague hasn't noticed or retained these messages. Gradually, he begins to see the boss as someone who is picking on him. His worldview isn't accurate; there isn't anything you can do to persuade him otherwise. He firmly believes the boss has it in for him.

Generalization

Generalization involves taking a few single examples and then building a worldview based on these. For example, your colleague Anne has an argument with the head of marketing. Later she has a run-in with the assistant head of marketing. Two days later, she has a heated discussion with the marketing co-ordinator. From this point on, she believes that everyone in marketing has a bad attitude.

Generalization isn't always a bad thing. In fact, it helps us learn. But when people don't challenge their own negative generalizations, conflict and disunity can emerge.

Fight-based perceptual distortion

When someone is communicating from a fight position, they will interpret the things you do and say as though you are fighting *them*. They will then try to defend themselves and this will lead to an escalation of their fight state. Here are some examples of distorted thinking that people in fight mode might experience.

▸ Picking up on emotional trigger words such as 'must' or 'have to' and pushing to assert their freedom to choose.
▸ Hearing questions as challenges rather than as requests for information.
▸ Interpreting your silence as a hostile move.
▸ Honing in on specific phrases in an email message and interpreting these as aggressive.
▸ Believing general comments are targeted directly at them.

Flight-based perceptual distortion

Perceptual distortions made from the flight position often involve interpreting events from the position of feeling like a 'victim' or a 'loser'. In other words, these types of distortions reflect a worldview built on low self-esteem. The following are some common examples of distorted thinking for people in flight mode.

▸ Interpreting feedback as a personal attack.
▸ Hearing laughter and believing it means people are laughing at them.
▸ Failing to recognize any compliments or positive feedback they receive.
▸ Assuming that because someone argued with them once, that person 'hates' them.
▸ Interpreting an invitation to speak up during a meeting as putting them on the spot.
▸ Thinking that making a mistake means they're a terrible person.

Spite-based perceptual distortion

When someone distorts perceptual information through the lens of a spite reaction, they interpret your words and actions as malicious. So, of course, they seek to keep themselves safe by attacking you. Here are some examples of perceptual distortion when in spite mode.

▸ Hearing double meanings in everything you say.
▸ Taking feedback as a scathing criticism.
▸ Finding negative meanings in positive statements – and then calling you a spin doctor.
▸ Seeing others' actions as evidence that a conspiracy is taking place.
▸ Taking offence at small behaviors that you're not even conscious of.

Handling perceptual distortion from alright mode

The best way to handle perceptual distortion is to gently challenge the evidence upon which the other person is basing their interpretation. For example, you might ask, 'What makes you think that?' or, 'Where did you get that information?'

When responding to distortions, it also pays to frame your message in neutral, non-judgemental language. Think carefully about the trigger words that may mean something threatening to the person who is distorting the message. It makes sense to avoid using these words during your dealings with highly reactive people. Stick to language that won't inflame the situation. You'll learn how to do this in the chapter on flameproof language, which you'll find in the next section.

▸ To find out more about deletion and generalizations, watch my video at http://difficultpeoplemadeeasy.com

Section summary

Congratulations. You now know how to assess what's going on when you're dealing with 'difficult people'. You understand how stress can trigger fight, flight and spite behavior. You can recognize the six toxic communication patterns people use to violate your personal boundaries.

These are:
▸ Verbal intrusions on your personal zone
▸ Heart/head mismatches
▸ Baiting
▸ Perceiving problems as personal attacks
▸ Interpreting difference as a threat
▸ Perceptual distortion

Now you're ready to learn how to respond to 'difficult people' from an assertive alright position.

In the next section of this book you'll see how to counteract the effects of toxic behavior. You'll learn how to build a SAFE conversational tone. Then you'll find out which words to use when responding to each of the toxic communication patterns.

WHAT YOU CAN DO TO COUNTERACT DIFFICULT BEHAVIOR ▸

CHAPTER THREE

TURNING TOXIC CONVERSATIONS INTO SAFE CONVERSATIONS

▶ If you are bitten by a snake, you quickly get to hospital and ask for the antivenin. If you accidently swallow a poison, you rush to an emergency clinic for the antidote. If you're exposed to toxic communication patterns, you get into a 'relationship clinic' as quickly as you can. Then you need to apply a verbal antidote to neutralize the effect of the toxic behavior.

So what, exactly, is a relationship clinic? It's the communication equivalent of a hospital. In everyday life, a hospital is a safe place, where patient wellbeing is the primary concern. A relationship clinic is also a safe place – a psychologically safe place. It runs according to four main principles, which I call SAFE.

What is a SAFE conversation?

A SAFE conversation is when people engage in trusting, honest and appropriate dialogue. In other words, it is a two-way conversation. During SAFE conversations, each person can express themselves honestly, appropriately and respectfully. When you are part of a SAFE conversation, you don't defend yourself if your viewpoint is questioned. Instead, you focus on listening and learning. You

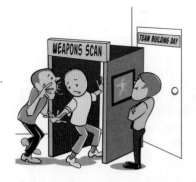

THE FACILITATOR HAD HEARD ABOUT THE TEAM'S DYNAMICS.

don't attack others' perspectives. Instead, you ask questions. This doesn't mean you abandon your own ideas and beliefs. You are true to yourself while respecting other people's point of view.

Being able to hold a SAFE conversation is a rare and valuable skill. Yet once you've mastered that skill, you'll be amazed that more people don't use it. You'll discover that keeping a conversation SAFE helps you sort out conflicts, stop power games and get better results from your conversations with people in fight, flight and spite modes.

There are four steps involved in building a SAFE conversation. First you start on a positive note. Then you ask about others' perspectives. Next you frame your own perspective. Finally, you explore options together

Start on a positive note

The words you use to open a potentially difficult conversation set the tone for the entire dialogue. If you want to keep the discussion harmonious, you need to use words that will resonate with other people. This means avoiding blaming or shaming language and being issue-focussed.

Identify one issue

It helps to identify **one** core issue that you want to discuss. This helps keep each communicator focussed. It also prevents you from biting off more than you can chew during a problem-solving conversation. If you're dealing with a complex situation, you need to separate the key issues and deal with them one at a time.

Resist the temptation to bundle up all your concerns into one statement. Instead, hone in on the single most important issue to address. Analyse that issue and think about what the other person is saying or doing when they are violating your boundaries. The following questions help you do this.

- What is the problem we need to solve?
- Why does this problem exist?
- What is contributing to this problem?
- What (if any) is the behavior I want to set a boundary around?
- What, specifically, is the other person doing or saying?

● On a scale of one (low impact) to ten (high impact), how seriously is the behavior impacting on me?

Describe that issue using neutral words

Next, you need to find a way of describing the issue in neutral language. Why should you do this? Because keeping your language neutral creates psychological safety. Neutral words are objective and unbiased. They describe what is happening without implying judgement. And they do not show any preference. The test for objectivity is that you can answer 'yes' to the question, 'Would the other person agree that this is a fair description of the problem?'

Here's an example. Members of an office team are in conflict over who should load the dishwasher each day. From the administrative assistant's viewpoint, the situation is that, 'Everyone on the team is lazy and assuming that admin team members are their slaves.' From a professional staff member's view, 'Cleaning the kitchen is a minor issue and not worth wasting my valuable time on.'

Neither of those descriptions of the situation is neutral. The professional staff are unlikely to agree that the word 'lazy' is a fair description of their mindset. Equally, the admin team members are probably not going to agree that the state of the kitchen is a 'minor' issue. To raise the issue in a way that will encourage everyone to help solve it, the team will need to agree on wording they can all accept. One way to frame the problem, for example, would be to say, 'The issue to be resolved is loading the dishwasher.'

Use this checklist to determine whether your description of an issue is objective.

☐ Language is unbiased.
☐ Wording does not suggest one party is to blame for a problem.
☐ No-one will be offended by the way the issue is framed.
☐ No judgemental words are used.
☐ Focus is on facts rather than opinions.
☐ Feelings of the person writing the description are not 'given away' by the words used.
☐ The statement is free of words that will trigger emotions.

Work out how to raise the issue

When you raise an issue, you draw someone else's attention to it. It is important that you do this in a positive, psychologically safe way. You can use the following phrases to create a positive note when raising issues.

- I'd like to discuss …
- I am concerned about …
- I have noticed …
- … is an issue we need to sort out.
- Have you noticed there's an issue with …?

Ask about others' perspectives

A SAFE conversation is all about sharing and respecting perspectives. If you want other people to listen to your point of view, it generally helps to listen to their opinions first. That's why the second step of SAFE is asking about what other people think rather than telling them your side of things. Sometimes this can be hard to do – after all, you want to get your point across as quickly as possible. However, you'll get less resistance to your ideas when you've shown respect for other people's perspectives first. Spending time exploring others' perceptions often speeds up the discussion overall.

There are many reasons why asking about others' views is a useful tactic. For starters, it can provide you with valuable information. It can also build rapport and minimize conflict. It gives you the details you need to understand a 'difficult person's' key needs and concerns. If a 'difficult person' is emotional or reactive, getting them to talk about their perspective will help them vent. And it buys you time to calm down as well, if you need to. Most importantly, asking about other people's views puts you in charge of the dynamic of the conversation and the direction it will take – towards a positive outcome. For this reason, most great negotiators open a dialogue by asking questions.

You can use the following questions as a starting point for drawing out others' perspectives on an issue.

- What do you think about this?
- How do you feel about this?

- What led you to say that?
- It sounds like you mean … Is that right?
- How is [issue] impacting on you?
- What do you think needs to happen to sort this out?
- What do you really care about in relation to this issue?
- What matters the most to you?
- What would it take for you to feel okay about this?
- Why is this issue important to you?
- What are you worried about in relation to this issue?
- Why do you worry about those things?
- What are you most concerned about here?

Of course, you don't want to sound like an interrogator. So avoid rapid- fire questioning. Make sure you ask your questions one at a time. Keep each question simple, short and clear. Avoid double-barrelled questions such as, 'What makes you say that? Is it because you don't understand the process? … Do you think we need to change the process? Did someone tell you the process wasn't working?'

Rambling sequences like this are confusing and send 'difficult people' into fight, flight and spite mode immediately.

It's also important to respect the other person's answers to your questions. When you're listening to the responses to questions, your job is to acknowledge what they say without becoming defensive. You don't have to agree with them. But you do need to show you're listening.

Frame your own perspective

Once you've thoroughly explored the other person's perspective, it's time to describe your own point of view. To do this, you need to identify your own thoughts and emotions. Then you need to put them into words. And if you want to avoid triggering a fight, flight or spite reaction, you need to choose neutral words. Here are some ways to do this.

Use 'and' to link your perspective to theirs

If you want people to listen to you, you need to grab their attention.
A highly effective way to do this is to link your opinion to theirs.
If possible, do this by agreeing with something they've said. For
example, instead of saying, 'I disagree' you could say, 'I agree with
what you said about ... and I have a slightly different view on ...'

'And' packs a lot of punch for such a small word. It builds bridges
and connects what you've said to what someone else has said. It
sends the message, 'I'm working *with* you, not against you.' So it's a
great word to use instead of 'but'. Here are ways to tap into the power
of 'and' when raising your perspective.

- I think that's a great idea. And I have a few questions. Is it okay if I ask them?
- I understand this really matters to you. And it also matters to me. Do you agree we need to sort it out?
- Yes. That's a great idea. And I'd like to suggest some other ideas too.
- I've listened to your perspective. And now I'd like to explain mine.
- I understand your views now. And so I'd like you to hear mine.
- Thanks for explaining your thoughts on this. And now I'm going to quickly explain mine.
- I agree we need to sort this out. From what I understand, you think _____. And I think _____.

Keep 'you' out of it

Framing your perspective means sharing what you think and feel.
There aren't really any 'good' or 'bad' thoughts or emotions. But there
are appropriate and inappropriate ways of expressing what you think
and feel. For example, imagine that a co-worker is feeling stressed by
her workload. She bails you up in the corridor and says, 'This is really
unfair. Because you're so disorganized, you've left both these projects
to the last minute. And now you're dumping them on me.'

Although this is an honest statement about what your co-worker
feels, I doubt you'd agree that it is appropriate. So how could your
co-worker get her point across without minimizing her concern?
She needs to stop using the word 'you' and start speaking from the
'I' position. For example, she could say, 'I'm confused about my
priorities this week. I've been tasked with drafting the annual report
and coordinating the customer conference on Friday. Each task will

require at least a week's work. Which one should I focus on?'

Framing her message this way helps her express the problem without casting blame or sending you into fight, flight or spite mode. Here are some examples of 'you'-based messages reworded as 'I'-based messages.

'You' Statement	'I' Statement
You should have told me …	I didn't know.
You're selfish.	I'd have liked input into that decision.
You don't know what you are talking about.	I see things differently.
Shut up!	I don't like that sort of joke.
You never listen to me.	I'd like you to listen to me.
You're too bossy.	I prefer to make my own decision about this.

Explore options together

You may need to cycle back and forth between asking about the other person's perspective and explaining your own. Finally, however, you will reach the problem-solving stage of the conversation. At this point, you need to work with the other person to generate ideas and options for resolving the issue. This involves using collaborative problem-solving techniques.

The aim of collaborative problem solving is to generate options for action. Some people find option generation easy. For others – especially those with very strong opinions or low levels of flexibility – the process of creating new solutions to problems can be challenging. You can use brainstorming techniques to help these people contribute. Brainstorming is a process for rapidly generating and listing options, without clarifying or editing them. Here's how to run a good brainstorming session.

Invite participation

Before you can run a brainstorming session, you need to persuade people to participate. When you're dealing with 'difficult people', this isn't always easy. They may refuse to participate or insist that there is only one solution to the problem – theirs. In these situations, you can use the following phrases to encourage participation.

- Do you agree we need to sort this out?
- I'd really like to clear this up. How about you?
- The benefits to you of solving this problem are _____. On the other hand, the costs of not solving it are _____. Can you afford not to participate in finding a solution?
- If we don't sort this out today, how much of your time/energy will this problem waste?
- I can see you really care about the issue. You've a lot to gain by working it out.
- So far we've agreed that _____. It won't take much effort to fully sort this out.
- If you don't want to participate in the brainstorm, who could represent you? We wouldn't want you to miss out on having a say in the solution.

Pose a focus question

It's important to start a problem solving session with a good question. This encourages everyone to step 'outside' the problem. For example, imagine that team of co-workers arguing about who is leaving mess in the kitchen. They won't find solutions while they're playing the blame game. They'll need to stop using aggressive tactics and take a collaborative problem-solving approach. Their first step is to frame a question they need to answer – 'how can we keep the kitchen tidy?'

Set guidelines for working together

Next you need to ensure you work co-operatively. To do this, it is useful to set some guidelines about how you're going to work together. Use these to keep the conversation positive and outcome-focussed. If you start criticizing each other's ideas as they emerge, your conversation will soon get bogged down. Criticism often sparks difficult and toxic behavior. You won't find solutions to the conflict if you're being critical, because you'll be back in the conflict. Don't resort to annoying behaviors such as nit-picking, nagging or unfairly criticizing. Instead, focus on solving the problem collaboratively.

You may find it helpful to think in terms of attacking the problem, not each other.

Generate as many ideas as you can

Step three of collaborative problem solving is coming up with as many ideas as possible. Think quantity, not quality. The more ideas you find, the more possibilities for positive action you create. You'll often find that your first ideas aren't very original. It takes time to get into full creative thinking mode. So take as long as you need to build a long list of options. Forget about logic at this point. Instead, focus on coming up with the wildest, most outrageous ideas you can. Just because you've thought of them, doesn't mean you have to put them into action.

Assess your ideas

Step four is to switch to logical mode. Now that you have a long list of creative ideas, you can use logic to identify the viable options. Assess the viability of each solution together. Compare your options in terms of costs and benefits for each side. Highlight the ideas that meet multiple needs. Select the options that get the best results for each person. And remember that you can use more than one option. Resist the temptation to cut your options list back to one idea. Instead, work out how to combine three or four ideas. This will build a truly creative action plan.

Example of how SAFE conversation works

Here's an example of a feedback conversation between a supervisor and a staff member that demonstrates the SAFE process in action.

Lucy: I noticed that the service desk opened ten minutes late today and yesterday because you arrived at work late both days. That meant customers were left waiting for the desk to open. The desk needs to open promptly every day. How can we make sure that happens?

Leo: This is all because you changed the roster without talking to me first. I have to drop my kids at preschool on Tuesdays and Wednesdays. Everybody knows that. When Anne was in charge of the roster, she never scheduled me to start at 9.00. She left you a note about it, so don't try to blame me. This is all because you've messed up the roster. I'm doing the best I can to be here on time, and I was only five minutes late each day.

Lucy: So you're saying Tuesdays and Wednesdays are bad days for you to open the desk?

Leo: Of course they are.

Lucy: It sounds like you thought I knew about your arrangement with Anne. So you must have been annoyed when you saw this week's roster.

Leo: Yes, I was.

Lucy: I'm happy to be flexible with the rostering, as long as the service desk is covered at 9.00 each day. My problem is that Jan is on leave for three months and the roster needs to be adjusted. How much flexibility do you have with dropping off your kids?

Leo: Well, I can change my drop-off days if I have a week's notice.

Lucy: So you need to know a full week ahead if you're going to be rostered on a Tuesday or Wednesday?

Leo: Actually, I can sort things out if I know by Thursday each week.

Lucy: Okay, I'll keep that in mind. You need to know your schedule by Thursday each week. And whenever possible, you'd prefer your 9.00 desk shifts to be scheduled for Mondays, Thursdays or Fridays.

In this scenario, Lucy did not fight back when Leo spoke to her in fight mode. Instead, she responded from an alright position.

How to prepare for your SAFE conversation

Planning ahead can help you keep a potentially explosive conversation SAFE. Here is a template you can use to plan what to say at each stage of SAFE.

1. What is the issue you need to discuss?

_____

_____

_____

2. Describe that issue in neutral words.

_____

_____

_____

3. Write down a sentence you can use to raise the issue without triggering a defensive reaction.

_____

_____

_____

4. List some questions you can use to draw out the other person's thoughts on the issue.

_____

_____

_____

_____

5. List some questions you can use to draw out the other person's feelings on the issue.

_____

_____

_____

_____

6. Write two sentences you can use to describe your own thoughts on the issue (without using 'you').

_____

_____

_____

_____

7. Write two sentences you can use to describe your own feelings on the issue (without using 'you').

_____

_____

_____

_____

8. List three sentences you can use to invite the other person to collaborate in solving the problem.

_____

_____

_____

_____

_____

_____

9. Write down a focus question you can use to start the brainstorming process.

_____

_____

_____

_____

CHAPTER FOUR

KEEPING BOUNDARIES HEALTHY WITH ACE STATEMENTS

▶ When you hold a SAFE conversation, you're being truly respectful. You're balancing respect for the other person and their boundaries with self-respect and a healthy regard for your own boundaries. But many 'difficult people' don't know how to reciprocate. They demand respect from you but seem unwilling or unable to extend the same to you. In situations like this, you need to know how to assert and maintain your own boundaries. This chapter teaches you how to do that, using a formula called ACE.

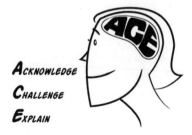

*A*CKNOWLEDGE

*C*HALLENGE

*E*XPLAIN

How to use ACE statements to assert your boundaries

You'll remember from Chapter Two that boundaries are markers of your personal territory. Asserting your boundaries prevents hard-to-handle people from invading your physical or emotional space.

You don't have to silently tolerate invasions of your physical or psychological space. Nor do you need to aggressively fight them.

By learning to set appropriate boundaries from the alright position, you can defend yourself from others' problem behavior. Healthy boundaries help define how you want to be treated by others. They keep you safe, both psychologically and physically.

For example, Tam works in the call centre of a software company. He and his co-workers deal with irate customers on a daily basis. Some of those customers can be downright abusive. They are demanding, critical and spiteful – quite willing to shout or threaten in order to get their own way. Most of Tam's colleagues find these customers difficult to deal with. Often, they'll be stressed and exhausted by the end of a long day on the phone. But Tam is different. He doesn't take his customers' difficult behavior personally. Even when a client resorts to abuse or hurling personal insults, Tam manages to stay relaxed and respond from an 'alright' position. He has a reputation for being a star performer and someone who is excellent at calming angry customers.

That's because Tam has healthy psychological boundaries. He doesn't take customers' words personally. He draws a distinction between his own and others' emotions.

When a customer says, 'What sort of moron are you?' Tam ignores the personal remark and listens for the customer's true message. That message might be, 'I'm not getting the answer I need' or, 'I just want a solution, quickly!'

Tam lets the insult pass and deals with the customer's real issue as quickly as possible. Not only does this calm the customer down, it helps Tam stay stress-free and maintain his assertive mindset. Tam is in control of how he feels and what he thinks. He decides when to verbally respond to boundary invasions and when to let them pass. And he knows how to use the ACE formula to speak up when he needs to.

▸ Find out more about using ACE statements in my video *How to set boundaries and limits* at http://difficultpeoplemadeeasy.com.

Using ACE statements to stop boundary invasions

ACE is a three-step process for setting and reinforcing your boundaries.

Because the three steps of ACE are easy to remember and use in high stress situations, ACE is useful in a wide range of situations.

When should you use ACE statements?

ACE is particularly useful for responding to other people who are highly critical, demanding, pushy or intent on getting answers to inappropriate questions.

You should use ACE statements whenever you need to set limits on another person's behavior. For example, you could respond to any of the following situations with an ACE statement.

▸ Someone blaming you for the way they're feeling.
▸ Dealing with an energy vampire who emotionally exhausts or drains you.
▸ Working with a seemingly 'difficult' boss who insists that things be done their way and then blames you when things go wrong.
▸ Receiving a request to borrow money from a 'difficult' co-worker, who you don't trust will pay you back.
▸ Being barraged with invasive questions about your personal life, which you really don't want to answer.
▸ Wanting to stand up for yourself, but feeling worried this will result in other people disliking you.
▸ Saying 'no' to others' demands on your time, when you have no time for yourself.
▸ Preventing other people from sapping your energy.

The purpose of asserting your boundaries in such situations is to reduce your stress and limit emotional or physical damage. ACE statements help you find the right words to deal with tricky situations, which in the past you might have handled from a fight, flight or spite position.

Remember that maintaining your psychological boundaries is crucial to building healthy relationships. It also prevents you from becoming enmeshed in dysfunctional relationships. It is vital for *negotiation* within relationships. For example, imagine that you are working in a professional role that requires a lot of skills. You believe your boss is taking advantage of you. He delegates complex tasks to you while he heads out for long lunches with his friends. You end up working back every night because of the excessive workload your boss throws at you.

Often, too, your boss assigns menial tasks to you, which you shouldn't really be doing – like going to the shop to buy his lunch, or picking up his laundry. You feel your expertise is being undermined. What should you do to deal with his difficult behavior? Set clear boundaries by saying something like, 'I feel uncomfortable doing your personal tasks, such as picking up your laundry. Can we talk about what's in the scope of my job and what isn't?'

Although this might seem confronting to do, it is a very important way of communicating your needs. As you 'draw the line', your boss will begin to rethink his behavior.

When dealing with upsetting behavior, boundary setting lets you separate your own thoughts and feelings from those of 'difficult people'. Having clear boundaries means you feel more in control of what you think, feel and do. You're able to communicate limits around what you're prepared to do, in an appropriate way. And you can respond appropriately to swearing or verbal abuse. Healthy boundaries are what you use to manage the expectations of highly demanding people. And you can use boundary setting to say 'no' from an alright position.

TREVOR HAD TAKEN BOUNDARY
SETTING TOO FAR.

How do you structure an ACE statement?

Because ACE statements consist of three parts, you structure them in three steps. First, you acknowledge the other person's positive intent. Second, you challenge their boundary-violating behavior. Third, you explain the behavior you'd prefer they use in future. Always remember to manage your own state of mind before wording your ACE statement. This will ensure that each part of your statement comes across as calm and assertive.

Here are some tips on carrying out each step of the ACE process.

1. Acknowledge positive intent

Step one of ACE is letting the other person know you understand where they're coming from. This doesn't mean you're agreeing with what they're doing or saying. It just means you're starting your statement from a positive position.

Aim to keep your message positive. Do this by acknowledging the *positive intention* behind another person's behavior. This is the reason why the other person is resorting to their challenging behavior. To you, their actions might not appear to be positive. But to them, their actions serve a purpose. This purpose is their intent.

For example, nagging is a behavior used by someone who cares about getting things done. By focussing on their positive intention, you can challenge their behavior in a palatable way. Thus, you might start your message with the words, 'I know you really care about getting this project completed on time. And I'm also committed to the deadline.'

Framing your message in this way allows the other person to maintain their dignity. Therefore, it minimizes the risk that the conversation will become inflamed.

To find the positive intent of any negative behavior, ask yourself the following questions.

▸ What result does this person want to achieve?
▸ If I were this person, what would my motivation be?

If your answer to either of these questions is something similar to, 'They want to hurt me', look beneath the surface and question the reason.

▸ What would 'hurting' me achieve for them?
▸ What will they gain from hurting me?
▸ How is hurting me useful for them?

This will reveal their true motivation, which is usually about self-protection. For example, hurting others is often a sign that someone has very low self-esteem. The benefit they gain from behaving hurtfully is that they feel powerful when their actions reap results. This isn't a positive result for *you*, but it is a positive result for them.

2. Challenge their behavior

In the second stage of the ACE process, you need to clearly describe the person's *behavior*. This keeps the conversation flameproof and neutral. Imagine you're holding up a mirror in order to show them exactly what they're doing. Make sure you use specific language here. Briefly outline exactly what the other person is saying or doing. Be careful to focus on what you saw or heard – this is evidence the other person can't dispute. Consider some ways to start your message.

- I saw you …
- I heard you …
- I noticed …
- When you …, I noticed…

It's crucial that you avoid using judgemental language during the challenge phase of ACE. For example, a non-judgemental message might be, 'I notice you often tell me about your problems with other members of the team.' This is a far more objective message than, 'You're always bitching about someone.'

The hard-to-handle person may not like hearing either message, but the factual statement is less likely to spark an amygdala reaction and send them into fight, flight or spite mode.

After you've described the problematic behavior, explain the consequences the behavior has *for you*. For example, consider saying something like, 'Talking about my colleagues behind their backs makes me feel uncomfortable.' Remember to also use non-judgemental words during this part of your boundary statement. Here are some phrases to use when doing this:

- As a result …
- This is causing …
- … makes me feel …
- I feel … when …

- What this means for me is …
- This impacts on me by …

Remember that when you challenge boundary invasions, you're giving feedback on *words* or *actions* that make you feel uncomfortable. The way you frame and deliver feedback has an impact on how 'difficult people' react to it.

It's wise to keep interpretive, emotional words out of the conversation. Instead, focus on spelling out the facts. Always distinguish between what is going on in your head (*interpretation*) and what is actually happening in the real world (*evidence*).

Interpretation	Evidence
John is trying to make me look stupid in front of the team.	When I made a suggestion at the team meeting, John said, 'That's a great idea' in a sarcastic tone of voice.
Maria is self-centred.	In the conversation that just took place, Maria did not seem to be listening to what I was saying because she looked at her watch three times.
Tam is overbearing.	Tam talked more than anyone else in the team meeting. He also interrupted me twice.

3. Explain the desired behavior

Finally, explain what you'd like the other person to do differently in future. Keep your message concrete and focussed on behavioral change. In other words, spell out what the other person can *do* or *say* differently. When someone is talking about a colleague behind that person's back, you might say, 'Please speak to Kim directly rather than telling me about your concerns around her behavior.'

Alternatively, you can outline how *you'll* respond to the difficult behavior in future, making sure you set a firm limit. You might say, 'I prefer not to have these conversations. So in future, if you talk to me about problems with Kim, I'll ask you to stop.'

Example ACE statements for handling fight, flight and spite behaviors

It's important to match your ACE message to the circumstance and to choose words that suit your context. Once you've mastered the basic structure of an ACE statement, change your words to suit your situation and your particular speech patterns. Sticking to a rigid script is rarely useful. Sticking to the intent of ACE – which is to keep the conversation assertive, respectful and solution-focussed – is what matters. Here are some examples of ACE statements that people have used in real-life situations.

ACE statements for dealing with fight-based behavior

- I know you're very concerned about this project. I have answered your questions about my progress three times today. This is preventing me from concentrating on the job. How about we agree on a specific time I can update you later today?
- I can hear that this is very important to you. It is hard for me to solve the problem while you are speaking so loudly and quickly. Let's sit down and discuss options for dealing with this issue.
- Thanks for bringing this to my attention. I can hear that there has been a long-standing issue and you want it sorted out. I'd like to find out what has happened, which will be easier if you answer a couple of questions. Is it okay if we talk through these?

ACE statements for dealing with flight-based behavior

- I know that speaking up in meetings can be challenging. And I also know you have lots of valuable ideas to contribute. I'd like to hear you giving more input during our meetings.
- I know you don't want to get into conflict with Jan. I've also noticed that you have asked me to approach her on your behalf three times now. How about we discuss ways you can raise issues with her yourself?
- I realize talking to angry customers can be challenging. And lately you've referred three customers to me when you could have sorted their issues out at your level. I'd like you to take more time with upset customers rather than diverting them to me straight away.

ACE statements for dealing with spite-based behavior

- I know you believe the new system will cause problems in workflow. I've noticed that you keep bringing up the same issues during team meetings. Since we've already created an action plan for dealing with these issues, I'd like you to contribute ideas for making the new system work rather than focussing on problems.
- I know you don't always agree with what I say in meetings. Lately I've heard you make disparaging remarks during customer meetings, which makes us look unprofessional. In future, I'd like you to keep your comments constructive when we're with customers.
- I can understand you like to do this task in a certain way. I'm finding your tone quite sarcastic when you comment on the way I do it. Since the task is now my responsibility, I would like you to stop commenting on the way I do it.

ACE statement planner

Think of someone who does things that violate your boundaries. Then think of a specific situation in which you felt your boundaries were violated by that person.

What, specifically, did the person do?

_____

_____

_____

Check your description of their behavior. Is it factual and non-judgemental? If not, reword your description to make it more behavior-focussed.

_____

_____

_____

Think of a benefit to *the other person* of their behavior. This is their 'positive intent'.

_____

_____

_____

How did the other person's behavior impact on you?

_____
_____
_____

What would you have preferred them to have done instead of what actually happened?

_____
_____
_____

Check your description of your desired behavior change. Is it factual and non-judgemental? If not, reword your description to make it more behavior-focussed.

_____
_____
_____

Now write an ACE statement you could use to discuss the person's behavior with them.

I'd like to talk to you about

_____

Perhaps you intended to

_____

What I saw/heard happen was

_____

And that caused me to think/feel

_____

So I'd like to request that in future, you

_____

CHAPTER FIVE

USING VERBAL ANTIDOTES TO DETOXIFY COMMUNICATION

▶ Now you've mastered the ACE formula, you're ready to learn some more advanced language patterns. These provide specific 'antidotes' to the toxic communication patterns described in Chapter Two. If you want to know exactly how to word your response to a fight, flight or spite attack, the verbal antidote patterns are for you.

How do verbal antidotes work?

Doctors wouldn't use spider antivenin to neutralize the effects of a snake bite. To get the right results, doctors choose the right treatments. And you need to do the same thing. To neutralize toxic communication patterns, you need to choose the right responses, which I call 'verbal antidotes'.

Verbal antidotes help you respond assertively to boundary violations, which are invasions of your emotional or physical space. For example, Susi was a middle-aged participant in one of my conflict management courses. She had a highly critical mother. No matter what Susi did, her mother would complain about it loudly.

This was driving Susi crazy. She was spending hours each day arguing with her mother, then staying awake half the night raging over the criticism. Susi's mother was violating Susi's right to make her own decisions and take autonomous action. Once Susi had mastered the verbal antidote pattern for giving feedback (the WISH statement pattern), she was able to address her mother's behavior from the alright position.

What is a verbal antidote?

A verbal antidote is a language pattern you can use to respond to a toxic communication pattern. You'll remember that there are six main toxic communication patterns. So there are also six verbal antidote patterns. You can actually use any of the antidote patterns in any conversation. However, you'll find it particularly handy to match your responses as follows.

Toxic communication pattern	Verbal antidotes
Verbal intrusion on your personal zone.	'I frames'.
Heart/head mismatch.	'You frames'.
Baiting.	WISH statement.
Personalisation of issues.	Flameproof language.
Perceiving difference as a threat.	Accord statements.
Perceptual distortion.	Spotlight questions.

Using 'I frame' statements to handle intrusions on personal space

When someone verbally intrudes on your personal space, you may be tempted to go into fight, flight or spite mode. Doing this, however, will only escalate the situation. If you want to deal with intrusions on your personal space, you need to speak up for yourself. 'I frame' statements are a tool for doing this assertively and appropriately.

What is an 'I frame'?

'I frame' statements help you tell other people what you think, feel or believe – without inflaming the conversation. They express your thoughts and feelings using first-person language. When you create an 'I frame', you use 'I'-based language. You avoid saying 'we,' 'they,' 'us' or 'you'. This puts you in control of how people perceive what you say.

 'I frame' messages usually open with the word 'I'. For example, any of the phrases below could be used to start an 'I message' when you're talking to someone in fight, flight or spite mode.

- I think …
- I feel …
- I want …
- I believe …
- I have noticed …
- I am concerned …

When should you use an 'I frame'?

You can use 'I frame' statements whenever you want to express confidence in your own position. They help you sound assertive without triggering fight, flight or spite reactions from other people. Even a tough message becomes more palatable when you deliver it using the 'I frame' formula.

Imagine, for example, that you work with a colleague, Tammy, who often operates in fight mode. You're annoyed by Tammy's habit of speaking as if she's representing everyone else's opinion, including yours. You decide to speak up using 'I frame' statements. Here's how the conversation might sound.

Tammy: Of course, no-one on the admin team supports this change..

You: I'd prefer to speak for myself on that, Tammy.

Tammy: You're not saying you agree with this stupid idea, are you?

You: I'm saying I'd like to explain my own position rather than having anyone else do it for me. What I think about the change is …

In this situation, using 'I frame' messages would help you redirect the conversation. It would also allow you to set a boundary without inflaming the situation. Here are some other examples of situations in which an 'I frame' statement would be a useful tool for managing a 'difficult person's' intrusion on your personal space.

▸ Speaking up appropriately when you don't agree with others' plans or ideas.

▸ Dealing with unfair criticism.

▸ Managing that hard-to-handle person who is never satisfied.

▸ Placing limits on the time you spend listening to or doing favors for others, especially those who don't ever help you.

▸ Interacting with someone who often leaves you feeling down.

▸ Expressing your feelings in situations in which you feel uncomfortable.

How do you structure an 'I frame'?

When speaking from the 'I' position, always remember to focus on describing what is happening for you. Talk about what you think, feel, see or hear. This keeps your language neutral and flameproof. There are only two steps involved in creating an 'I frame' message.

1. First, you describe what you think or feel.
2. Second, you either outline why you think or feel that way, or you describe the implications of your thoughts and feelings.

The basic structure of an 'I frame' message therefore follows one of two simple patterns.

1. I think/feel ... because ...
2. I think/feel ... and so ...

▸ See a demonstration of 'I frame' messages in my video *Speak assertively with 'I' statements*. You'll find it on the video page at http://difficultpeoplemadeeasy.com

---

Here are some examples of how these two 'I frame' structures could be used in real life.

- 🗨 I think we need a longer deadline for Xero because we've lost two team members in the last month.
- 🗨 I think some data is missing from this report and so I'd like to review it before we send it to senior management.
- 🗨 I feel unsure about that option because it assumes interest rates will stay the same for the next three years.
- 🗨 I feel worried about implementing these changes because the team has not been trained on the new system yet.

Of course, it's fine to modify the basic 'I frame' structure. As you become more confident in speaking from the 'I' position, you'll vary your language. For example, any of these following phrases can be used to speak from the 'I' position.

- 🗨 I'd like to add something to that.
- 🗨 What I'm thinking is ...
- 🗨 I believe ...
- 🗨 I've noticed ...
- 🗨 My feelings are ...

- My perspective on this is ...
- My opinion is ...
- My experience is ...

Example 'I frame' statements for handling fight, flight and spite behaviors

Always remember that 'I frame' statements are a tool for speaking from the alright position. Your tone of voice and body language will impact on how any 'I'-based message is received. If you shout, point your finger and use blaming intonation while using 'I' language, you will sound as if you're coming from the fight position. So keep your body language congruent with your verbal message.

'I frame' statements for responding to people in fight mode

- I'd prefer to discuss this in a meeting room because we're disturbing other people by talking here.
- I'd like to explain my perspective on this because this is a serious accusation you're making.
- I feel uncomfortable answering you right now because those questions are quite personal.
- I think this needs more discussion because my viewpoint is very different to yours.

'I frame' statements for responding to people in flight mode

- I'd like your opinion on this because you have a lot of expertise in this area.
- I'd prefer you to make your own decision because I have other tasks to attend to.
- I'm uncomfortable hearing so much detail about your personal relationships. I'd prefer we talk about something else right now.
- I prefer not to give advice on personal problems because I'm not qualified to do so.

'I frame' statements for responding to people in spite mode

- I don't feel comfortable listening to jokes about religion. I'd prefer to discuss something else now.
- I believe my weight is a personal matter. So I'd like you to stop commenting on it.

- I felt embarrassed by the comments you made during my presentation. In future, I'd like to receive feedback in private.
- I'm unsure how to take that comment because you sound a bit sarcastic. What are you trying to say?

'I frame' activity

Write an 'I frame' message you could use in the following situations.

1. Your colleague has just asked you how much you earn. You're not comfortable revealing this information.

_____

_____

_____

2. This morning, your boss shouted at you in front of a customer. You don't want this to happen again.

_____

_____

_____

3. Your teammate keeps calling you 'Einstein'. You know he is implying you are stupid.

_____

_____

_____

4. Your co-worker is complaining about your boss. You don't want to continue the conversation.

_____

_____

_____

Using a 'you frame' statement to handle head/heart mismatches

When there is a mismatch in the language two people use, it is difficult to communicate from both perspectives. So if you are speaking in head-based language and your colleague is speaking from the heart position, the relationship can become strained. To stop this happening, you need to show empathy for your colleague's position.

Empathy is the ability to accurately assess and respond to another person's opinions or feelings. Making an empathic statement involves verbally acknowledging the other person's thoughts or emotional state. You don't have to agree that their thoughts or feelings are justified – you simply have to communicate that you've understood them. Using the word 'you' when empathizing makes it clear that you are *acknowledging* the other person's feelings or perspectives rather than supporting them. That's why I suggest using 'you frame' messages whenever you make an empathic statement.

What is a 'you frame'?

A 'you frame' message is a sentence that acknowledges what another person thinks or feels. It is used to express empathy. When you empathize with someone else, you tune into their reality. Doing this helps you connect and build rapport with them. Empathy helps you detect and understand the mindsets or emotions that drive problem behaviors.

Paraphrasing the speaker's own words is the key way to create an empathic 'you frame' statement. For example, an angry customer says, 'This is the third time I've asked you idiots to sort this problem out.' There are a couple of ways you can respond to this comment. You can paraphrase the facts they've communicated by saying, 'You've called us three times and the problem still hasn't been solved.'

Or you can make your response more deeply empathic by reflecting back the *emotion* expressed by the customer. Thus, your response becomes, 'You've called us three times and the problem still hasn't been solved. You're frustrated by the lack of action and want it sorted out now.'

By using a 'you frame' statement, you can create a climate that supports collaborative problem solving, thus minimizing the other person's need to act out anger, frustration or anxiety by resorting to fight, flight or spite power modes.

▶ You can see me demonstrating 'you frame' statements in *How to make reflective statements*. It's on my video page at http://difficultpeoplemadeeasy.com

---

When should you use a 'you frame'?

When empathy is lacking during a difficult conversation, things can rapidly spiral out of control. For example, imagine that you have a problem with your phone bill. You've been overcharged by several hundred dollars. You call the phone company and spend ages on hold. Finally, you speak to a customer service representative. After a long, complicated conversation – during which you are placed on hold several times – you are told the problem has been 'rectified' and the erroneous charge removed.

A week later, your phone is cut off. You call the phone company again. After another long wait, you speak to someone who explains that your account was suspended 'due to non-payment'. Following another long, frustrating conversation, you are informed that the problem has been resolved. Your phone will be working again tomorrow. The next day, your service is still not working. How will you react when you call and speak to yet another customer service representative who appears to take no interest in you as a person? There's every chance you'll become a 'difficult customer'.

This situation demonstrates the danger of neglecting the feeling component during difficult conversations. When people are treated like numbers, they become frustrated and resort to using difficult behavior in order to get their point across. Great communicators know this and avert poor behavior by empathizing before people step into fight, flight or spite mode.

Here are a few examples of specific situations in which you will find 'you frame' messages help you build rapport.

- Someone else is very angry or upset.
- The other person keeps repeating their opinion and insisting they are right.
- You are discussing a problem that is impacting on how the other person feels.
- Feelings such as frustration, sadness or confusion are being expressed by another person.
- You're dealing with someone who finds it hard to express what they're thinking.
- You disagree with what the other person is saying, but want to maintain a respectful relationship.
- The other person has a very strong opinion and you need to acknowledge this.

When I teach people how to use empathic statements in business contexts, someone often asks, 'Why should I empathize with someone who is clearly wrong?'

This question reflects that the speaker is confusing *validation* and empathy. When you validate someone's perspective, you state that it is right. When you empathize with it, you acknowledge that it exists. So empathizing with someone is very different from agreeing with them.

When you make an empathic statement, you're not saying the other person is right to feel or think the way they do. You're simply saying that you *recognize* their emotions or thoughts. At a practical level, there are many reasons why you might choose to empathize when others resort to challenging behaviors.

Remember that empathy is also different from sympathy. The key difference lies in where you place your boundaries. When you empathize with someone else, you draw a clear line between your own feelings and theirs. When you sympathize with them, you fail to make the distinction. This results in you 'catching' the other person's feelings. You experience the same emotions that they do.

When you're dealing with highly emotional or opinionated people, sympathizing with them can cause problems. For example, if your problem boss is stressed and you 'catch' their stress, this isn't healthy for either of you. So it's important that you empathize rather than sympathize.

Remember that when you empathize with someone, you maintain your own perspective while, at the same time, communicating your desire to understand *their* perspective. When you sympathize with someone, you are 'infected' by their feelings. There is no boundary between your feelings and theirs. To ensure that you maintain healthy boundaries with 'problem people', you need to master the art of showing empathy. This is very different to sympathizing or agreeing with them.

How do you structure a 'you frame'?

To create a 'you frame' statement, it helps to divide what you say into two parts. Your first statement should acknowledge what the other person feels or thinks. Your second should communicate that you understand *why* another person is feeling that way. Put together, you get the formula for a basic empathic statement.

▸ **You** feel [emotion] because [description of situation].
▸ **You** think [summary of their opinion] because [description of facts].

Sometimes, you'll need to empathize with someone who has told a long and convoluted story. In this situation, you can use a summarising statement to reflect the key points they've made. Do this by starting your statement with, '**You're** saying ...'

As you've just seen, you can use 'you frame' statements to acknowledge feelings, thoughts or essential facts. Which element you target will depend on the context. If someone is highly emotional, empathize with their feelings. If they're expressing an opinion, reflect back the main facts they've talked about. When they're telling a complicated story, mentally sort out the relevant facts from the non-essential details. Then summarize the key point their story communicates. Here are some examples.

They say	You need to acknowledge	You can say
I can't believe Jan didn't invite me to the Awards Night, after all I've done for her team.	Feelings	You feel hurt because Jan left you off the invitation list.
There have been a lot of holdups on the technical side of the project. To meet the brief, we'll need another month.	Thoughts	You think we need an extra month to complete the project because of the technical problems we've encountered.
Penny won't have enough people on staff next week. Bill's on holiday overseas. Julie is still on secondment. She'll be away for another three weeks. And Roxanne is working the evening shift.	Essential facts	You're saying Penny will need extra staff next week because of staff movements.

As the above examples show, the structure for a 'you frame' statement is formed in two parts. Part one acknowledges what the other person is feeling, thinking or believing. Part two acknowledges *why* they're feeling, thinking or believing that. Here are some phrases you can use to structure your empathic statements.

- I imagine you feel … because …
- Right now, you're thinking … because …
- You believe … because …
- Your opinion is that … You think this because …
- When [event] happened, you felt [emotion].
- Let me check that I understand how you feel about …
- Sounds like when … happened … you felt …
- I have a sense that you think/feel … because …
- You must be feeling …
- Am I right in understanding that you feel/think …
- Part of you wants to [action] but another part of you wants to [action].
- That feels really …
- It seems to me that …
- I imagine that would feel/be …
- I can see that you are [emotional state].

Example 'you frame' statements for handling fight, flight and spite behaviors

It's important to match your message to your listener and to choose words that suit your context. So once you've mastered the basic structure of a 'you frame' statement, you can change your words to suit your situation. Here are some examples of 'you frame' statements people have used in real-life situations for the different fight, flight and spite modes of communication.

'You frame' statements for responding to people in fight mode

- Because you haven't received a confirmation email, you're worried that your application has been lost.
- You feel left out because you weren't invited to join the working party.
- You're angry because Meredith left her work unfinished when she went on holiday and now you have to do it.

'You frame' statements for responding to people in flight mode

- There's been so much going on, you feel overwhelmed.
- You're confused about which product to buy because there are so many.
- You believe Geoff is bullying you because he frequently criticizes your written work.

'You frame' statements for responding to people in spite mode

- You don't really sound like you think that's a good idea even though you said 'great idea'.
- Because you've ignored my greeting three times this week, I'm getting the sense you're upset with me.
- Because you rolled your eyes when I asked you to do that task, I'm getting the impression you don't want to do it.

'You frame' activity

Write a 'you frame' statement to empathize with the speaker's *feelings* in the three situations below.

1. Margaret has gone on leave without finishing her work. And now I'm expected to pick up after her.

You feel

_____

_____

because

_____

_____

2. I've been offered a promotion at work. I'd like the extra pay. But I don't want the extra stress.

You feel

_____

_____

because

_____

_____

3. Carlos is a total control freak. He's always telling me what to do.

You feel

_____

_____

because

_____

_____

Write a 'you frame' statement to empathize with the speaker's *thoughts* in the three situations below.

1. We need to get organized. Let's decide on the venue for the end of year party this week. Otherwise all the good places will be booked.

You think

_____

_____

because

_____

_____

2. The website layout is too confusing. It needs to be redesigned so that customers can find the products they need with only one click.

You think

_____

_____

because

_____

_____

3. A direct mail campaign will cost too much. We'll get twice the results for half the price if we concentrate on digital marketing. But management are stuck in the past, so they're insisting we use direct mail.

You think

_____

_____

because

_____

_____

Write a 'you frame' statement to summarize the _key points_ the speaker is making in the situation below.

1. We need someone to cover the reception desk next Monday and Tuesday because Jo and Sara are going to a conference. It turns out the casual can't come in because he's working on an assignment. Normally we could ask the accounts staff to help out, but they have a team planning day on Monday and on Tuesday they'll need to catch up with Monday's enquiries. Maybe I should change my roster and take Friday off instead of Monday?

You're saying

_____

_____

_____

Using WISH statements to handle baiting

As you'll remember, baiting is a form of psychological game-playing. The point about psychological games is that they are based on predictable patterns of behavior. The 'difficult person' delivers their message, expecting you to react in a way that maintains the game. Here are some examples.

Bait	Anticipated Reaction
Your co-worker criticizes you.	You become upset and defend yourself.
Your boss makes a sarcastic remark about you arriving late.	You arrive on time in future.
A customer screams at you when you set a boundary based on your organization's policy.	You ignore policy and give them what they want.
Your colleague complains that they have no time to process a task with a tight deadline.	You 'rescue' them and help them complete the task.

It's worth noting that game-playing behavior is very easy to deal with. If you fail to give the anticipated reaction, you'll interrupt the game. So when someone baits you, aim to interrupt their game by giving an unanticipated response. This will prevent the game continuing.

For example, an irate customer wants a refund of goods that he's already used. He shouts that he is going to report the situation to Consumer Affairs. His words are designed to trigger the flight reaction. He's expecting the shop owner to react by backing down and giving him what he wants. If she doesn't do this, the store owner will have interrupted the customer's game. Here are some alternative reactions the store owner could use in this situation.

- Agreeing that the customer has every right to make a complaint and handing him the store's complaint form.
- Giving the customer Consumer Affairs' phone number and web address, and at the same time outlining the basis on which claims can be made.
- Giving the customer three alternative options for dealing with the situation.
- Inviting the customer to leave the store now and return when he's willing to talk more collaboratively.
- Telling the customer she doesn't care what he does next.

Obviously, some of these responses will de-escalate the situation and others will inflame it. The point is that all of them would disrupt the customer's game-playing.

What is a WISH statement?

A WISH statement is a sentence structure for expressing your perspective, needs, feelings or concerns. It helps you speak from the 'I' perspective. The aim of speaking from this position is to prevent other people being triggered into fight, flight or spite reactions. WISH statements tell other people where you're coming from, without blaming or shaming them or inflaming the situation.

An effective WISH statement has four parts. It has the added benefit of being easy to remember because WISH is a mnemonic for the first word used in each section of the statement. A WISH statement uses the formula:

'When _____ happens, it causes [me to feel or _____to happen].

So I'd like _____. How can we achieve this?

WHEN...

IT CAUSES...

SO I'D LIKE...

HOW CAN WE...?

WISH statements help you speak up in tough situations. For example, if someone is baiting you into an argument by criticizing you unfairly, you can use a WISH statement to let them know you want them to stop. Or if someone is attempting to make you feel guilty so they can manipulate you into doing what they want, you can assertively expose their game playing.

▸ Watch my video *Speaking assertively with 'I' statements* to find out more about WISH. Go to the video page at http://difficultpeoplemadeeasy.com

---

When should you use a WISH statement?

If you dread having tough conversations in order to handle baiting behavior, you're not alone. Most people feel nervous during a conversation that may create conflict or trigger emotions such as embarrassment or anger. These nerves may sometimes cause you to procrastinate and move into flight mode rather than sort out an issue. In all of these situations, however, it is far wiser to act than to rationalize.

For example, imagine your colleague, Tony, is causing some problems. He makes lots of personal phone calls from his desk during work hours. During these calls, he seems to be fighting with his wife.

He becomes highly agitated, raises his voice and swears. When he hangs up, he starts complaining to you about how stupid his wife is. He obviously wants you to take his bait and ask what is wrong.

You feel embarrassed to be overhearing such personal conversations. You're offended by Tony's language and feel anxious about the way he is speaking to his wife. You're also angry that his conversations are distracting you from your work. It's time to speak up. But you're worried that if you say something, Tony will turn the force of his aggression on you.

There are a million and one ways you can rationalize staying silent in this situation. A rationalization is a story you tell yourself about why you are doing something (or not doing anything). When you rationalize, you explain your behavior or decisions in ways that justify them to yourself. For example, someone who is on a diet might rationalize eating a large slice of cake by thinking, 'It's only one piece. And I didn't each much for lunch today.' They know they shouldn't eat the cake, but they find a reason to do it anyway.

Rationalizations help you feel good about yourself. They are normal. But they can also reinforce the passive thinking associated with being in flight mode. When you rationalize about staying silent, you are making a decision to put up with bad behavior. The most common rationalizations I hear people using for not speaking up about boundary violations or baiting behaviors are listed below. When you find yourself thinking any of these, it is time to make a WISH statement.

▸ I don't want to hurt his/her feelings.
▸ He/she won't listen to me anyway.
▸ He/she has a really bad temper. I'd better not risk setting off a tantrum.
▸ I can't stand up to my boss. I'll get sacked if I do.
▸ Saying something would be rude, so I can't say anything.
▸ I spoke up before and it didn't work.

When you think about it, long-term exposure to baiting is far more damaging to you than the temper tantrum a 'difficult person' *might* throw when you speak up. You need to stand up and speak out.

WISH statements are a great tool for speaking up assertively when someone is baiting you or your boundaries are being invaded. Most importantly, they help you communicate your thoughts, feelings, needs and acceptable boundaries. Using a WISH statement is all about speaking up for yourself without invading someone else's boundaries.

You are the expert on *you*. This means you know what you need or want better than anyone else does. No one else can read your mind. By communicating your needs and desires assertively, you are letting 'difficult people' know that you are your own person.

Using the WISH formula to structure self-disclosure statements stops you being 'struck dumb' when 'difficult people' bait you in order to test your boundaries. It enables you to know what to say to stand up for yourself, even in high stress situations. When you use WISH statements, it's easier to prevent 'difficult people' reacting badly when you speak your mind. WISH statements keep your language neutral and objective so you don't shame or blame anyone when speaking about what matters to you. Mastering WISH statements will build your reputation as a highly skilled communicator – someone who speaks up assertively when boundaries are crossed.

WISH statements can be used to raise problems or give feedback in a safe way. They can also be employed to clearly communicate your 'inner perspective'. By sharing your feelings and thinking processes, you allow others – including 'problem people' – to have more understanding about you as an assertive person. You can use WISH statements for raising touchy issues, explaining your position during conflicts, giving feedback and setting boundaries with 'difficult people'.

How do you structure a WISH statement?

WISH statements work best when you express your position using the principles of a SAFE conversation. Keep your focus on behaviors and actions, not attitudes or personality characteristics. Be honest about what you feel and think – but also keep your message respectful and appropriate. Never make someone feel you are shaming them.

Your WISH statement starts with a behavior-focussed description of what is happening. It then outlines the consequences of that behavior (which can be either feelings or practical implications). The third section of the WISH statement is a description of what you want to happen to address the problem. This can either be a specific solution, or a request for a problem-solving discussion. The final segment of the WISH statement invites input from the other person (because involvement in creating solutions promotes buy-in to actioning them).

Here's a bit more information about what to do in each part of your WISH statement.

Note: There's also a WISH statement planning template at the end of this section, which you can use to prepare for tough conversations in advance.

1. Part one: When

The opening phrase of the WISH statement describes – in objective language – the issue that concerns you. It's important to keep this part of your WISH statement specific and non-judgemental. Remember to focus on describing things you can *see* or *hear* because this keeps your language flameproof. Let's go back to the imaginary problem with Tony (the colleague who is abusing his wife over the phone during work hours). You could say, 'When I can overhear your personal phone conversations ...'

2. Part two: It causes

In the second section of the WISH statement, you describe the impact of the issue on you or other parties involved in the situation. Choose whether to outline the practical or emotional consequences based on your context. For example, you might describe the practical consequences of Tony's behavior by saying, 'It causes me to lose focus on my work.' Or you might outline your feelings about the situation by saying, 'It causes me to feel uncomfortable.'

You can use the following phrases to start this part of the WISH statement.
- It causes me to feel ...
- It causes us to look ...
- It causes problems because ...
- It causes other persons/other team members problems because ...
- It causes disruption to ...

3. Part three: So I'd like ...

This segment of the WISH statement describes your ideas about how to sort out the situation. You can either suggest a specific course of action, or request that the other person meets with you to discuss the issue. For example, you could say to Tony, 'I'd like to suggest you take your phone outside when you're making personal calls.' Or you might request that Tony collaborate with you to solve the problem by saying, 'I'd like us to discuss ways you can carry on your conversations without me overhearing them.'

You can use the following phrases to get the third section of your WISH statement right.

- I'd like to suggest ...
- I'd like to sort this out by ...
- I'd like us to discuss ...
- I'd like you to consider ways we can ...

4. Part 4: How can we sort this out?

The final part of your WISH statement invites the other person to work with you in resolving the situation.

This is an important step because it ensures commitment to the action plan. Remember that good communication involves dialogue and this section of your WISH statement makes this clear. For example, you could say to Tony, 'How can we make time to sort this out?' This signals to Tony that you don't want to tell him what to do, but you're serious about solving the problem.

Here are some other effective phrases you can use to finish off your WISH statement.

- How can we sort this out?
- How do you think we should do this?
- How can we make time to discuss this?
- How can we get a positive outcome here?
- How can we resolve this?

Example WISH statements

In high stress situations, you don't want to sound like a computer spitting out a formulaic response. So you can play with the wording of your WISH statement. As long as you stick to the intention – being honest and appropriate in expressing your perspective – you can rearrange the parts of your WISH statement to fit your context. Here are some examples that my students have created during workshops on dealing with difficult behavior at work.

WISH statements to use with fight-based communicators

- **When** I am interrupted halfway through what I'm saying, **it takes** the conversation off track. **So I'd like** to finish what I have to say before taking comments. **How can** you keep track of your questions so you remember them at the end of my presentation?
- **When** arguments happen during team meetings, **it causes** us to lose focus. **So I'd like** us to be more collaborative about resolving differences of opinion. **How can** we address our concerns without arguing?
- **When** my work is criticized in front of the team, **it causes** me to become so anxious that I can't understand what you want. **So I'd prefer** to meet with you once a week and talk through your feedback rather than receiving it on the run. **How can** we set up a way to do that?

WISH statements to use with flight-based communicators

- **When** we're brainstorming and only two or three people contribute, **it causes** us to lose momentum. **So I'd** like to hear you contributing more. **How can** we make sure you feel comfortable doing that?
- **When** I find out at the last minute that a critical task won't be completed to deadline, **it means** I can't adjust our schedule. **So I'd like** to receive early notice when a task is behind schedule. **How can** we ensure this happens?
- **When** more than three angry customers are referred to me during a shift, **it causes** me to get behind with my admin tasks. **So I'd like** you to deal with customer complaints at the counter rather than sending them to me. **How can** we get you trained up to do this?

WISH statements to use with spite-based communicators

- **When** the service desk opens late**, it causes** customers to be inconvenienced. **So I'd like** the desk to open punctually each day. **How can** we achieve this?
- **When** reports containing spelling mistakes are circulated, **it causes** the department to look unprofessional. **So I'd like** to review our checking process. **How can** we eliminate errors in future?
- **When** email messages are being written during team meetings, **it causes** us to lose focus. **So I'd like** you to put your phone away during meetings. **How can** you make sure you're not distracted by your phone from now on?

DENISE FINALLY THINKS OF A PERFECT RESPONSE TO ZACK'S POINTED COMMENT.

WISH Statement Planning Tool

What is the behavior or situation you want to address?

For example, you're having to clean up the kitchen because no one else does so.

_____
_____
_____
_____
_____

List the other person's actions or words that concern you.

For example, when they finish lunch, your colleagues leave their plates and cups in the sink. At the end of the day, the dirty dishes are still there.

_____
_____
_____
_____
_____
_____
_____

Describe the issue or behavior in neutral and non-judgemental words.

For example, 'When dirty dishes are left in the sink after lunch ...'

When ...
_____
_____
_____
_____
_____

Outline the impact of the situation or behavior.

For example, '... it causes a mess in the kitchen, which needs to be cleaned up at the end of the day.'

It causes ...
_____
_____
_____
_____
_____

**Suggest a solution to the problem
or request co-operation in solving it
together.**

For example, 'So I'd like us to discuss
ways to keep the kitchen tidy.'

So I'd like ...

_____
_____
_____
_____
_____

Ask for input.

For example, 'How do you suggest we
do this?'

How can we do this?

_____
_____
_____
_____
_____

Using flameproof language when someone personalizes issues

Have you ever tried to solve a problem with someone in fight mode, only to have them fly off the handle? Perhaps they even tried to blame you for their state of mind, claiming that your words were the trigger for their temper tantrum. This is a classic example of what happens when people personalize situations or events.

Personalising a problem involves someone interpreting neutral information as an attack. It happens when people with poor emotion-control take neutral situations personally. They allow messages intended for the professional communication 'zone' to penetrate their personal boundaries.

You may remember that the innermost circle on this diagram represents someone's private psychological space. No-one else is entitled to intrude on this space – it is a fully personal zone. The middle circle symbolizes the emotional space the seemingly 'difficult person' shares with friends or loved ones. It is inappropriate for workplace messages to enter this space.

The outer circle signifies the communication space the 'difficult person' shares with colleagues and customers. The information exchanged within this space is impersonal and neutral. Problem-solving discussions at work should *always* occur within this zone. When you raise a problem with someone who has poor boundary control, however, they may not hear the issue at this level. Instead, they will allow your message to penetrate their personal zone. This will result in a fight, flight or spite reaction.

Defensive reactions are probably a sign of a 'difficult person's' poor self-control. But it is possible to prevent professional messages entering the personal zone in the first place. It's called using flameproof language.

When you use flameproof language, you are speaking from the alright position. You're able to minimize communication barriers and improve work relationships. You convey respect, thus increasing your chances of getting a good outcome in tough situations. Talking to 'problem people' becomes more comfortable. You brand yourself as a person of integrity, authenticity and honesty.

When you start using flameproof language, you'll find it easier to get your point across with power and conviction. You'll know how to say 'no' in an appropriate way. You'll have the skills you need to sort out workplace conflicts without escalating them to management. This will do wonders for your reputation as a skilled employee – it might even lead to a promotion.

What is flameproof language?

Flameproof language is non-inflammatory language. It prevents tempers sparking and conflicts exploding. Flameproof language allows you to say what you perceive, think or feel in ways that are psychologically safe for your listener. When talking to people who are in fight, flight or spite power mode, make sure you focus on one issue at a time and deal with each issue objectively. Keep your language neutral and free of blaming or judging words. Speak about observable facts rather than generalizing or labeling. The more precise your language is, the less likely it is to combust.

Flameproofing your communication works because it enables you to apply that key rule for holding SAFE conversations: avoid shaming and blaming. As you know, many hard-to-manage behaviors are caused by low self-esteem. People with self-esteem issues can be highly reactive to comments they hear as critical, attacking or controlling. Flameproof language is neutral and safe – so it is less likely to trigger a stress reaction in someone with a low sense of self-worth.

Flameproof language is clear, honest, unambiguous and assertive. It comes from an alright position. It is respectful of everybody's boundaries. After all, people who speak from an alright position balance sharing their own views with exploring the views of others. They enjoy sharing their own point of view, as well as finding out what other people think. They are fair, inclusive and respectful in their use of language.

When should you use flameproof language?

Flameproof language can be used to set boundaries on inappropriate workplace behavior, such as bullying. It's also useful when you want to give feedback without triggering defensive reactions. Overall, mastering flameproof language will mean you can express your opinion with appropriate honesty and authenticity.

You can use flameproof language whenever you need to do one of the following.

▸ Deliver feedback – particularly on 'touchy' issues.
▸ Make requests that may trigger defensive reactions.
▸ Express your opinion in situations in which it differs from the majority opinion.
▸ Tell others how you feel.
▸ Present your ideas.
▸ Ask someone to stop a behavior that is violating your boundaries.

How do you structure a flameproof message?

Creating a flameproof message involves using five principles for keeping your words neutral and non-judgemental. You need to avoid trigger words, describe rather than judge, eliminate verbal minimizers, balance honesty and appropriateness and know how to say 'no'.

1. Avoid trigger words

Have you ever witnessed a customer being 'set off' by something a service provider said? Or seen a staff member responding emotionally to a message from their manager? If you have, then you've observed the power of trigger words. Yes. Words are very powerful. Language not only expresses emotion, but it also *triggers feelings*. Some words and phrases are a lot more emotionally charged than others.

For example, notice your reaction when you read the words 'pain' or 'sorrow', or 'joy' or 'love', or 'freedom'. Each word carries a different emotional meaning. As you read each word, you may experience a change in your mood or state of mind. This may only be a sense of warmth or tightness, but it is there at some level.

So words can carry emotional meanings and trigger changes in a person's state. For example, the following phrases will often upset customers.

- Our policy is …
- You made a mistake.
- You have to …
- You can't …
- The computer says I can't do that.
- That's not possible.
- We don't …

All of these phrases convey meanings or implications that can trigger fight or flight reactions. For example, a customer who is triggered by the phrase 'our policy is …' may quickly become enraged. They may think, 'I'm not going to be told what to do by a sales assistant.' They will then begin shouting and arguing – all because the phrasing used by the sales assistant triggered a fight reaction.

To some extent, trigger words are unique to each individual. After all, the meaning assigned to a word depends on someone's mindset.

However, some words are more likely than others to trigger negative states. You'd be well advised to avoid using these in heated situations. Equally, there are words that carry positive connotations for many people – these can be used deliberately to keep conversations running smoothly.

Here are some examples.

Negative triggers	Positive triggers
No	Yes
But	And
Penalty	Solve
Mistake	Resolve
Must	Choice
Have to	Can
Should have	Help/assist
Can't	Immediately
Transfer you to	Discount
Policy	Free

Overall, remember to use positively-packed words and avoid negatively-packed words.

2. Describe, don't judge

Communicating from the alright position often involves exchanging feedback. And effective feedback is concrete and specific. It describes exactly *what* someone is doing or saying – without passing judgement on *why* they are doing or saying it. For example, there's a big difference between saying, 'You're so disorganized' and, 'You've arrived late to team meetings three weeks in a row.' The first statement is hostile and comes from a fight power position. The second is fact-based and honest. It comes from the alright position.

To make your feedback useful, focus on describing two things. Start with a description of what you see or hear happening now (present state). Then describe what you'd like to see or hear in the future (desired state). For example, 'When you were speaking to that irate customer, I heard your voice speeding up and getting louder. That seemed to irritate them. In future, you might find it helps to keep your voice at a normal pace and to speak in a calm tone.'

Notice that the above feedback was clear and specific. It described exactly what was going wrong, as well as providing concrete steps for change. It was helpful feedback, not criticism. The difference between feedback and criticism is that feedback can be actioned. It clearly spells out what *behavior* needs to change. It also provides tips for how to change.

Always keep your feedback neutral, concrete and specific by talking about observable behaviors – what you *saw* happen or *heard* the 'difficult person' say. Don't use 'summary' words, which interpret behaviors and imply that you are judging the other person's behavior.

Summary words include generalizations such as 'poor attitude', 'sloppy', 'rude', 'negative', 'arrogant' or 'poor team player'. These are not useful words to use in feedback because they do not describe the person's actions. They are vague and non-specific. Good feedback is concrete and addresses observable actions. For example, 'poor attitude' might involve observable actions such as 'leaving difficult tasks unfinished' or 'arguing in meetings' or 'raising problems without suggesting ways to solve them'.

To keep your language factual, try starting your sentences with the following phrases.

- I saw …
- I heard …
- I felt …
- I noticed …
- I'd like to explain how this impacts on me …
- When I heard/saw …, I got the impression …
- When you said …, I felt …

3. Eliminate verbal minimizers

Words like 'only' and 'just' and 'it would be great if …' are verbal minimizers. They undermine the significance or meaning of your message, implying that what you're saying isn't really important. This can destroy the effectiveness of your message. It can make people switch off and fail to listen to you. Even when people do listen, they are unlikely to take your message seriously if it contains a lot of minimizers.

For example, imagine your boss giving you this feedback.

'There's just one thing I'd suggest might make you a better team player. It would be great if you could try to improve your punctuality and time keeping. Maybe you could put some effort into arriving earlier. Perhaps you can catch an earlier bus or something.'

Would you know what you're expected to change? You're much more likely to understand the situation – and take it seriously – if the boss says, 'I would appreciate you being on time for meetings in future.'

Stand by your opinions and statements. Other people can take advantage of you if you seem to lack self-confidence and self-assurance. Remember that there are no 'ifs and buts' in the language of an assertive communicator. Aim to speak directly and to give the impression you are confident in what you say. Speak from the alright power position. Here are some minimizing phrases to avoid if you want to speak from an alright position.

- Perhaps …
- Should we …
- This is just a suggestion, but …
- Sorry to interrupt, but …
- Maybe …
- How about trying …
- You might have already thought of this, but …
- Maybe this is a silly idea, but …

4. Balance honesty and appropriateness

To speak from the alright position, you need to be both honest and appropriate at the same time. An honest message is one in which you tell the truth. But you need to be careful about how you word 'honest' statements. Honest messages that are short or abrupt can come across as fight-based communications. They can sound too direct or pushy, thus triggering other people to react with difficult behavior.

This is why it's important to combine honesty with *appropriateness* when you're talking from the alright position. Imagine, for example, that someone who often shouts in order to get their way asks you, 'Do you think I am aggressive?' An honest answer would be, 'Yes, I do'. However, this answer may seem abrupt or critical. You would be better off giving a more appropriate and behavior-based answer. In other words, you would be well advised to give flameproof feedback.

An appropriate message is framed in a way that fits your context. It also matches the needs of the person you are talking to. It is honest – but it is also respectful of others' boundaries. An appropriate answer to the question, 'Do you think I am aggressive?' might be, 'When you get excited, you speak very loudly. Often it sounds like you're shouting, which can seem aggressive. How do you want to sound?'

Appropriately honest messages turn generalizations into specific, behavior-based content. Doing this involves five steps.

First, you make a mental note of your overall impression. Then you observe what you see or hear that creates that impression. Next, you describe those details to the other person. You then explain the impression their behavior creates. Finally, you let them decide what to do with your feedback. Here's an example of applying this process to a tricky question.

Example of response to *that* question, Does my bum look big in this dress?	
Your overall impression	Yes, her bum does look big in that dress.
What you see or hear that creates that impression	The fabric is bunched at the waist and hangs badly from the waist down.
Description of details	'The fabric is bunched at the waist and billows out at the back ...'
Description of impression	'... which makes your backside look larger than it is. The cut seems unflattering to me.'
Handover	'What do you think?'

Always remember that messages that start with 'you' can easily sound critical, judgemental or negative. Many people will hear them as blaming statements – and go straight into fight, flight or spite mode.

For example, consider the reaction a team member would receive if she said to her boss, 'You always cut me out of cross-department meetings.' This sounds whining and accusing. Now consider the flameproof version of this same message: 'I'd like to be included in visits to other departments because I have information to share with them.' This is much more likely to gain a positive reception from the boss.

Here are some useful phrases to get your message across.
- 🗩 I'd like to make a request …
- 🗩 I have some thoughts about this.
- 🗩 I see things differently.
- 🗩 From my perspective, …
- 🗩 I feel concerned about …
- 🗩 I'd like to work out a way to …
- 🗩 I have an idea I'd like to discuss with you.
- 🗩 I've noticed something that concerns me.

5. Know how to say 'no'

Have you ever agreed to do something you really didn't want to do? Or taken on too much because you felt bad saying 'no'? If you do this too often, you will come across as passive, weak or timid. So you need to say 'no' in a confident way. But before you say 'no', you need to believe you have the right to say it.

If you feel uncomfortable turning down requests, remind yourself that saying 'no' to one task makes room to say 'yes' to something more important. For example, saying 'no' to an interruption may give you time to say 'yes' to writing an important report.

Get into the habit of making your 'no' clear and direct. Avoid making excuses or saying, 'I can't' or, 'I shouldn't'. Instead, say, 'I'm not able to fit that in' or, 'I have decided not to …'

Here are some useful phrases for delivering simple, straightforward 'no' messages.
- 🗩 Thanks for asking. I'm not able to take that on right now.
- 🗩 At the moment, I have other priorities.
- 🗩 I can't fit this in right now.
- 🗩 My schedule is too tight to fit this in.
- 🗩 I'll have to say 'no' because I'm working on something else.

In tricky situations, such as saying 'no' to your boss, you can use the 'negotiated no' formula. This lets the other person have input into the final outcome of the discussion while taking into account your workload and priorities. The aim of negotiating the 'no' is to reach an agreement about what will be a workable load for you to carry. You're effectively saying, 'If I take on this new task, I'll have to drop an existing job.' Here are some examples of how to open this type of negotiation.

What to say	When to say it
I'm working on ... right now. Which task would you prefer I do?	Someone in authority has given you two conflicting priorities and you don't have time to work on both.
I can't do this, but I *can* ...	You are short for time, but would like to help out.
My schedule is very tight. As you know, I'm working on Project X and Project Z. So I can't take that on without dropping something else.	You don't want to accept a task or a meeting request.
I don't want to let you down by not meeting the Project X deadline. So I need to say 'no' to this new task.	You are being asked to take on a complex task or project that will involve more time than you have available.
I can do ... if you do ...	The other person is really responsible for the task they are asking you to do.
I'm unable to commit to this because I'm working on ...	You are being asked to do something that is low priority, or urgent but not important.
Now is not a good time. As you know, I'm working on the budget this week. Can it be done by ... ?	The task does need to be done by you, but you don't have time to do it today.
That's not my area of expertise. A better person to help you with this is ...	Someone asks you to do a task that is not your responsibility.

If the other person argues after you've delivered your message, reinforce your 'no' by repeating it politely. Sometimes people need to hear your message three times before they digest it. Try saying, 'So I need to say 'no' to your request' or, 'I can't help you this time'. Show your respect for the other person's request and their right to make it. Doing this firmly but politely helps you uphold your boundaries.

Examples of flameproof language to use with people in fight, flight and spite mode

No matter how another person is behaving, you can always respond from the alright position. Keeping yourself calm and resourceful helps you find exactly the right words to fit your specific situation. You won't find scripts useful when dealing with fight, flight and spite tactics. But you will find it helpful to stick to neutral, non-inflammatory words. Here are some ideas about how to do this.

When to use flameproof sentences	
When people are in fight mode	I think we should sort this out right now. Let's find a meeting room and sit down. This is an important issue. Let's talk about it now. I can help you with this once I fully understand the problem. Please talk me through what has happened.
When people are in flight mode	This is an important project. I'd like to hear your thoughts on the implementation plan. Let's take a moment to think this through together. There are two ways we can improve this report. Let's discuss them now.
When people are in spite mode	I'd like to talk about what happened during the meeting just now. I am always willing to listen to feedback when it is constructive. What's on your mind? Although you say this doesn't matter, I believe it does. Either we can sort it out together or we can ask HR to help us.

Flameproof message planner

Think of something another person has said or done that upset you. Use this as an example for trying out ways to use flameproof language.

List two or three words that might trigger a negative reaction from this person – these are words you'll avoid in your flameproof statement.

_____

_____

_____

List two or three words that are likely to *appeal* to this person – you'll use these words in your flameproof statement.

_____

_____

_____

Write a short description of exactly what the other person said or did.

_____

_____

_____

_____

Read over the description you wrote above. Cross out any words that imply you're judging the other person.

Next, cross out any words that might trigger a fight, flight or spite reaction.

Check that your description communicates what the other person has said or done in purely factual language.

Choose a phrase to start your flameproof statement from the 'I' position:

- I'd like to make a request.
- I've noticed …
- I feel concerned about …
- I've noticed something that concerns me.
- I'd like to give you some feedback.

Now write down exactly what you'd say if you were giving feedback to the other person. Remember to start with the phrase you selected from the previous list and include some of the words that will appeal to the other person.

_____

_____

_____

_____

Check that you have not used any words that might trigger a negative reaction.

Using accord statements when someone perceives difference as a threat

Racism, sexism and ageism are all examples of mindsets that kick in when people perceive difference as threatening. When you're dealing with people with mindsets like these, there's no point in launching into a lecture on diversity. This will only make matters worse because it will increase their insecurity. So you need to be smart. Tackle their offensive behavior from the alright position. And, whenever possible, highlight ways in which you're similar to them. Accord statements help you do this.

What is an accord statement?

Accord statements are sentences that highlight areas of agreement. They work by drawing attention to common ground and are particularly useful for dealing with people who use 'us and them' style thinking. For example, during labor negotiations, a union representative might say, 'Management have shown no interest in maintaining a safe working environment for staff.'

In response, management's representative might say, 'In fact, we agree that health and safety are primary concerns. Let's discuss how we can provide a suitably safe environment and reach our productivity targets as well.'

Did you notice the way this response was structured in two parts? First, the management representative expressed agreement with the union representative's key concern (health and safety). Then she moved into solution-seeking mode. This redirects attention and sets a new course for the negotiation.

When should you use accord statements?

You can use accord statements whenever you're dealing with someone who feels threatened by difference. You can also use them to reduce conflict or calm down people who are complaining about problems or perceived inequities.

For example, one Saturday morning I saw an events co-ordinator dealing with a very angry customer. The customer had misread his course enrolment paperwork. This meant he'd missed the first Saturday of the two-day course he'd enrolled in. He'd turned up on day two, thinking it was day one.

Rather than simply attending that day's session – which he was perfectly entitled to do – the customer wanted a full refund of course fees on the spot. The events co-ordinator was not authorized to issue refunds. Since it was a weekend, the request could not be escalated until Monday. The events co-ordinator suggested the customer fill in a special circumstances form, on which he could record his request for a refund.

The customer slammed his fist on the reception counter and shouted, 'This is ridiculous. I'm not filling in anything. It was a genuine mistake. I'm entitled to a refund.'

His enraged tone suggested that he wasn't going anywhere until he got that refund. But the events co-ordinator's response was made from the alright position. She looked the customer in the eye and said, 'I agree. It was a genuine mistake. On Monday, I will let my manager know I spoke to you about it. If you'll help me out now by writing down what happened, I'll add a note to the end of your form.'

Suddenly the customer realized he was better off keeping the events co-ordinator on-side. He abruptly stopped shouting and filled in the form. Ironically, the course he had enrolled in was my program on dealing with 'difficult people'.

If you ever find yourself dealing with customers like this, you should use accord statements as often as possible. You don't have to agree with everything they say. But they'll calm down if you use the words, 'I agree' early in the conversation. There are many other situations in which you'll find accord statements useful.

▸ Handling wild generalizations, such as, 'Women aren't suited to work like this'.
▸ Replying to 'us and them' statements.
▸ Managing divisive behavior in a team.
▸ Letting someone know that you expect to have a say in the way a situation is resolved rather than simply doing what they want.
▸ Responding to complaints from internal customers.
▸ Handling bombastic statements such as, 'This is outrageous'.
▸ Assertively setting boundaries around how a problem will be handled.

How do you structure accord statements?

The simplest way to make an accord statement is to say, 'I agree ...' There are many other words you can use to express accord. Here are a few to get you started.

- I see.
- Yes.
- Okay.
- You're right.
- That's correct.
- Exactly.
- Absolutely.
- Of course.

Remember that you don't have to agree with *everything* the other person has said. You just need to agree with part of their statement. Then redirect the conversation towards 'safe space' or common ground. You do this by structuring your accord statement in two parts. Part one expresses agreement with some part of what the other person has said. Part two redirects the person and leads into introducing a new perspective.

I agree that _____ and _____.

Here's an example of a manager using accord statements to calm his direct report, a team supervisor, who expresses sexist opinions about one of his team members. The accord statements are highlighted in bold text.

Supervisor: Jane is getting to be a bigger problem every day. I told you a woman wasn't suitable for this role.

Manager: **I agree.** You did say that. And we had a conversation about appropriate language at the time. So let's talk about what's going on. You sound really angry. Has something happened between you and Jane?

Supervisor: She keeps interfering with everyone else's work. On Monday, she told Bob to stop working on the Pizazz project. I only found out today. Now we're three days behind on our deadline for stage one.

Manager: **Yes.** I can see why you're upset. So Bob stopped working on Pizazz without talking to you first?

Supervisor: Exactly! Can you believe it? I don't know how we're going to get back on schedule.

Manager: **I agree.** It's a real problem that Pizazz is three days behind schedule.

Supervisor: It sure is. And it's all Jane's fault.

Manager: **Of course.** You must feel really angry, since you think Jane is responsible for delaying Pizazz. And now you'll have to manage the situation.

Supervisor: Jane is a stupid cow. She just won't accept that I got the supervisor's job and she didn't.

Manager: **I agree** it might be frustrating to work in those circumstances. And at the same time, I'm not comfortable with Jane being referred to as a cow.

Supervisor: Well, she's really causing problems. You should see the way she glares at me every time I ask her to do something. She's impossible to control.

Manager: **Yes.** I have seen some hostile looks between you and Jane. Now let's talk about how to improve your relationship.

Example accord statements for handling fight, flight and spite behaviors

Yes, it can be challenging to express agreement with someone who has said something offensive. So it's important to keep your aim in mind when using accord statements. Your aim is to focus attention on the concerns, ideas, feelings or perspectives that you share with the other person. At the same time, you're directing attention away from points of difference. This approach helps you build a SAFE way to address touchy issues.

Accord statements for responding to people in fight mode
- I agree that's an important issue. And we need to sort it out.
- Yes. That's something we should discuss.
- Of course I'd like to talk this through with you.
- That's a good point. Let's discuss the whole issue this afternoon.
- I agree with what you said about ... And I also think ...

Accord statements for responding to people in flight mode

- I agree it isn't easy to talk about this. And until we sort things out the problem will persist.
- I agree. This is an uncomfortable situation for you to be in. Let's talk it though.
- Yes. This isn't an easy decision for you to make. And I am not in a position to help you make it.
- I agree it's important to respect others' opinions. At the same time, I would like to hear more about what you think.

Accord statements for responding to people in spite mode

- I agree that it's good to share jokes at work. And I'd also like those jokes to comply with our appropriate workplace behavior policy.
- Yes. That cartoon might be funny to some people. And some of the team could find it offensive.
- I agree that your opinion is important. And I'd also like to have my ideas recognized.
- Yes. Working with different types of people can be challenging. And we need to master that challenge.

Accord statement activity

Write down an accord statement you could use in the following situations.

1. Your colleague makes a dismissive joke about an issue you care about deeply.

I agree

_____

_____

And

_____

_____

2. You are a member of a recruitment panel. Another panel member remarks that the applicant you've just interviewed is 'too old for the job'.
Yes

_____

_____

And

_____

_____

3. Your colleague, Jess, refuses to talk to the newest member of your team, Bronwyn. Jess has told you this is because 'people like Bronwyn lack any sense of morality.' Bronwyn has just asked you to send her a sample template for formatting her work. Jess makes a big show of taking you aside. She whispers, 'Don't give it to her. She'll just steal all your ideas and take the credit for them.'
I agree

_____

_____

And

_____

_____

Using spotlight questions to challenge distorted perceptions

No doubt you have met plenty of 'problem people' who whinge, whine and come across as energy vampires. These are people who always seem to have a problem. If something good happens, they'll find a downside to the situation. If they walk into a freshly painted room, they will find the one blemish on the ceiling. Or, if you're enjoying yourself, they'll use a smart remark to put you in your place. It seems as though they're wired to see problems.

The unfortunate truth is that many people do love having problems. In fact, some will even seek out or create problems. They divert the conversation. Why? So they have something to complain about or so they get attention.

But you don't have to put up with this sort of problem-focussed behavior. You can challenge other people and redirect the conversation towards positive outcomes. How? By asking a special sort of question – a spotlight question. This is a question that shifts the focus of conversation from blaming and shaming towards spotlighting solutions. Spotlight questions force people to take a collaborative problem-solving approach rather than dumping problems or issues onto you.

What is a spotlight question?

Spotlight questions are used to shift attention away from *having a problem* towards *solving that problem*. For example, think about a problem you have right now, or used to have in the past. Now imagine having a conversation in which someone helps you solve that problem. Instead of telling you what to do, they prompt you to build a solution for yourself. That's a solution-focussed conversation. It is a conversation in which spotlight questions become a tool for change and positive action.

These power-packed questions are based on the principle of being solution focussed. This is a brilliant approach to take when dealing with hostile or negative behavior because it prevents other people from engaging in blaming and shaming.

The benefit of asking spotlight questions during tough conversations is that they prevent people fixating on negatives. Spotlight questions also give a clear focus for problem-solving conversations. Because they take the emphasis off who is to blame or what is 'wrong' with people, spotlight questions encourage collaborative problem solving. When you focus the beam of someone's attention on solutions, it's very hard for anyone to maintain a negative mindset. Instead, you'll be showing them how to create new options and solutions.

▸ Find out more about asking useful questions in my video *Solution-focussed questions* available on my website: http://difficultpeoplemadeeasy.com

---

When should you use spotlight questions?

Spotlight questions are highly versatile. You can use them to redirect a conversation away from negative topics and towards positives. You can also use them to gently challenge the assumptions behind others' statements or mindsets. And during problem-solving discussions, you can ask solution-focussed questions to keep the conversation on track.

How do you structure a spotlight question?

Spotlight questions always address one key theme: how can this problem be solved? So they focus on the future rather than the past. And they always imply that solutions can be found. To get your spotlight questions right, use future-focussed, positive and active language. Here are some examples.

Don't ask	Instead ask
What will stop us achieving our goal?	How will we overcome any barriers to success?
Why did this problem happen?	What can we do to solve this problem?
What's the solution?	How many solutions can we find?
Who is to blame for this situation?	Who can help find the best solution?

Use your spotlight questions to draw forth as many options as possible – even if some of these options seem not to be sensible at first. Remember that your language can make or break problem-solving efforts. For example, there is a huge difference between asking, 'What way can you solve this problem?' and, 'How many ways can you solve this problem?' The first question can prompt the response, 'There is no way.' The second question requests a list of suggested solutions.

Aim to broaden the thinking of other people by asking really good questions. There are five key principles to keep in mind when asking spotlight questions.

1. Don't disguise advice as a question
Giving advice to people who are in fight, flight or spite mode is useless. They won't take it anyway. But they may have lots of ways to argue with it. Don't give 'problem people' the chance to reject your ideas. Instead, ask them to find solutions for themselves. Because they aren't solution-focussed, avoid questions that start with the following phrases. Really, these questions disguise advice in a question format.

▸ Why don't you …
▸ Have you tried …
▸ Have you thought of …
▸ Could you …
▸ What about …

2. Do imply that all problems can be solved
Hard-to-handle people – particularly those who operate from flight position most of the time – often act as though there are no solutions to their problems. You need to challenge this behavior. Make sure that your spotlight questions imply that solutions can be found – even when a problem seems impossible to deal with. Avoid questions that limit possibility, such as, 'What will you do if you can't solve this problem?' Instead, ask questions that expand the potential for option finding. An example of this sort of question would be, 'How will you move towards a solution if you hit a barrier to success?'

3. Don't ask 'why'

Good spotlight questions start with 'what', 'how' or 'when'. They rarely start with 'why'. In fact, asking 'why' questions can create a trap. 'Why' questions focus minds on the reasons a problem exists. This can lead to someone providing long-winded explanations and rationalizations that do nothing to help solve the problem.

'Why' questions take attention away from ways to solve a problem because they focus on history. Asking 'why' is a great way to reaffirm a problem and reinforce difficult behavior. Don't encourage people to go around in circles when you can go straight to solutions. Ask 'how' questions in place of 'why' questions. That way, you'll encourage 'problem people' to discover new ways of thinking or doing things.

Here are some examples of 'why' questions transformed into 'how' questions.

Don't ask 'why?'	Change to 'how?'
Why did you say that?	How did that comment come about?
Why are you so determined to do things that way?	How will doing it that way help us get a good outcome?
Why should I do this?	How many ways can I do this?

4. Focus on the future, not the past

Under stress, many people will bring ghosts into a conversation. Ghosts are past experiences that are used to haunt present endeavors. For example, 'Barbara never did it that way' or, 'We tried it before and it didn't work.' Once people have raised these ghosts, they passively give up on problem solving. Don't let them get away with this. Instead, ask a spotlight question that shifts the focus of the conversation onto the future.

For example, imagine two colleagues who have worked together for eight years. Each of them is stuck in spite mode. And their story goes back five years. Way back then, they had a conflict about how to restructure their workloads. To this day, they won't speak to each other. Their attention is well and truly focussed on the past. To overcome this problem, they need to focus on the future. A mediator working with this pair could help them shift their attention to the future by asking questions such as the following.

- What needs to change for this relationship to work better?
- If you had a good relationship, what would be different?
- How can you change the way you communicate in future?

5. Finish with a goal

Setting goals will ensure that your spotlight questions lead to action. Goals are descriptions of the 'difficult person's' desired future state. In solution-based therapy, the strategy of setting goals is used to guide clients towards positive and resourceful action. When setting goals, it is useful to keep three assumptions in mind.

The first assumption is that there is always more than one solution or option for action. Acting from this assumption helps 'problem people' feel powerful and in control of their own destiny.

The second assumption is that solutions are *constructed* not discovered. Believing this means that a 'difficult person' can build the solution that will work for them. They don't have to do what works for someone else.

The third assumption is that you should always add choice – never take it away. Don't ask 'difficult people' to give things up. Instead, add more options to expand the range of choices available.

How do you sequence spotlight questions?

Spotlight questions need to be carefully sequenced. You can use them to break a huge problem into smaller parts. You can also use them to steer the direction of a conversation. You need to actively manage which parts of a discussion you illuminate by selecting your questions carefully.

For example, imagine you're walking through an unfamiliar environment late at night. You're not sure of the territory in front of you. Luckily, you've brought along a good torch. You can expand the beam of that torch, to show you the terrain that lies far in the distance. Or you can narrow the beam, to focus on the ground directly in front of you. Both perspectives are useful. You decide when to expand or narrow the beam, depending on the view you need to move ahead safely.

Spotlight questions are like that torch. You can use them to gain an overview, or to hone in on specific details.

In general, there are seven steps involved in sequencing spotlight questions.

1. Spotlight the precise issue you need to address

Before you begin asking questions, be absolutely clear about what problem you're trying to solve. For example, someone talking from a fight position might shout, 'You've cut me out of every single decision in this team.' The benefit of this abrupt and abusive communication style is that it makes the person's concerns obvious. The issue you need to address is who to include in decision making.

2. Check your assessment is correct

Use a 'you frame' statement to check that you've accurately interpreted what the 'difficult person' is saying. For example, say, 'You think I don't value your opinion. Is that right?'

3. Focus your beam on data

During the third stage of spotlight questioning, you're aiming to gather facts about the problem. You're narrowing down the beam of your torch so that it shines on what already exists. Ask questions about what's going on right now. For example, what evidence is there that a problem exists? When does it happen? How does it manifest? What makes it worse? What reduces its severity? What impact does it have? Whom does it impact? What has already been done to try to solve it?

   Be careful not to step into interrogation mode during this part of the conversation. Keep your voice warm and curious as you ask probing questions.

- What makes you say that?
- What, exactly, have I done that shows I don't value your opinion?
- When, specifically, did I seem to disregard your views?
- What leads you to think I'm not interested?

4. Gain commitment to solving the problem

People are much more likely to find solutions when they're aware of what they're supposed to be doing. Don't assume another person understands that your aim is to solve the problem. Instead, tell them outright. Highlight the benefits *to them* of solving the problem. Then ask a spotlight question that leads them directly into solution-finding mode. Here are some examples of how to do this.

- That sounds like a big problem. No doubt you'll be much happier when it's sorted out. How about we take time to solve it now?

- I agree that we have a problem here. Both of us can benefit from solving it. What can we do about it?
- So the problem is _____. Fixing this problem will help you _____. Are you willing to put some time into solving it now?
- You think there's a problem in relation to _____. How interested are you in solving this problem? Okay, how many solutions can we find?
- I'm sure we can find a fair solution to this issue. One that will let you meet your need for _____ and me to meet my need for _____. Let's put our heads together. What solutions will work here?
- This issue impacts on both of us. We've both something to gain by working it out. What can we do to sort this out?

5. Shine light on your desired goal

Having gained agreement to sort the problem out, you'll probably be keen to start generating ideas. But it pays to slow down. Take time to define what your end goal is before you rush into deciding how to get there.

Beware of the trap of moving straight into brainstorming mode. Brainstorming is a creative thinking tool. Without a well-defined sense of what you're trying to create, you will lose momentum. So pause and discuss your answers to the following big-picture level questions before you begin considering detail-level actions to take in relation to the problem.

▸ When the problem no longer exists, how will things be different?
▸ What will change when the problem is gone?
▸ If you woke up tomorrow and the problem had been resolved, what would be different?
▸ How would you like things to be in future? What would be different? What would stay the same?
▸ What benefits will you gain from solving this problem?

6. Narrow the beam on to options for action

Now you can begin thinking creatively and developing ideas for action. Encourage the other person to keep their ideal, big-picture outcome in mind while thinking of concrete actions that can be taken. Guide the other person towards *creating the solution* rather than getting rid of the problem. Foster creativity by pointing out that all that is happening at this stage is idea generation – mentioning an idea does not mean you are committing to actioning it. Putting this frame around ideation can help controlling personalities let go of the need to argue about the viability of every option that emerges.

Here are some questions that may be useful when eliciting options for action.

- What are all the ways you can reach your ideal state?
- What are all the possible options for action?
- What needs to happen in order to create your ideal future?

If a 'difficult person' gets stuck during this stage of the conversation, try asking these questions to shift their mindset.

- What will happen if things stay the way they are for the next five years?
- What would your best friend do in this situation?
- What would Einstein do?
- What's the most outrageous way to generate your desired change?
- What can you do to make the problem even worse? What does this suggest you need to keep in mind when solving the problem?

It can be productive to use brainstorming techniques at this stage of solution finding.

7. Light up the *workable* solutions

During the final stage of the spotlight questioning sequence, you're using your question torch to select items from your listed options. Point the torch at each option, one at a time. Decide whether or not each option will work. Work collaboratively with the other person to identify *all* the workable options. Avoid trying to narrow down to a single solution – doing this simply leads to arguments. Instead, stress the value of combining multiple options when building a blueprint for action. Use 'yes, and' language patterns – 'yes, this option *and* that option' instead of 'this option *or* that option'.

Some of the following questions can help to steer conversation at this point.

- Which options will work?
- Which options can you modify in order to make them more workable?

- If you had ten points to allocate amongst all these options, how would you distribute them?
- Which options do you want to action?
- How can you combine those options to create a viable action plan?
- What is your action plan?
- What steps need to be taken?
- What sequence do these steps need to be taken in?
- What resources will you need?
- How can you obtain those resources?

Example spotlight questions

Spotlight questions are problem-solving tools. They help people think beyond their existing mindsets. They draw upon theories of problem solving and creative thinking. These theories suggest that collaborative problem solving involves working through three main stages.

- Identifying what's happening now.
- Imagining a new, better future.
- Working out how to create that better future.

Here are some examples of useful 'what', 'how' and 'when' questions for prompting people to solve problems rather than dwell on them.

'What' questions
- What is the current situation?
- What makes the situation better?
- What makes it worse?
- What, specifically, is problematic about this situation?
- What have you tried in terms of solving this problem?
- What haven't you tried?
- What would be a better/preferable situation?
- What needs to happen for this problem to be solved?
- What steps can you take to address this problem?
- What action do you need to take to solve this problem?

'How' questions
- How, exactly, is the problem impacting on you?
- How does the problem manifest itself?

- How have you tried to solve it?
- How would the ideal situation differ from your current situation?
- How can you get a better result?
- How can you solve the problem?
- How can you take positive action in this situation?
- How can you get the resources you need to solve the problem?

'When' questions
- When does the problem get worse?
- When does it get better?
- When will you obtain the resources you need to support action for change?
- When will you take action?
- When will you take the first step towards solving this problem?

Spotlight question activity

Write three spotlight questions you could use to prompt each of the speakers below to take a positive approach to their situation. Remember to start each question with 'what', 'how' or 'when.' And avoid 'why'.

1. I've had to work back late every night this week. My boss keeps giving me more tasks. But I need to work on the budget because it is due next Monday.

_____

_____

_____

_____

2. Greg never gets the data to me on time. He's supposed to have it ready on Tuesday so I can prepare the team report for Friday. The earliest he ever finishes, though, is Wednesday afternoon.

_____

_____

_____

_____

3. My exercise program isn't working. I've tried to go to the gym two nights every week and I'm still the same weight I was when I started six months ago.

_____

_____

_____

_____

_____

_____

4. That's a stupid idea. We tried it before and it didn't work.

_____

_____

_____

_____

_____

5. Gina always butts in when I'm talking to customers. Then she tries to put her name against my sales so she gets all the commission.

_____

_____

_____

_____

_____

6. I'd really like to buy an investment property. But I can't afford the mortgage repayments.

_____

_____

_____

_____

_____

HOW TO HANDLE REAL-LIFE SITUATIONS ▸

CHAPTER SIX
APPLYING EMOTIONAL FIRST AID

▶ Just like a doctor varies a treatment approach to fit the unique make-up of a patient, you need to adapt your responses to the person in front of you. A doctor assesses and stabilizes a patient before administering specific treatments. And you need to do the same thing by applying 'emotional first aid'. First, you need to objectively assess what you're dealing with. Next you need to stabilize the emotional state of the other person. Finally, you need to apply your verbal antidotes at the right time and in the right quantity. Use the acronym AIR to help you remember these three steps.

*A*SSESS
*I*NSTALL CALM
*R*ESPOND

Assess the power mode

Being able to detect someone's dominant power mode helps you to predict their behavior. This makes it easier to plan ahead for challenging conversations. It also takes the surprize factor out of your interactions with chronically hard-to-manage people. After all, knowing what you're up against is the first step in dealing with it. You'll find that tracking power modes helps you quickly spot any patterns in someone's challenging behavior.

Knowing what power mode you're dealing with helps you respond confidently to toxic tactics. It also helps you choose the best way to communicate from an alright position – so you can be assertive during challenging conversations. When you track power modes, you can work out what 'belongs' to the 'difficult person' and what 'belongs' to you – so you don't take on guilt trips or succumb to manipulative tactics. And this means you can stay calm and set boundaries when someone's behavior becomes unacceptable.

What is behavioral assessment?

Behavioral assessment involves closely observing what someone says and does. The aim is to work out, from their behavior patterns, what power mode they are operating from. When you do this type of assessment, you use cues (such as words or gestures) to gather information about what someone else thinks, feels or perceives. This information helps you plan your response, so you can get the best possible results from the conversation.

How to do a behavioral assessment

There are three main steps you need to take when assessing difficult behavior. During each step, you will answer a series of questions that are designed to pinpoint the exact problem you're facing. Let's first explore how the steps fit together. Then you'll discover what to ask yourself at each stage of the assessment process.

1. Pinpoint the specific problem behavior

The first step of behavioral assessment is identifying the specific behaviors that are causing problems. This involves being clear and objective so you can work out exactly what actions or verbal patterns are involved in the challenging behavior. Once you know exactly what you are dealing with, you are better equipped to make intelligent choices about your responses.

Assessing difficult behavior involves mentally stepping back, so you can get a 'fly on the wall' perspective about what is really going on. This helps *you* stay cool, calm and collected, even when other people are upset or heated. Being objective is easier when you focus your attention on sensory-based evidence (things you can see, hear and feel) rather than generalizations or interpretations. Here are some examples that highlight the difference between sensory-based evidence and interpretations.

Sensory evidence	Interpretation
Jane is speaking loudly, swearing and pointing at you.	Jane is out of control.
Your manager says that Brett blamed you for a mistake you know Brett made himself.	Brett is a lying, manipulative person.
Millie cries when you ask her to call back a customer who was very angry this morning.	Millie is trying to get out of handling tough customers.
You did not receive the email invitation to the end of year party.	The team has deliberately excluded you from the party.

To pinpoint the behavior that is causing problems, answer the following questions.

1. Which type(s) of problem behavior does this person display?
▶ Verbal.
▶ Physical.

2. What is your overall impression of this person's behavior (e.g. arrogant, hostile, playing victim)?

3. What, specifically, have they said or done that gives you this impression (e.g. they talked over me, they shouted at me, they wasted my time telling 'poor me' stories)?

4. Describe their actions or words using **neutral**, **behavior-focussed language** (e.g. they began talking when I was in mid-sentence, they raised their voice when giving me feedback, or they spent thirty-five minutes yesterday telling me about their problems with their spouse).

2. Map the behavior to a power mode

The second stage of behavioral assessment involves identifying which power mode the other person is operating from. To do this, you map the person's patterns of behavior against the key cues for each power mode. Here is a chart you can use to do this.

Fight	Flight	Spite
☐ Shouts.	☐ Avoids eye contact.	☐ Uses sarcasm a lot.
☐ Talks over you.	☐ Speaks very quietly.	☐ Makes pointed jokes.
☐ Uses patronising language.	☐ Rarely contributes.	☐ Spreads malicious rumors.
☐ Criticizes excessively.	☐ Waits to be told what to do.	☐ Deliberately makes mistakes.
☐ Humiliates you in public.	☐ Plays the victim.	☐ Body language expresses contempt.
☐ Micro-manages.	☐ Wants you to solve their problems for them.	☐ Refuses to talk to you.
☐ Threatens violence.		☐ Sulks.
☐ Throws or smashes objects.	☐ Always says 'yes'.	☐ Drags out simple tasks deliberately.
☐ Insists they are right.	☐ Does not solve their own problems.	☐ Withholds information.
☐ Demands you do things their way.	☐ Fails to speak up in meetings.	
	☐ Is afraid to try new things.	
Total number of ticks:	Total number of ticks:	Total number of ticks:

▸ You can complete a more comprehensive checklist on the questionnaire page of my website http://difficultpeoplemadeeasy.com

3. Identify whether the behavior is chronic or reactive

Your next step is to assess whether a difficult behavior is chronic (persistent) or reactive (short-term and triggered by a one-off stressor).

Knowing this helps you decide how to set appropriate boundaries and create a plan for managing your situation. Use the tool below to assess the behavior of the person you are dealing with.

Chronic	Reactive
☐ The difficult behavior occurs daily.	☐ The difficult behavior occurs once a month or less often.
☐ The person has a reputation for being a 'difficult person'.	☐ The behavior is confined to a specific situation.
☐ Others try not to 'set off' this person because they are known to be hard to deal with.	☐ Duration of the behavior is short.
☐ The person cuts themselves off from normal social interaction.	☐ Difficult behavior is 'out of character' for this person.
☐ There is often a conflict happening in this person's life.	☐ Behavior is sudden and infrequent in onset.
☐ When the person talks, they often use negative language and express negative opinions.	☐ Problem behavior is clearly associated with an upsetting or negative event in the person's experience.
☐ The person's communication is frequently erratic or irrational.	☐ The difficult behavior is quickly over and done with.
☐ The person often fixates on small issues and makes a big deal out of them.	☐ The person apologized for the behavior and has not repeated it.
Total number of ticks:	Total number of ticks:

Install a calm state

Step two of the AIR process is all about leading the other person into a calm state. Being calm means everyone can think straight and talk through problems rationally. This is why you need to focus on installing calm states as quickly as you can during difficult conversations.

During tough conversations, you will often need to calm yourself first. Then you'll work to shift the other person into a relaxed, resourceful state. Essentially, this means stepping into an alright position yourself and then encouraging the other person to join you.

Being in an alright state involves making assertive choices about your own perceptions, thoughts, feelings and actions. Assertive choices respect both yourself and the other person. Remember, the more control you have over your own physical and emotional state, the more control you have over the situation.

What is a calm state?

So what, exactly, is a calm state? It is the way you think and feel when you have no worries or anxieties. In a calm state, your mind is fully absorbed in the moment. Your body is relaxed and comfortable. You are relaxed, but also fully alert and aware. You are not distracted by any mental chatter. You realize you are okay and you see other people as okay instead of labeling them as 'difficult'.

Calm states are marked by physical and mental indicators. Your physical indicators of a calm state may include a deep, relaxed breathing pattern and your heart beating at a normal rate. In a calm state, you'll experience minimal muscle tension. You'll feel relaxed and comfortable in your own body. At the same time, your mind will be tranquil, serene and focussed. You will be aware of feeling fine both physically and mentally – even when you're faced with problematic situations.

How do you access a calm state yourself?

Calm states don't just descend upon you by chance. You can actively *create* them all by yourself. How? By using 'state management' processes. These are techniques from applied psychology that help you manage yourself physically or mentally. The aim of state management is to move you from limiting states (such as feeling anxious or angry) to resourceful states (such as feeling calm or confident). You can do this by changing your physical state or your thinking patterns. To change your physical state, you can use a **controlled breathing process**. To shift your thinking patterns, you can use the **sensory shift process**.

Controlled breathing process

Your breathing plays an extremely important role in managing your physical state. Think about what happens to your breathing when you're dealing with 'problem people' and their annoying behaviors. It probably speeds up and becomes shallow. This is a sign of stress and it happens whenever you experience a fight, flight or spite reaction. If you want to tackle toxic behavior assertively, you need to manage that stress. Controlled breathing is a simple but truly effective way of doing this.

Controlled breathing techniques give you the ability to manage your physical state when dealing with 'difficult people', tough situations and conflicts. This is because they calm the automatic fight or flight reaction of your body. This puts you in control physically and emotionally. It also helps you think rationally, so you can make wise choices about what you do and say in response to the toxic tactics 'difficult people' may use.

When you're learning to breathe deeply, it helps to imagine you have a coffee plunger inside your chest. Each time you breathe in, imagine the plunger pushing deep into your belly and taking the air down with it. As you breathe out, imagine the plunger rising to the top of your chest, followed by the air. This internal imagery helps you really breathe deeply. The deeper you breathe, the calmer you become. And the calmer you are, the better you are able to handle 'difficult and toxic' people.

To breathe effectively, make sure you close your mouth and breathe in through your nose. Focus completely on the breath you are taking in. Push that breath deep into your belly and count to three as you do so. Pause. Open your mouth and release the breath through it. Focus completely on the breath you are exhaling. Push all the air out of your lungs and count to three as you do so. Pause. Breathe out fully before taking in another lungful of air and repeating the entire process.

Don't wait until you're face to face with a 'difficult person' before you try this technique. It will work much better if you're used to breathing this way. Put aside ten minutes every day to practise your breathing exercises. You'll find they help you feel calm and resourceful. If you have trouble sleeping – perhaps because you're worrying about 'difficult people' and the things they've said or done – do your breathing exercises just before you go to bed. You'll be amazed at how easily you slip into a relaxing sleep once you've primed your body to relax.

▶ To help you master controlled breathing, I've created a podcast called *Breathe and relax*. You can buy a copy at my shop: http://difficultpeoplemadeeasy.com

---

Sensory shift process

This technique works by shifting what you place your attention on. It is based on the idea that your body responds to what you do with your mind. If your mind is focused on negatives, your body enters fight, flight or spite mode. If you shift your attention to more positive aspects of your reality, your body will go into alright mode. Follow the steps below to do this.

1. Notice what you're noticing

Where you place your attention influences how you feel. So the sensory shift process starts by tracking how you're thinking. Start by assessing your 'inner reality' – the way you are representing your situation right now. You create your inner reality by using your senses – what you are seeing, hearing and feeling 'about' the situation you are in or the person you are dealing with. Use the steps below to track your reality.

▶ Check what you see in your mind's eye right now. Notice the pictures that are appearing inside your mind. Pay attention to their content as well as their size, brightness and color schemes.
▶ Notice how your internal pictures are impacting on how you are feeling.
▶ Check what you hear in your internal 'soundtrack'. Notice the sounds you are focussing on – perhaps the 'difficult person's' voice.

Or perhaps your own internal dialogue. Pay attention to the volume, tonality and pace of those sounds.

▸ Notice how that internal soundtrack is impacting on what you feel right now.
▸ Check which physical sensations you are aware of. Pay attention to the temperature of your skin, any muscle tension you're experiencing and the pattern of your breathing.
▸ Make a note of how these physical sensations are impacting on what you feel right now.

2. Work out what needs to change

Step two involves changing the parts of your sensory experiences that are contributing to your limiting state. If you're stressed, it's likely that some of your internal experiences are associated with a stress reaction. These are the parts of your current reality that you need to change. Changing these elements will help you handle difficult behavior assertively. To work out which parts of your internal reality you'd like to change, answer the following questions.

▸ Which parts of my internal pictures are unhelpful?
▸ Which parts of my internal soundtracks are unhelpful?
▸ Which of my physical sensations are causing discomfort?
▸ Which parts of my sensory experience do I want to change?

3. Change your internal pictures, sounds and feelings

The pictures, sounds and feelings you experience in your mind are not real. You can change them whenever you want to. Doing this helps you experience reality in a different way. And as your sense of reality changes, so does your state.

So step three of the sensory shift process involves changing your focus of attention. To shift your focus, use the following questions to prompt you.

▸ How can I make my internal pictures more resourceful? What happens when I change the size of those pictures? What happens when I shift my focus? What happens if I imagine the pictures getting smaller... or larger? What happens if I make them duller or brighter? Which visual changes make me feel the most resourceful?
▸ How can I make my internal sound track more resourceful? What happens if I change the direction the sounds are coming from? What

happens when I make the sounds louder or quieter? If I change the tonality of the sounds in my head, what difference does that make? Which auditory changes make me feel the most resourceful?

▶ How can I make my physical sensations more resourceful? What happens if I relax any muscles that are tense? If I imagine the temperature of my skin cooling down, what difference does that make? If I imagine myself becoming warmer, what happens? If I change the pattern of my breathing, what results do I notice? Which changes to my physical sensations make the most positive differences to my state?

The sensory shift process can really help you calm down quickly. It works best when you have learned to complete each step automatically. After all, when you're dealing with 'difficult people', you can't pull out a list of questions and start answering them internally.

▶ To help you use the sensory shift process, I have created an audio file called *Be calm under pressure*. You can purchase it at http://difficultpeoplemadeeasy.com

---

How do you calm someone else?

Of course, you can't really make someone else feel calm. Their feelings are their responsibility. But you *can* influence someone else's ability to change states for themselves. Sadly, some people never learn the basics of self-management. They don't know how to calm themselves down in stressful situations. Instead, they fight or retreat until the threat subsides. If you can reduce someone's sense of threat, you can reduce the intensity of their difficult behaviors.

Here are five key steps you can use to help calm someone down when they're in fight, flight or spite mode.

1. Give them time to calm down

Remember what you learned about the amygdala in Chapter One? It is the emergency response system of your brain. When it detects danger, it triggers the fight, flight or spite reaction. It also sparks the release of stress hormones into the body. It takes *at least* ten minutes for the physical impact of these hormones to subside. In many cases, it takes a lot longer. This is why you need to work slowly when managing difficult behavior. You need to provide breathing space so that the person you're dealing with can calm down. Otherwise, they won't be able to think rationally or tackle problems and conflicts logically.

Yes, it might feel frustrating to allow time for someone else to calm down. You might just want to resolve the issue and finish the conversation. After all, dealing with difficult behavior isn't much fun. But this attitude won't help. In fact, it will often make things worse. So focus on how you're reacting to the problem behavior. If you feel frustrated or keen to move the conversation along, focus on managing your own state. If you want difficult behavior to stop, keep in mind that you need to give people time to calm down.

2. Remove or reduce the threat

Always remember that difficult behavior will persist until the trigger goes away. The fight, flight or spite reaction will continue until the person feels safe and secure. The quickest way to move someone from an aggressive, passive or passive-aggressive mode is to remove any sources of fear or anxiety. Here are some ways to do this.

▸ Avoid behaviors that can be perceived as threatening. These include arguing, defending yourself, standing over the other person or adopting aggressive body language.
▸ Eliminate visual or auditory triggers for the stressed state. These include signs that limit choice (e.g. 'no handwritten applications will be accepted'), flickering lights, jarring color schemes, sudden loud noises, irritating background sounds and harsh voice tones.
▸ Show that you are listening and taking the other person's concerns seriously. You can use empathic responses and 'you frame' messages to do this. These techniques are described in the toolkit section of this book.
▸ Agree that the problem exists and that it needs to be managed. By doing this, you remove the need for the 'difficult person' to repeat themselves over and over again. You don't have to agree with every demand they make. But you can find a way to acknowledge that the situation needs to be resolved.

Remember that difficult behavior stems from feelings of distress. Someone who is distressed is primed to react defensively. So it is important to help 'difficult people' see that you're not a threat.

3. Get them using the neo-cortex

When their behavior is driven by the amygdala, a 'difficult person' is being controlled by the oldest, most primitive part of their brain. The amygdala controls instinctive reactions. Its key role is to identify sources of trouble and allow people to react without thinking. For example, if you unexpectedly see a snake, you'll jump away from it without consciously thinking about it. That's your amygdala protecting you.

When other people perceive *you* as a threat, they will react in an equally instinctive way. Their actions will be driven by preverbal, defensive modes of behavior. Your challenge is to get them to respond at a more sophisticated level. Your aim is to switch on the newer part of their brain called the neo-cortex. The neo-cortex manages logical thinking, language, imagination and problem solving. Obviously, it is a very important part of the brain when someone is dealing with problems, conflicts and tough situations.

The simplest way to switch on someone's rational mind is to get them talking. The longer they talk, the more they are accessing the part of their brain responsible for logical thinking. Ask them to tell you about their opinions, thoughts and feelings. Encourage them to describe their own perspective in detail. Remember that as upset people talk, they tend to calm down. Allow at least ten minutes of venting time for very distressed people to settle. You will notice their problem behavior drops away as they regain a state of calm.

4. Help them find solutions

Once you've calmed someone down, you need to move them into solution-focussed mode as quickly as possible. Solving problems and working out action plans help 'difficult people' feel in control. This means they're less likely to become stuck in a fight, flight or spite power mode. The best way to focus someone else on problem solving is to ask spotlight questions. You may recall that you can ask questions like these.

● What is the main issue we need to sort out?

- What, specifically, are you concerned about?
- What do you think needs to be done?
- How could this problem be solved fairly?
- What will it take for you to be satisfied?
- How can we find a solution that will work for everyone?

In response to your questions, some people may initially suggest solutions that will work for them but are not agreeable to you. In this situation, avoid arguing or debating. Simply write the suggestions down and follow up by asking, 'What else could we do?' Or you can gently challenge a proposed option by saying, 'How will this idea sit with other people involved in this situation?'

5. Influence their breathing patterns

You can calm down someone else by getting them to slow their breathing. To do this, you can use tracking and matching techniques. Start by tracking the other person's breathing patterns. Watch their shoulders and belly to determine how deeply and rapidly they're breathing. Then listen carefully, noticing how their speech patterns reflect their breathing habits. You may even be able to hear them inhaling or exhaling.

Next, begin to match their breathing pattern. Do this by copying the speed, rhythm and depth of each inhalation. If matching with your breath feels very uncomfortable, try matching the breathing pattern with a movement of your foot or fingers. You'll get quicker results, however, when you match the other person breath for breath.

Continue matching the person's breathing for around five minutes. This creates an instinctive state of synchronisation, which primes the 'difficult person' to follow changes to your breathing patterns. Then, gradually shift your breathing into 'relaxed' mode. In other words, draw each breath deep into your lungs. Pause for a second before exhaling slowly. Establish a slow, steady rhythm of breathing.

Now monitor the other person's behavior. If their breathing begins to slow down, you have successfully influenced them. In this case, continue to breathe slowly and deeply. If the other person does not follow your lead, simply match their breathing for another five minutes. Then repeat the process of moving into a relaxed breathing pattern.

Once the other person is matching your relaxed breathing pattern, watch for signs that their state is becoming more resourceful. For example, you may see them sit back in a relaxed posture or uncross their arms. You may hear their tone of voice change, or notice that they use more positive language.

▸ You can find out more about matching in my video *How to build rapport and trust*. View it on my video page at http://difficultpeoplemadeeasy.com

---

Respond from the alright position

1. Manage your physiology

Step one when responding to difficult behavior is to manage your body language. Check that you are standing or sitting in an appropriate posture. Next, try inviting the 'difficult person' to sit down. This helps *them* to calm down and puts *you* into a more relaxed physical position. Sitting will also help balance out any height differences that can contribute to a sense of one person dominating the conversation.

2. Identify the cause of the difficult behavior

Difficult behavior is always a reaction to something. If you can find out what triggered the reaction, you can remove that trigger for challenging verbal or behavioral patterns. For example, difficult behavior is often triggered by a sense that someone's position has not been understood or respected.

You can quickly calm down someone who feels this simply by demonstrating that you want to understand. Use 'you frame' messages to do this. Ask spotlight questions to draw out the other person's story. Demonstrate your understanding of their answers by reflecting back both the emotional and factual content of what has been said. You can even write notes, so they can see you're taking the situation seriously.

3. Empathize with their position

As you learned earlier, empathy is the ability to detect and acknowledge someone else's situation, perspective and feelings. Empathic responses demonstrate that you are listening respectfully to someone, regardless of their problem behavior. Even if you don't agree with their position, you can still seek to understand it. And empathic responses communicate that this is what you are trying to do.

Empathic responses are particularly useful in situations in which 'difficult people' become very emotional. Your empathy creates a safe space in which their negative emotions can be expressed and released. This then allows them to relax and recover from their amygdala's hyperactive state. Useful phrases for expressing empathy include some of the following statements.

- This is a real problem for you.
- Sounds like this is really [emotion: worried, anxious, distressed and so on].
- You must be feeling [emotion].
- If I understand you correctly, the problem is [summary of problem].
- That sounds very [emotion].
- What you're saying is [summary of their story].
- That must have been a very [emotion] experience for you.
- I imagine this is a very [emotion] situation.

4. Gang up on the problem

Show that you want to work *with* the other person rather than against them. Verbally mark out your intention to take a collaborative problem-solving approach, by saying, 'Let's work out what we can do about this problem.' Position yourself next to the other person, rather than adopting the more aggressive face-to-face position. This signals that you want to co-operate and work together in resolving the situation. Taking this approach removes any element of conflict from your interaction. The other person will no longer feel compelled to resort to problem behavior because they sense that you are on their side.

5. Discuss options

Talking through options helps people feel in control. It also expresses a co-operative mindset. A useful technique is to jot down a list of possible options and ask the 'difficult person' for their opinion on which will work best. This helps them understand that their position is respected and that they have a say in what happens next.

6. Agree on an action plan

Close the conversation on a positive and affirming note by summarising what is going to happen next. This helps the 'difficult person' to feel confident that they have been taken seriously. It also provides you with a chance to reiterate any agreements that have been reached.

When you know how to respond from the alright position, you can show respect for other people, even when you hold very different beliefs or opinions to them. At the same time, you can express your needs and concerns in ways that actually get through to 'difficult people'. Your communication skills reach an advanced level, so you're able to handle even the toughest situations masterfully.

CHAPTER SEVEN

USING PAIR WITH PEOPLE IN FIGHT MODE

▶ This chapter explains how you can adapt the basic AIR model to handle the tactics used by people in fight mode. This involves adding an extra step to the three-part AIR process. Remember what AIR stands for: assess the power mode, install calm and respond from the alright state. To handle people in fight mode, you start with an additional step: preventing escalation of the aggressive state.

Key points to remember about fight mode

For many people, there's something about the fight reaction that is overwhelming. You may even find it downright scary to handle someone who is in a full-blown rage. That's because the threat of physical violence lies behind their aggressive language and nonverbal behavior.

But the good news is that *most* people operating from a fight power mode don't resort to physical force or violence. Keeping this in mind can help you install calm, so you can tackle their toxic tactics effectively. Yes, you do need to handle those tactics promptly instead of ignoring them. When aggression is ignored, it continues.

If you don't challenge someone in fight mode, why would their fight-based behavior change? The other person is already getting exactly what they want. If you want them to stop treating you badly, you have to do something new. That means speaking up from an alright power position and actually *using* the techniques you've learned. When you do this, you'll get amazing results.

Here's an example. Emily was a student in one of my assertiveness classes. The class ran over two months and met weekly. Each week, Emily would talk about her experiences dealing with her boss, Dave. At the start of the program, you could hear anger and frustration in her voice every time Emily talked about Dave. From her perspective, Dave was an aggressive, power-hungry attention seeker. He took credit for Emily's work. He never invited her to important meetings. He dumped boring tasks on her and kept all the good ones for himself. The list of Emily's frustrations seemed endless. Her 'Dave stories' had become a regular feature of the class.

Although Emily said that she wanted Dave's behavior to change, she was reluctant to speak to him about it. She was a master of rationalization. Whenever her classmates offered advice on how to handle Dave, Emily would say, 'That's a great idea, but I can't do it because …' One week, another student drew this pattern of behavior to Emily's attention. He pointed out that if Dave threw a temper tantrum when Emily raised her concerns, it wouldn't be Emily's fault. It would just be more evidence that Dave had a problem.

The next week, I taught the class about WISH statements. One of Emily's classmates joked, 'You should tell Dave you WISH he'd pull his head in, Emily.' Emily didn't respond. But the next week she came back and told us a new story about her dealings with Dave. This was a very different type of story. Instead of casting herself as the victim, Emily was playing the part of a confident and assertive young woman. She told us how she *had* used a WISH statement to raise her concerns with Dave. And he'd been shocked to hear how his behavior was coming across.

WHEN…
IT CAUSES…
SO I'D LIKE…
HOW CAN WE…?

Dave explained that because Emily was very quiet in meetings, he'd thought she didn't like attending them. Hearing Dave's side of things helped Emily see their communication in a different light. She was also relieved to find that Dave took her perspective seriously and didn't react aggressively to her feedback. She was able to have a SAFE conversation with him and they developed a plan for working together in new ways. Emily had just learned the value of speaking up even when she was afraid to.

START ON A POSITIVE NOTE

ASK ABOUT OTHERS' PERCEPTIONS

FRAME YOUR PERSPECTIVE

EXPLORE OPTIONS

What's the moral of this story? That change won't happen until you do something new. If you're someone who stays quiet when 'difficult people' rage, try speaking up and starting a SAFE conversation. If you're someone who usually screams back when others shout, try listening deeply for a change. When you do, you'll experience the benefits of being an assertive communicator. You'll prevent conversations spiralling out of control.

Remember that aggression is a form of *behaviour*. It is not a personality trait. This distinction is important. Yes, people may be powerless to change their personalities. But they do have the power to change their behaviour. People who resort to aggressive or bullying behaviour can stop any time they want to. They are not 'born' aggressive. And they are not 'made' aggressive by other people. So don't accept responsibility for their unacceptable behaviour.

Handling fight-based behaviour can be challenging. Hostile people can seem very intimidating. They may intrude on your personal space, violate your boundaries, force their opinions upon you and make unreasonable demands. Their language is threatening, offensive or plain illogical. And all of this can trigger your amygdala reaction. So it's very important to manage your own state before dealing with someone in fight mode.

PAIR process

To deal with people in fight mode, I add an extra step to the AIR model. This turns it into the PAIR model.

PREVENT
ASSESS
INSTALL CALM
RESPOND

The extra step is important for several reasons. It reduces the number of fight reactions you need to deal with in the first place. This benefits you because you no longer have to manage the stress that comes from exposure to aggression. Prevention strategies can also reduce the severity of any fight reactions that do occur. This means that even if a 'difficult person' goes into fight mode, you'll be able to calm them down more quickly. And, of course, the conversation will have less of a negative impact on you.

I also like PAIR because it stresses a significant point about dealing with people who are talking from fight mode. Battling their attitude gets you nowhere. But *pairing up* with them against a common problem changes the way you interact. It builds a SAFE conversation and allows you to sort out issues rather than engaging in toxic games. So let's explore how to use PAIR when dealing with someone in fight mode.

Prevent fight behavior escalating

In communication, just like in medicine, prevention is better than cure. Often, it's possible to nip a fight reaction in the bud simply by removing potential triggers. For example, I once worked in a customer service area where people came in to dispute their library fines. There was no private space to which we could take customers who needed to talk about personally sensitive issues. Customers felt like everyone in the service queue was listening to their private information. And this often triggered hostility and aggression. We set up a screened-off space to deal with these matters and levels of customer aggression immediately went down.

Another way to prevent the people you work with from slipping into fight mode is to audit your own behavior, at a personal level. You may be doing things that reactive people interpret as attacks, without being aware of it. Many years ago, for example, my boss gave me feedback about the way I was standing during training sessions.

What for me was a natural posture – standing with my hands on my hips – came across to some group members as aggressive. It didn't matter whether I *felt* hostile. I *looked* hostile and that increased the chances that group members would 'act up' during my sessions. Quitting that posture took a fair bit of effort (it's amazing how easy it is to fall back into a habitual stance), but it paid off over time.

You might be doing things that accidently send negative messages to other people. Think about the way you stand and speak when you're stressed. Is there anything you do that might set off a fight reaction in a 'difficult person'? You can use the following checklist as a starting point for reflecting on this question. If you're unsure about whether you use any of the behaviors on the list, ask someone you trust to complete the checklist for you.

☐ Using blaming language or body language.

☐ Making critical or shaming comments.

☐ Invading someone's personal space.

☐ Making assumptions about what another person thinks, feels or does.

☐ Speaking in a patronising tone of voice.

☐ Telling someone what they 'have' to do, or what they 'can't' do.

☐ Using jargon another person doesn't understand (this makes them feel at a disadvantage).

☐ Suggesting someone's feelings or actions are 'wrong'.

☐ Trivialising another person's problems or concerns.

☐ Laughing – even if you aren't laughing at them, someone else might hear it that way.

Focus on cutting out these ten behaviors for just one week. You'll find that other people react to you differently. After all, it's easier for other people to be calm when you are confident, calm and respectful yourself.

Finally, remember to keep your language flameproof – otherwise conflict will flare up. Think of yourself as a professional translator. Your job is to translate the language of abuse into flameproof language. Why? Because when you translate insults into neutral language, they become a lot less insulting. This makes it easier for you to stay calm and redirect the conversation towards problem solving. For example, 'I'm fed up with your crap' can be rephrased as, 'I'm frustrated by your behavior.' You can reinterpret, 'Can't you ever get anything right?' as, 'I think you've made a mistake.' Or, 'I have a different opinion' can be a better way of saying, 'That idea stinks.'

Once you've identified the issue beneath the baiting behavior, check that you've accurately understood what the other person is trying to say. To do this, combine a 'you frame' message with flameproof language. For example, in responding to the statement, 'I'm fed up with your crap', you can say, 'You want me change my behavior.'

After the other person has confirmed you understand what they perceive to be the problem, let them know you're willing to negotiate. Some helpful reframed responses can be very simple.

🗩 Let's discuss this.

🗩 I'd like to hear more about what concerns you.

Remember, at this point, you are communicating your willingness to talk. This does not mean you're agreeing that you'll change your behavior.

Assess the level of risk posed by aggressive behavior

When you're dealing with someone who is having a fight reaction, you may feel intimidated or frightened. This is because fight-based behavior alerts your brain to the potential for violence. Although it is very rare that an aggressive person will resort to violence, in some jobs you need to take this risk seriously. For example, security personnel, mental health workers and medical staff work in higher risk environments than most of us.

If you work in such a role, it's important to watch and listen out for signs that aggression is escalating. These early cues are warnings that you need to calm the other person down. When you see or hear the following behaviors, focus on ensuring everyone is safe and call for assistance.

Early cues
▸ Speaks very belligerently.
▸ Refuses to co-operate, even with senior people.
▸ Speaks or argues irrationally.
▸ Swears constantly.
▸ Repeats the same point over and over again.

Escalation cues
▸ Paces or moves around restlessly.
▸ Gestures in wild or threatening ways.
▸ Refuses to obey laws, policies or procedures.
▸ Verbally threatens to hurt someone.
▸ Claims they are being victimized.
▸ Tells you they have a weapon.
▸ Chants or speaks extremely quickly.

Crisis cues
▸ Comes right into your personal space.
▸ Throws things.
▸ Destroys furniture or property.
▸ Draws a weapon.
▸ Physically assaults someone.

Remember that it's much better to act early than to find yourself stuck in a situation that is becoming out of control. Never stay alone with a potentially violent co-worker, customer, boss or supplier. If you must be around a potentially violent person, make sure there are others in the room and nearby at all times. If possible, get aggressive people to sit down. This reduces the risk that they will erupt into sudden violence.

Carefully consider the time and venue of any meetings you have with potential aggressors. Never meet with them alone or in isolated venues. Check your meeting room and remove anything someone in fight mode could pick up and throw. Seemingly innocent items like potted plants or ornaments can do a lot of damage if they're hurled your way. It's also wise to avoid taking hot drinks into a meeting with anyone who may become violent.

Make sure that you have direct access to an exit. In meeting rooms, sit next to the door. Never let a potentially violent person get between you and the only exit point. If you drive onto a site where you may be dealing with aggressive people, face your car towards the exit. This ensures you can drive out quickly if you need to.

Also assess any risks that others' behaviors pose for your psychological wellbeing. This is particularly important if you're exposed on a daily basis to someone who displays a repeating pattern of fight-style behavior. For example, if you're dealing with a person with a very damaged personality, they might actually *want* to hurt or demean you. This is because making you feel bad makes them feel good. Triggering feelings of powerlessness in you makes them feel powerful.

Obviously, people with this mindset have very low levels of self-esteem. They usually need professional help. If they won't get it, you need to work out how to minimize their impact on *you*. After all, their behavior amounts to emotional abuse. Signs that you might be facing an emotionally abusive, aggressive person include the following.

▸ They frequently make fun of you or put you down in public.
▸ They inappropriately attempt to control what you do, say and spend.
▸ You feel you need their permission before taking any action or making any decision.
▸ They often ridicule or dismiss your feelings or opinions.
▸ Your boundaries – physical or emotional – have been repeatedly violated by this person.
▸ You are harshly criticized but never praised or given positive feedback.

▸ They set you up to look foolish or to take the blame for their actions.
▸ You feel frightened to speak up for yourself because you fear this person will punish you for doing so.

Refuse to tolerate abusive actions that have gone beyond the norms of acceptable workplace behavior. If a very aggressive person refuses to change their behavior, be prepared to walk away. Remember that it's okay to walk away from conversations that pose a risk to your psychological or physical wellbeing.

If you do need to remove yourself from an unsafe conversation, do it from the alright position rather than from a spite position. Explain what you're about to do and why. Then let the other person know you're willing to resume the conversation once their behavior has changed. You might say, 'I feel frustrated because I'm repeatedly being interrupted. So I'm going to finish this conversation for now. When you're ready to listen to me, let me know. Then we can continue working on how to sort this problem out.'

Installing calm when people are in fight mode

When people feel agitated, they are unlikely to be able to think clearly. And agitation can be highly contagious. Of all the communication modes, fight mode is the most likely to spark agitation. This is why it's crucial to calm everyone down before dealing with situations in which aggression is playing out.

Remember the basics of installing calm. You need to manage your own state before you try to influence others' states. Here are some ideas about how to install calm, specifically in the context of dealing with an aggressive person.

Respect their personal space

A common trigger for aggressive behavior is someone feeling that their personal space has been violated. Angry people won't think twice about fighting back if they feel you're too close. For example, I was once involved in debriefing a team of librarians after an incident with an angry client. The client had an exam the next day and wanted to borrow a study guide to help him prepare. He was told he couldn't borrow the book because he had a large fine outstanding. He then went into a rage state. He threw the book at a staff member and then he started to run out of the building.

Unfortunately, he tried to go out the 'in' door. A passing staff member (who hadn't seen the start of the incident) stepped into his path and put a hand on his arm. The client reacted by punching the staff member. When security arrived, the client's version of the events was that the staff member had hit him first and so he was defending himself by fighting back. It's quite possible that this wasn't simply a cover story.   When someone is in fight mode, their perceptions are distorted. The lightest touch can seem like a physical attack. The moral to this story is: give people who are in fight mode plenty of room. Stand back and never touch them.

Manage space

People in fight mode often use stand-over tactics to gain power. You can quickly diminish their sense of control by shifting the physical set-up for your communication. For example, if an aggressive boss stands over you and shouts, don't passively remain in your seat. Stand up and say, 'I'd prefer to have this conversation in a private meeting room.' Doing this puts you in charge of the communication dynamics – which undermines the boss's sense of having power over you.

Act as though this is a negotiation

It often helps to frame the situation as a negotiation. Never act as though another person has the right to tell you what to do. Instead, insist on finding solutions that will work for both of you. For example, imagine that you and a co-worker have different views on how to do a particular task. Your colleague is adamant that you should do the task his way. He starts criticizing and shouting at you. You, however, want to try out a new way of getting the job done. Signal that you want to negotiate a solution to the problem by saying, 'Let's sit down and talk this through.'

Next, formalize the discussion. Start by saying, 'What's the problem we need to solve?' Once you've defined the issue in neutral language, write it down on a piece of paper. Put the paper between you, to signal that the two of you are PAIRing up against the problem. Ask your colleague to talk you through his perspective and draw out his key needs and concerns.

Then explain your own views logically and politely. Invite your co-worker to brainstorm options for doing the task with you. This approach signals to your colleague that the conversation is a negotiation. Rather than being a situation in which he can dominate or control you, it is a SAFE conversation.

Pace the conversation

Pacing is very important when you're dealing with fight-based behaviors. Once someone is upset, their amygdala is in control. Their body is full of stress hormones. It will take time for those hormones to subside. Until their stress reaction has died down, the other person will remain highly emotional. They won't be able to think logically, so don't expect them to take a reasonable approach to finding a solution straight away. Instead, give them time to relax. Ask about their perspective and let them know you want to work with them to sort out the situation.

Respond with the right words

When you're dealing with someone in fight mode, tiny words and actions matter. If you want to keep the conversation on an even keel, you need to speak from the alright position and use flameproof language. If you move into fight, flight or spite mode, the conversation will quickly turn toxic. No matter how hard the other person tries to turn the discussion into a fight, you need to remain solution-focussed. Here are some tips for doing this.

Find something to agree with

Often it helps to use 'words of accord' when handling someone in fight mode. These include words such as 'I agree', 'This is very important' or 'I'm sorry'. However, you need to use these expressions carefully. You are using them for their calming impact, not necessarily to signal total alignment with what an aggressive person is saying. So you need to be artfully vague about what you're agreeing about and what is important. Here are some sentences you can use to do this.

- 🗩 I agree this is something we need to sort out.
- 🗩 I agree this must be a problem for you.
- 🗩 I agree we need to talk about this.
- 🗩 This is very important and we need to sort it out fairly.
- 🗩 This is very important to you.
- 🗩 This is very important for us to deal with.
- 🗩 I'm sorry you feel this way.
- 🗩 I'm sorry you think that.
- 🗩 I'm sorry what happened came across that way to you.

Use questions to redirect

When an aggressive person is going on and on about a problem, you need to shift their attention towards solutions. The following spotlight questions can be useful when you're encouraging people in fight mode to move into solution-finding mode.

- 🗩 How do you suggest we solve this problem?
- 🗩 What would have to happen for you to feel better about this?
- 🗩 What options do we have for sorting this out?
- 🗩 What needs to happen now?
- 🗩 What do you want?

Managing common fight-based behaviors

If you work with someone who uses fight based behavior frequently, you probably want some practical tips for dealing with them. Here are some tactics you can use with specific fight behaviors.

Handling someone who shouts at you

How many of these characters are familiar to you?

- ▸ Bosses who raise their voices unnecessarily.
- ▸ Co-workers who throw tantrums.
- ▸ Customers who come to your service point and scream – all the

while watching the other customers in line to make sure they have an audience.

▸ Callers who hurl abuse at the top of their lungs.

All of these aggressive types use shouting as a power play. They have learned that shouting is a great tactic – it gets them what they want. A cosmetics sales representative, Sam, once told me about a 'notorious' customer his team had to deal with. For years this woman had been bullying whoever was assigned to managing her account. She purchased a lot of product, so everybody tried to keep her happy. Finally, Sam did something about it.

The woman was on the phone, shouting that the accounts team had made a mistake on her last invoice. Sam was tempted to shout back. But he didn't. He dropped his voice. This is counter-intuitive, but it works. Most people who shout expect you to shout back, or to at least begin defending yourself. So lowering your voice catches them off-guard.

Next, Sam repeated the customer's name three times. Names are powerful words. They break through emotional static and capture attention. Hearing her name made the customer stop shouting. She was silent for the first time in five minutes.

Next, Sam told the woman that he was not prepared to be threatened, using the WISH formula. This broke her stand-over tactics. People who shout often get a psychological boost because they feel in control of the situation. So you need to balance your position in relation to them. When on the phone, you can do this by using a WISH statement, like Sam did. When you're in the same room as the aggressive person, you can balance out power by shifting your physical position. If you're sitting while they're yelling, stand up immediately. If you're standing and they're taller than you, step towards them.

Finally, Sam set a clear boundary. He calmly explained that he'd cancel the customer's account if she ever raised her voice to him again. The customer went dead silent. She never shouted at him again. And she later told Sam's boss, 'I knew shouting worked on your people, so I kept doing it until it stopped working with Sam.' It was all just a game to her.

If you're like Sam and want to stop screamers in their tracks, you need a process for responding to shouting from the alright position. Here it is.

1. Lower your own voice.
2. Say their name until they stop shouting.
3. Break their stand-over position.
4. Set a clear boundary (using a WISH statement).

When you're using this process, it helps to have some assertive phrases to draw upon. Here are a few suggestions.

- When I'm listening, I find it easier to understand if everyone speaks at a conversational volume. So I'd like to ask that you lower your voice.
- I find it easier to understand you when you lower your voice.
- I'd like to focus on what you're saying. But at the moment I'm a bit overwhelmed by your voice. It would help if you spoke just a bit softer.
- I'm listening. So please take your time and tell me, in a normal speaking voice, about what's bothering you/what the problem is.
- We can't change what happened in the past. But we do have choices about what happens next. Let's focus on finding solutions to this problem. What can we do to resolve it?

Responding when someone is critical or complains too much

Have you ever worked with someone who sets you up to take credit for their mistakes? Or have you had to put up with a boss who assigned blame without checking their facts? Perhaps your customers blame you for problems they create themselves. Or you've been frustrated by a disorganized supplier who made mistakes and then said you filled in a form incorrectly. If so, you've come across people who play the blame game. Not only are they annoying, but they can also damage your reputation. So what can you do about their behavior?

You can learn from Darwin's experience. Darwin was a really nice man. He was polite, positive and a hard worker. But he was having trouble with his friend, Don.

Don was a chronic complainer. Whenever Darwin went out socially with him, Don kicked up a stink about something. No matter how good a meal was in a restaurant, Don was sure to find something to dislike. Not only that, he'd make a big scene, first complaining to the waiter, then to the manager.

Don's behavior embarrassed Darwin. Darwin wondered whether he should speak up – and how he could do so without sparking Don's anger. He worked through his situation in five steps. You can use the same steps if you're ever dealing with a highly critical person.

1. Assess whether to challenge the behavior

Darwin started by thinking through the impact of Don's behavior. He realized that a lot of people were avoiding Don these days. Don's ex-wife refused to talk to him when he collected his children on weekends. His old friend Raj never answered Don's calls. Work colleagues avoided being assigned to projects with Don. Darwin himself was considering skipping future lunches with Don. The situation was serious enough to require action.

Darwin's cool assessment ensured that he made a measured response to Don's behavior.

If you're ever concerned about the impact of someone else's criticism, you should follow Darwin's lead. Ask yourself whether you really need to take the other person's words seriously. In general, it's only worth rebutting a critical statement if any of the following are true.

▸ The criticism will damage or end an important relationship.
▸ The statement has the potential to do *severe* damage to your reputation or that of your business.
▸ Your job may be at risk if the statement is believed by other people.
▸ There may be legal consequences attached to a mistake or event you're being accused of being involved in.
▸ Workplace bullying is taking place and the blaming behavior is associated with it.

If none of the above criteria apply, you might be wiser to do nothing than to expend energy refuting a trivial statement.

2. Work out what they're filtering for

Darwin started by thinking about what prompted Don's actions. He quickly realized that Don was just as critical of himself as he was of everyone else. His low self-esteem drove him to work too hard and to second-guess himself every moment of the day. He was constantly criticizing himself and finding things he needed to do better. Don was filtering for imperfections. Inevitably, he picked up on imperfections because those were what he filtered for.

3. Acknowledge their positive motivation
Understanding Don's mindset gave Darwin a way to connect with him. The next time the pair were organizing to go out for lunch, Darwin said, 'Don, I know you expect the restaurant to deliver a flawless meal. I remember you said that to the manager at Café Blu when you complained about how long your coffee took to arrive.' This statement helped Darwin build rapport with Don before challenging his nit-picking behavior.

4. Challenge the usefulness of the criticism
Darwin's next step was to gently challenge Don's mindset. He said, 'For me, our conversation is far more important than the restaurant's service. I didn't think it was worth complaining about the coffee.'

His statement was a great example of reframing – or giving an alternative meaning to – a difficult situation. Darwin was asking Don to consider what mattered most: the coffee or their friendship.

5. Request that they stop complaining
Darwin's next move was to politely request that Don change his behavior. He looked Don in the eye and delivered a WISH statement, saying, 'When complaints are made about small details like that coffee, I don't enjoy our time together. So what I'd like is for us to ignore any small issues so we can enjoy our time together. How will that work for you?'

At first, Don resisted the idea of staying quiet when he saw things going wrong. Darwin spent time listening and then explained again how uncomfortable the complaints made him feel. Finally, Don agreed to consult with Darwin before raising an issue with café staff. Their next lunch was complaint free and Darwin made sure he thanked Don for the change in his behavior.

Darwin's strategy was simple but effective.
1. Assess whether you need to challenge the behavior.
2. Work out what they're filtering for.
3. Acknowledge their positive motivation.
4. Challenge the usefulness of the criticism.
5. Request that they stop complaining.

The next time you're facing someone who complains or criticizes too much, try Darwin's steps for yourself. Here are some additional phrases to try.

- What makes you believe I did/was responsible for ...?
- I'm not sure why you're blaming me for ... Can you explain?
- What, exactly, are you saying I've done?
- How do you know that claim is justified?
- I don't believe this is a big issue. So I'd prefer to leave this matter here.
- When feedback is given in such a general way, it confuses me. So I'd like to ask you for more detail. How do you want me to change?
- I feel a bit overwhelmed by that feedback. Can you explain what I need to do differently?
- I appreciate feedback when it helps me improve. Right now, I'm unsure how your comments can help me. I'd like you to give me feedback on things I can change rather than my personality.

Responding to threats

Threats come in myriad forms. A boss might threaten an employee's job security. Workplace bullies might threaten apprentices or minority groups. Irate customers might insist on getting a service officer's name and then imply they'll hunt them down. Grudge-bearing employees might threaten to make a claim of harassment – when they themselves are experts in using inappropriate workplace behavior. Threats can be physical or psychological. They can be verbal, physical, written, texted, painted on your door or delivered in any number of ways – but they're always a boundary invasion.

Should you take threats seriously? In order to decide, it helps to understand the psychology behind threatening behavior. Many people experiencing a fight reaction will use threats to defend themselves. But most of them won't follow through. Threatening behavior is generally a reaction to feelings of fear. Not knowing what to do with these feelings, people in fight mode resort to threats and verbal attacks. They might threaten to harm you, your reputation, your job security, your friends or your family. But when they calm down, they realize that follow-through would be foolish.

Remember that threatening behavior is typically a reaction to pain or fear. Seemingly 'difficult people' threaten you because they feel weak. They want to reassert their power. And they believe that when you toe the line, they will feel okay. Unfortunately, when you give these people what they want, their feelings of satisfaction are short-lived. They need to assert their power again. That means they start to threaten and bully you again. So the more you comply, the more they will threaten you.

Here's an example. Lissa has a reputation as a workplace bully. She's currently targeting Halima. She started by verbally abusing Halima. Next, she started pushing her whenever their paths crossed in the hallway. Two weeks ago, Halima began finding abusive notes on her desk. Halima has decided to ignore the notes even though they upset her. She has thrown them all away.

Now Lissa is upping the ante. She's started leaving pornographic photos on Halima's desk. Reacting in flight mode, Halima throws the photos away. She interprets the photos as a threat that she's going to be attacked. So she arranges for her husband to collect her from work every day. Halima feels anxious and jumpy at work. And now she's having trouble sleeping at night. If she continues to stay silent, the threats will continue. But speaking up seems too hard to do.

Unfortunately, situations like this still occur in many workplaces. If you're exposed to similar threatening behaviors, here's a process for dealing with them.

1. Assess the likelihood that threats will turn into action

Halima is in a tough situation. She can't really be sure who is making the threats against her. However, the severity of their intimidating actions is escalating. She needs to take the situation seriously. Signs that can indicate levels of risk are increasing include the following.

▸ A sustained pattern of threatening behavior has emerged over time. Originally, incidents were trivial and annoying. Now, however, you are feeling frightened or anxious.

- Damage has been done to your property or your personal items have been stolen. For example, your work tools have been interfered with.
- A weapon has been flashed. For example, the aggressor has shown you a knife that they carry in their bag.
- You have been subjected to minor physical attacks. These might include pulling your hair, pushing, barging into you or slamming a door in your face.
- The aggressive person has mentioned that they know your home address, or you have seen them standing outside your home.

If any of the above behaviors take place, report the situation to your HR team, the police or security. Remember that many people are all talk and no action. They have a lot of pent-up emotions and their threats are usually a way of making themselves feel powerful. Pause and assess how likely it is that they will follow through with threats. Then, if the threat really does seem real, take action to protect yourself.

2. Tell them to stop

Do not ignore threats in the hope they'll stop. They won't, because you're sending a message that you are prepared to live with the situation. In Halima's case, for example, ignoring Lissa's verbal threats enabled the situation to escalate.

If you find yourself in a similar situation to Halima, it's important to send a single, clear message to the person menacing you. Tell them you want their behavior to stop. For example, if you're receiving threats by email or text, reply once with the message, 'I do not want to receive any more emails like this.'

After this, never reply to their threatening messages again. Hooking you into an email conversation makes the person issuing threats feel powerful. Therefore, replying repeatedly will escalate the situation. And of course, you should never match threat for threat as this will trigger more aggression.

If you're being threatened verbally say, 'If you continue to threaten me, I will report your behavior.' After that, walk away. Avoid being alone with the person who has made the threat. If they do find an opportunity to make another threat, immediately write down exactly what was said and when the threat was made.

3. Save the evidence

Halima has made a big mistake. Destroying the notes and the pornographic photos that were left on her desk leaves her with no evidence of the harassment. She has also disposed of the material that might be used to confirm that Lissa is the person victimizing her. When threats are made, it's important to keep the evidence intact.

If you ever receive threatening messages by email or text, print them out and make a hard copy file. Also save the messages on the device that you received them on. Don't go back and read the saved messages repeatedly – this will just upset you. The reason you've kept them is that you may need to provide evidence of the aggressor's actions, not so you can torture yourself.

4. Report the problem

Halima needs to report her situation immediately. The sooner she does, the sooner she'll receive the help she needs. People she can talk to include her line supervisor, a manager, her Human Resources team, a union representative, the organization's security team or the police.

If you find yourself in Halima's position, you should never allow threats to continue for longer than one week without being reported. The aggressor is usually violating workplace policy and is also often breaking the law. Report the threats to your manager, Human Resources department or the police. If you're not satisfied with the response your report receives, contact a lawyer.

In summary, there are four steps for dealing with threatening behavior.

1. Assess the likelihood that threats will turn into action.
2. Tell them to stop.
3. Save the evidence.
4. Report the problem.

Here are some phrases that might come in handy when dealing with threats.
- I'd like to report some behavior that is causing me concern.
- Recently, I've been the target of some threatening behavior.
- I need the way _____ is behaving to be dealt with.
- I'm worried about some threatening emails/texts/notes I've received.

Dealing with someone who brags excessively

Believe it or not, bragging is a form of fight-based behavior. This is because it involves boundary violations. For example, a team member who incessantly talks about their five investment properties is violating your boundaries by refusing to stop going on. The boss who drives you crazy droning on about his magnificent tomato plants is violating your boundaries in a similar way. The problem co-worker who keeps on about her wonderful grandchild is infringing your boundaries by distracting you from your work. Tiring and draining, braggarts can be extremely annoying to work with.

If you have a chronic bragger in your workplace, you may find them easier to deal with once you realize they're damaged goods. People brag when they are insecure. When a 'difficult' colleague brags, they want you to think of them as superior. And why would that matter to them? Well, they want to compensate for personal weaknesses that distress them. So they start playing up their strengths – or their imagined strengths. They may also put you down in an attempt to seem better than you. It's all part of the same psychological pattern.

For example, Lee's co-worker Marcia has a narcissistic streak. She constantly talks about how well she is performing. Whenever the talk turns to someone else's success, Marcia quickly takes over the conversation. She brags about the smallest success while ignoring the fact she has several areas of weakness. The more vulnerable she feels, the more she brags. Listening to her constant 'me' talk is wearing Lee down. When he sees Marcia approaching, his muscles tense and his heart starts pounding. He needs to stop Marcia's behavior impacting on his physical and mental wellbeing.

1. Keep your success stories to yourself

Lee has noticed that when he talks about his own achievements, Marcia becomes defensive. She immediately begins listing her own successes and strengths. The more threatened she feels, the more outrageous her bragging becomes. There is no end to her attention-seeking tales. Lee can minimize his exposure to this behavior by keeping all conversations with Marcia strictly neutral. If Marcia begins talking about herself, he should end the conversation. Most importantly, he should never match her claim-for-claim.

Yes, braggarts are annoying people. Maybe you'd love to put them in their place by pointing out your own successes. But that will only make things worse. Resist the temptation to put them down. Remember that bragging is often a sign of low self-esteem. Putting a braggart in a one-down position will only make them engage in even more difficult behavior. Avoid getting into competitive situations with someone who brags a lot. Competition will make them feel insecure and therefore trigger the bragging reaction. Keep your successes to yourself and don't set off a bragging war. Do you really have time to be involved in that?

2. Go on a jealousy fast

Why do you think Lee gets so upset by Marcia's bragging? It is obvious Marcia's just talking hot air. Deep down, though, Lee is comparing himself to her. He's worried that even if only a small proportion of Marcia's claims are true, she's better off than he is. This is faulty thinking.

Lee needs to remember that bragging sometimes prompts jealousy or self-criticism. If Marcia brags about the size of her investment portfolio, for example, he might wish his finances were in a better state. However, beating himself up isn't much use. He needs to focus on building his own financial success rather than envying Marcia's.

You need to take this approach to braggarts, too. If you're angry about someone's bragging because it makes you feel inferior, work on building your own self-esteem. Notice your own feelings. Do you feel jealous or inferior? If so, stop comparing yourself to others. Go on a jealousy fast. Instead of feasting on jealousy, focus on your own strengths and abilities.

3. Close down the conversation

Marcia is in full performance mode. But Lee doesn't have to be her audience. She'll soon stop bragging if there is no-one listening. So Lee needs to close the conversation down. Because bragging is a boundary violation, his best bet is to respond to Marcia's boasts with a WISH statement. For example, he could say, 'When you're talking about your investments, it causes me to lose focus on my work. So I'd like to ask that you hold off on describing your portfolio. Let's just work on the project brief for now.'

If you're ever faced with an annoying colleague like Marcia, concentrate on setting limits on how much you're willing to hear. Let the braggart know that you like them as they are. Explain that you will respect them regardless of what they own, where they live or who they have met. Emphasize that you know the braggart is very capable of doing well. Then point out that they seem to talk about themselves quite often and request that they cut back on praising themselves.

Remember to keep the conversation SAFE while using the three key steps for handling excessive bragging.

1. Keep your success stories to yourself.
2. Go on a jealousy fast.
3. Close down the conversation.

Use lots of WISH statements so you set clear boundaries. Here are a few examples of WISH statements my students have used successfully with bragging co-workers.

- When I'm listening to stories about your grandchildren, I become distracted. So I'd like to ask for some quiet time to concentrate on my work right now.
- While I know your garden is important to you, I'm getting behind with my work. If I could have an uninterrupted hour to work on the ABC report, I'll be able to finish it for you today.
- I know you're very proud of your achievements. And you've mentioned them three times so far today. I'd like to focus on my work now, so I am going to ask you to go back to your desk.

▸ To help you deal with excessive bragging, I've created a mind programming audio session called *Respond to braggarts*. You can buy your copy through my shop at http://difficultpeoplemadeeasy.com

---

Reacting assertively to controlling or pushy behavior

The aim of controlling behavior is to prevent mistakes or inconveniences. Have you ever come across one of these people at work?

▸ The boss who insists you copy them into every email you send.
▸ The supervisor who monitors every call you make to customers and then criticizes what you've said.
▸ The colleague who gives you instructions about how to do your job – even though you're perfectly competent.
▸ The manager who questions every decision your team makes.

If you have, then you know how annoying controlling behavior can be. In everyday conversation, we tend to label people who use lots of controlling tactics as 'control freaks'. Beneath the surface, these people don't trust anyone, so they desperately try to dominate and micro-manage.

Neil came to me with a classic example of this. Neil was irritated by his colleague, Sara, who kept giving him unsolicited advice. Because he'd never asked her to stop this annoying behavior, it had escalated over time. The final straw came when Neil was working on a client proposal. Neil left his draft proposal on his desk while he was at lunch. Sara took this opportunity to read it. When Neil returned from his break, Sara bailed him up in the meeting room. She insisted he should drop his price by 10 per cent. Neil knew that quality, rather than pricing, was his client's prime concern. He told Sara this, but she kept on insisting that he follow her advice.

Luckily, Neil had a coaching session with me that afternoon. We talked through his situation and developed a strategy for addressing it from the alright position. Here's what Neil decided to do.

1. Acknowledge positive motivation

Behind every controlling action is a positive intent. Yes, really. Neil didn't want to believe this at first. But eventually he admitted that Sara might have a good reason for her behavior. Perhaps she wanted to make sure things got done the right way. Or maybe she was terrified things would go wrong with the client contract. Recognising this would help Neil address Sara's behavior in a positive way, he decided to open their conversation by saying, 'I know you're keen to offer this client a great deal.'

2. Connect with 'and'

I asked Neil what he was going to say after his opening statement. He thought for a moment, then said '... but this client isn't concerned about price.' I pointed out that 'but' is a very powerful word. It activates the fight reaction because it implies that you're about to criticize the other person's perspective.

I suggested that Neil say 'and' instead. This would create the impression he was working with Sara instead of against her. For example, he could say '... and I agree it's important to give this client a great deal. I've spoken to him about his needs and he says quality is more important than price-point to him.'

Framing his challenge this way would keep Neil in charge of the conversation. By using 'and' instead of 'but' he would prevent an argument developing. You, too, can tap into the power of 'and' in similar ways. When you're talking to someone who wants control, always use 'and' to introduce your own perspective.

3. Thank them for their input

Just like 'and', the word 'thanks' can wield a lot of power. I suggested that Neil disarm Sara before requesting that she leave him to make his own decisions about the proposal. I reminded him that by saying 'thanks', he wasn't agreeing he'd take Sara's advice on board. He was simply keeping the conversation SAFE. Neil decided to keep his message short and respectful by saying, 'Thanks for taking the time to give me your thoughts.'

4. Assert your freedom to choose

The next step in Neil's planned process would be the most important. It involved explaining that he wanted to make his own decisions. My advice was that Neil should use a simple 'I'-based message to do this. For example, he could say, 'I prefer to keep pricing consistent, so I'm charging this client our standard fee.'

Neil could then follow up by talking Sara through his rationale for making this decision. He could also explain that he knew what he was doing and that Sara could trust him to get a good result. If Sara still seemed anxious, he could offer to take full responsibility if anything went wrong. No matter what, he needed to end this stage of the discussion assertively.

5. Refuse to be manipulated

Neil was worried that Sara wouldn't accept his message without a fight. So I explained that when boundaries are set, many people will test them. Yes, Sara might react in fight mode by arguing with Neil. Or she might react from a spite position by trying to manipulate him into doing things her way. But Neil didn't have to let these tactics throw him off course. He could simply reassert his message by saying, 'I know you would do it differently. I'm choosing to do it this way.'

The day after our coaching session, Neil emailed me an update. Sara had pushed back when he made his first challenge statement. They talked for about twenty minutes. Neil was careful to keep the conversation SAFE and listen to Sara respectfully. He also made it clear that he wanted to make his own decision. Finally, Sara agreed that his decision was sound. An unexpected bonus of the conversation was that she also agreed to let him make his own decisions in future.

Would you like to get a similar result when dealing with a pushy or controlling person? Then follow Neil's five-step process.

1. Acknowledge positive motivation.
2. Connect with 'and'.
3. Thank the person for their input.
4. Assert your freedom to choose.
5. Refuse to be manipulated.

Here are some useful phrases to use when dealing with controlling types of people.

- I know you're keen to get this done the right way.
- You really want this to go right. And so do I.
- I know getting this done well matters a lot to you. It also matters to me.
- I know _____ has worked for you in the past, so you want me to do it, too.
- Thanks for your suggestion. I prefer to do this my way.
- Thanks for your concern. I'll keep your comments in mind.
- Thanks for giving me your input. I still prefer to _____.
- I'd like to be free to make my own choices about this. How about I come to you if I ever need advice? Otherwise I'll complete the task myself.

- When I'm working on _____, I prefer to do things my own way.
- What I'd like is to be left to complete this task by myself. How about we work out a process for discussing any procedural changes at team meetings rather than on the job?

Reacting to arrogant remarks

Arrogance is a fight-based behavior because it is based on having *power over* you rather than building an equal relationship. Here are some signs that you're dealing with arrogant behavior.

▸ Nasty put-downs.
▸ Demeaning comments.
▸ Statements designed to highlight the speaker's superiority.
▸ Rude and demanding instructions.
▸ Inappropriate use of power or authority.

Although arrogant statements and gestures can be annoying, they are relatively easy to deal with. The key to success is managing your own thinking. After all, it's not what the other person says or does that matters, it's how you *interpret* their words or actions. You can view a 'difficult person's' raised eyebrow as an insult. Or you can choose to see it as evidence of their poor social skills.

For example, Karol was a student in my course *Dealing with Difficult People*. She irately told me about one of her customers, Mr Quigley, and his consistently 'insulting' behavior. Apparently, Mr Quigley refused to speak to anyone but the CEO. This was a problem because the CEO had instructed all frontline staff that she would only meet with Mr Quigley if he made an appointment first.

A few days after attending my course, Karol called to thank me. Mr Quigley had visited her workplace again. This time, however, she handled him differently. The CEO was out when Mr Quigley arrived. Karol offered to help him. He replied, 'I'm paid $400,000 a year. I don't deal with juniors.' In the past, Karol would have reacted defensively to this comment. This time, she stayed calm and used three simple steps to sort out the situation.

1. Picture their words as bait

During Karol's course, I'd mentioned that arrogant behaviors are a form of bait. People who use them want to hook you into a state of low self-esteem. They lose their power the instant you refuse to take their bait. Karol had taken this metaphor one step further and developed a creative technique for keeping herself calm.

In her mind's eye, Karol pictured Mr Quigley's words as bait strung on a hook. Then she visualized herself as a fish swimming past the hook. She found that 'seeing the bait' this way helped her switch into an alright mode for the first time ever with this customer.

2. Identify the real issue

Beneath every arrogant statement lies a need. In Karol's case, the customer's need was to receive advice from a senior staff member. Realizing this brought two benefits to Karol. It helped her stay calm because it reframed her situation. It also helped her work out how to satisfy Mr Quigley as quickly as possible. After all, difficult behavior stops when needs are met.

Identifying key needs involves listening very carefully to what the 'arrogant person' has said. As Mr Quigley spoke, Karol asked herself three key questions.
1. How many parts were in his message?
2. Which parts were intended as an attack?
3. Which part/s expressed Mr Quigley's real need or desire?

She realized that there were two parts to the customer's message. The first part was, 'I'm paid $400,000 a year.' This sentence carried a hidden attack message – 'I earn more than you, so I am better than you.' Karol chose to ignore this part of the message. Then she turned her attention to the *real substance* of the customer's message. This was that he wanted to see the CEO.

3. Give choices when you can

Karol was no longer distracted by Mr Quigley's bait. So it was easy for her to address the real issue: the customer wanted to see the CEO, but he'd need an appointment. She assertively stated, 'The CEO is not available. If you won't accept my help, you'll need to make an appointment with the CEO. She'll be available next week. Would you prefer to speak to her by phone or make an appointment to come back next week?' At this point, Karol was applying another idea I'd mentioned in the course – you should always try to give pushy people choices. This makes them feel powerful, which makes it more likely they'll drop their difficult behavior.

The technique worked on Mr Quigley. After a moment's silence, he decided that making an appointment would involve too much hassle. For the first time ever, he agreed to be served by Karol.

Karol's story is a great example of how to use three key steps to stay calm when dealing with seemingly arrogant people.

1. Picture their words as bait.
2. Identify the real issue.
3. Give choices when you can.

The next time you're faced with annoying, arrogant words or actions, make sure you use these steps yourself.

Here are some useful phrases for redirecting the conversation when dealing with arrogant behavior.

- It sounds like you're concerned about…
- What you want is…
- I realize you'd like…
- Let's focus on how to sort this out.
- So the issue is…
- I agree, this needs to be dealt with.

Planning how to handle YOUR situation

Think of someone who operates from fight mode when under stress. Use the questions below to plan how to deal with them assertively in future.

1. What behavior does this person use when they are stressed?

_____

_____

_____

2. What triggers this person's difficult behavior?

_____

_____

_____

3. How can you reduce or eliminate those triggers?

_____

_____

_____

4. Rate the level of risk the behavior poses to your physical and mental wellbeing on a scale of one (low risk) to ten (high risk).

_____

_____

_____

5. If necessary, create an action plan for ensuring your personal safety.

_____

_____

_____

_____

6. List four or five statements you can use to help calm the person down when they are stressed.

_____

_____

_____

_____

7. Write down the steps you will take to respond to their behavior the next time it happens.

_____

_____

_____

_____

CHAPTER EIGHT

USING STAIR WITH PEOPLE IN FLIGHT MODE

▶ In this chapter, you'll find out how to manage people who are in flight mode. On the surface, their behavior might not seem problematic – after all, flight mode results in submissive, non-assertive communication. However, failure to speak up or confront conflict can create a difficult dynamic in the workplace. If you need tips for talking assertively with flight-based communicators, this chapter is for you.

Key points to remember about flight mode

When someone operates from flight mode too often, they can become detached from other people, or even come across as aloof and unfriendly. Others might dismiss them as being shy or unconfident. And they might find more aggressive people taking advantage of their quiet style of communication.

Flight-based communicators can try too hard to avoid conflict rather than dealing with it and sorting it out. This can sometimes lead to others exploiting them. For example, other people may believe that a passive communicator's feelings, thoughts and needs aren't important. People who act from flight mode a lot have a tendency to put other's needs before their own. This can earn them the reputation of being 'people pleasers'.

If you work with people who operate in flight mode frequently, you'll know that they can be very hard to communicate with. Some find it hard to contribute to everyday conversations, let alone problem solving or conflict-management sessions. You may also find it impossible to get them to take the initiative or solve problems for themselves. But the good news is that you can learn how to work with them more effectively.

You already know that AIR stands for Assess the situation, Install calm and Respond from the alright state. Now let's explore how you can build on the AIR process as the foundation for handling flight-based behavior.

STAIR process

To deal with people in flight mode, it helps to add two extra steps to the AIR model. This turns it into the STAIR model.

SEPARATE YOURSELF FROM THEM

TAKE IT SLOWLY

ASSESS THE SITUATION

INSTALL CALM

RESPOND FROM THE ALRIGHT POSITION

The acronym STAIR also helps you remember the most important point about communicating with people who are coming from the flight power stance. You need to break the communication into steps and work through these steps slowly. This prevents the other person being pushed too far outside their comfort zone and being flooded with stress hormones. In other words, it helps them stay in an alright state and keeps the conversation SAFE. Here are some more details about how to use each step of the STAIR process.

Mentally separate yourself from the other person

It's easy to get caught up in 'rescuer' games when you're dealing with a flight-based person. For example, when a colleague plays victim and asks you to solve a problem for them, you may feel sorry for them and take on the extra work. Or you might spend hours giving career advice to a passive co-worker who has no intention at all of following it. They just want someone to listen to their 'poor me' story about how they haven't been promoted in over five years.

When you see someone worrying or feeling low, it's natural to want to help them by doing whatever you can to relieve their stress. But in the long term this exacerbates their problem. Someone who avoids taking risks doesn't learn. They become dependent on other people thinking and acting for them. So you need to be sure of your boundaries. Don't allow yourself to be contaminated by the other person's feelings. Instead, clearly separate yourself from them.

This is simply a matter of setting robust boundaries. Strong boundaries protect you from experiencing guilt when a passive person acts helpless. They keep you calm when tears are shed. They also prevent you from being hooked when a passive person plays victim. When you're setting boundaries with someone in flight mode, you'll feel very different to the way you feel when drawing a line with fight or spite behaviors. You may have to keep your own desire to be helpful or nice in check. Do this by reminding yourself that taking an assertive stance will force the other person to learn new coping skills.

Always set clear boundaries around what you can and cannot do for people who adopt a passive stance. Be particularly vigilant about protecting yourself from the mind games they sometimes play. If you feel guilty, protective or outraged on their behalf, it's very likely that you've been hooked into a 'rescue me' game. Don't react by trying to help. Instead, say to yourself, 'I'm not responsible for their feelings.'

Some people find it helpful to use visualization techniques to build a clear separation between themselves and passive people. One way to do this is to imagine you're directing a film. You're watching footage of the flight-based communicator playing the role of a helpless character. As you watch, you're scripting the commentary for a voiceover. This focuses on describing the specific behaviors the character is using and how these behaviors contribute to the 'victim' role.

For example, imagine you're talking to a colleague who often takes on a victim stance. As she tells you about how hard-done-by she feels, she begins crying. You have a sense that her tears are designed to hook you into fixing her problems for her. Looking down your imaginary camera lens, you say to yourself, 'Notice how she looks out the corner of her eye to see if she's hooked anyone into playing rescuer. She's a real expert at getting attention through tears.'

▸ If you want to get better at setting boundaries, buy a copy of my mind programming audio session *Setting boundaries and limits*. It's available on my shop page at http://difficultpeoplemadeeasy.com

---

Take it slowly

When dealing with people in flight mode, you need to take into account their physiology. Remember that they may very well be susceptible to flooding with fear hormones. Once their fear reaction has been triggered, it will be hard for them to respond from the alright position. Therefore, you need to work with them gently and slowly. Keep your movements calm and steady. Make your gestures small. Avoid approaching a fearful or anxious person too quickly or suddenly. Give them ample warning if you want to discuss touchy or difficult issues.

Your agenda is to help flight-based communicators solve their own problems. But you need to do this carefully. Avoid pushing them to change too quickly or leap into unknown territory suddenly. Instead, help them to gradually extend their personal comfort zone by asking lots of questions and encouraging them to think for themselves. Model rational thinking by using spotlight questions to prompt them to break down problems and find ways to generate solutions.

Here are some examples of useful spotlight questions for this situation.

- What needs to happen now?
- What can you do?
- Where can you get help dealing with this?
- What support do you need?
- Who can support you with this?
- Where do you need to go from here?
- What are you going to do next?

If the other person is unable to come up with their own ideas, gently make some suggestions. Make sure, though, that you avoid telling them what to do. Offer options and choices rather than directives. Remember that sometimes the best option is for the other person to consult a human resources practitioner, doctor, counselor or support service. If so, help them connect with a suitable practitioner. If they are very distressed, offer to call and make an appointment for them.

Remember that stress hormones can cloud thinking, so you need to help people in flight mode access the logical centres of the brain. Don't rush them. It can take a long time for someone to feel comfortable talking about their own thoughts, ideas or feelings. This means you may have to work hard to build rapport. Resist the temptation to push for insight or change. Instead, let them work things out at their own pace. When you are listening, it's important to resist filling in pauses. Silence gives the other person an opportunity to reflect and develop new ways of thinking about problems. Nod to show you are listening, but don't interrupt or answer your own questions on their behalf. Simply *remain silent*.

When the other person does finally speak, empathize with their perspective. Use a 'you frame' statement to reflect back the meaning of what they've said. If necessary, gently challenge feelings of helplessness or powerlessness by implying they are transitory. Do this by labeling feelings as being the emotions someone is aware of 'right now'. This implies that their emotional state may change in the future. Here's an example.

Carla: I know the new computer system will be too hard for me to learn. I've never been good with technology. I can't believe they're getting rid of the old system just when I'm feeling okay using it.

Nathan: You're feeling overwhelmed by the thought of learning a new system right now.

Be prepared to spend a long time drawing out the other person's perspective. If necessary, give a flight-based speaker 'time out' to think of responses to your questions. You can do this by suggesting they think about an issue for a couple of hours before telling you their thoughts. However, always make sure you follow up. Otherwise, they're likely to see the pause in conversation as a way of avoiding taking action.

BRENDA WAITS PATIENTLY FOR HER PAY RISE.

Never underestimate the importance of creating a SAFE environment when you're dealing with someone in flight mode. They're unlikely to speak up if they feel threatened. Help them open up by creating a comfortable space for communication. Speak to them in a private place where you won't be interrupted or watched over.

Assess the level of risk posed by flight-based thinking

When you're assessing the behavior of someone who appears to be in flight mode, keep an eye out for signs of depression or anxiety. Both of these mental health issues are quite common and can lead to subdued or non-assertive behavior. Of course, it isn't your role to diagnose mental health problems. But it can be useful to recognize signs that someone needs help.

Here are a few pointers on cues that can indicate that depression or anxiety underlies passive behavior. These can be a useful starting point for identifying whether you need to talk to someone about the possibility that they need support or assistance in dealing with depression or anxiety.

Cues that can indicate depression

Someone who is depressed will frequently experience emotions such as sadness, disappointment, loneliness, hopelessness, self-doubt or guilt. They may have physical symptoms too – fatigue, muscle pains, headaches and stomach problems can be associated with depression. Here are the main cues to look out for if you think someone at work is experiencing depression.

▶ Frequent absences from work.
▶ Arriving late and/or leaving early on a regular basis.
▶ Seeming to be overly sensitive.
▶ Crying or becoming upset a lot of the time.
▶ Losing their temper over minor issues.
▶ Becoming rude, socially withdrawn or distant.
▶ Finding it difficult to get going in the morning.
▶ Withdrawing or disengaging from team conversations.
▶ Not wanting to participate in social or team events.
▶ Being very quiet and uncommunicative.
▶ Taking little care in their personal appearance.
▶ Having trouble concentrating.
▶ Forgetfulness.
▶ Speaking in very negative or critical ways on a regular basis.
▶ Talking a lot about death or illness.

Cues that can indicate anxiety

Have you ever worked with someone who is jumpy, moody or irritable most of the time? Or have you noticed that one of your co-workers seems extremely passive, shy and compliant? This could mean you've worked with someone who suffers from high levels of anxiety.

Anxiety causes nervousness, fear and apprehension. These are normal feelings that everyone can experience from time to time. Feeling anxious before a big exam, during a job interview or when you're giving an important presentation are all natural reactions. However, when anxiety becomes relentless, extreme and out of proportion to your situation, it is a problem. This is what happens when someone has an anxiety disorder.

There are many different types of anxiety disorders, so actual diagnosis requires a professional assessment. But here are a few cues you can watch out for if you think difficult behavior may stem from a problem with anxiety.

▸ Frequently arriving late for work. Or arriving very early.
▸ Complaining about having trouble sleeping.
▸ Regularly talking about worries and concerns.
▸ Seeming to be preoccupied with what might go wrong.
▸ Appearing to lose concentration very easily.
▸ Irritability or restlessness.
▸ Seeming to be overly concerned with cleanliness or safety (e.g. constantly washing hands or checking doors and locks).
▸ Avoiding social situations (e.g. skipping meetings, being extremely passive in group situations, making excuses for not being able to attend social events or avoiding answering the phone).
▸ Requiring things to be done in very specific ways and becoming upset if usual routines change.
▸ Taking a long time to complete tasks.
▸ Avoiding interaction with co-workers or customers.
▸ Staying silent during team meetings.
▸ Crying or being overly emotional in response to reasonable feedback.
▸ Taking sick leave to avoid anxiety-provoking situations, such as public speaking.
▸ Failing to take the initiative or solve problems.

Like depression, anxiety presents in different ways for different people. However, these cues can be a useful starting point for working out whether someone needs professional help. See the final chapter of this book for tips on how to handle situations when a person may require professional help.

Install calm

Working with extremely passive people can be stressful. For example, you may feel irritated by their need to be given detailed instructions about how to do the simplest task. You may find it exhausting to talk to them because you need to work so hard to draw them out. You may also resent a colleague's inability to get through their own work without needing help from you. When they fail to deliver and you end up carrying their load, it's tempting to be angry. But what you really need to do is install calm.

When you're dealing with someone in flight mode, it's essential that you stay calm. Your behaviors send a clear message about your frame of mind. Many non-assertive people are highly sensitive to the meta-messages your body language communicates. If you are stressed or irritated, they will pick up on this and experience a fear reaction. The more fearful they become, the more heightened their flight reaction will be. So you need to manage both your thinking and behavior.

1. Shift your self-talk

Manage your self-talk. Sometimes passive behavior can trigger anger. Sometimes it sets off feelings of guilt or the desire to rescue. If the voice in your mind is critical, change what it says. Make it say something constructive, as in the following examples.

▸ They're doing the best they can, given who they are.
▸ This is a minor issue and not worth worrying about.
▸ The behavior is annoying, but the person is worthwhile.
▸ What are they doing that I *like*?
▸ The best three things about this person are …
▸ Three options I have right now are …

Also check that your internal dialogue isn't encouraging you to play rescuer. You're in rescuer mode if it's saying, 'they should do this…' Remember that you don't have to fix the other person's problems. Nor are you responsible for how they feel. You can use the following statements to replace any self-talk that suggests you should help a passive person feel better or solve their problem.

▸ When I take over, they lose the chance to learn.
▸ They are capable of sorting this out for themselves.
▸ I am leaving this to them.
▸ They feel … I choose to feel calm.
▸ Helping in the short term damages in the long term.
▸ They are not weak or helpless. They can deal with this.
▸ This is their choice, not mine.
▸ The best help I can give is a referral to a professional.

2. Visualize your boundaries

Remember that healthy boundaries keep you psychologically safe. You need to separate your own emotions from those of the person who is in flight mode. If you feel sorry for them or want to stop their pain, it's time to set a firm boundary. You may find this challenging at first, especially if you value helping others. Keep in mind that by rescuing someone you prevent them from learning to stand up for themselves. To help you detach from the other person's feelings, use this easy visualization technique.

Make believe there's a wall standing between you and the other person. Picture your words of advice or consolation as brightly-colored balls. Imagine yourself throwing those balls at the wall and having them bounce back at you. Then picture the other person's feelings as arrows leaving their body and flying towards the wall. Imagine each arrow hitting the wall and rebounding, returning the feelings to their rightful owner.

Remind yourself that many flight-based communicators can have self-esteem problems. They may try to shift the burden of their negative feelings onto you. They may imply that you are responsible for their misery. Or they may believe you're being cruel if you don't try to fix their problems. But you don't have to buy into their mindset. Let them deal with their own feelings instead of acting as though you're responsible for them.

Once you've got your boundaries firmly in place, you can tackle the task of influencing the 'difficult person's' state. You can use both verbal and nonverbal techniques to do this.

3. Empathize, don't sympathize

People in flight mode often feel overwhelmed by their feelings. Talking about their feelings can overcome this problem. After all, labeling and expressing troublesome emotions helps people deal with them. Here's a real-life example of the power of empathic listening.

I was teaching a course on communication skills, which involved a lot of student participation. One of the students was very subdued throughout the morning's activities. As we went to lunch, she mentioned that she had travelled from the country to the city to attend the course. She was staying in a five-star hotel and treating herself to a weekend away as well. I asked, 'How are you finding it?' She explained that she was feeling guilty. This was the first time she'd been away by herself since her young daughter had been diagnosed with a serious illness.

The woman opened up and told me about the conflicting emotions she was feeling. I didn't try to make her feel better or give her advice. I just used lots of 'you frame' statements to show I was listening. Twenty minutes later, the woman sighed loudly and said, 'I feel much better now. Thanks for listening.' Both her mood and physical state were visibly different that afternoon. She began to participate in activities with a new level of energy. She started to ask questions and contribute to group discussions. Her problem hadn't gone away, but her state had changed for the better.

4. Influence their physiology

Sometimes physical activity shifts people out of low, negative or 'stuck' states. In fact, doctors advise people with depression to exercise as a way to improve their moods. Exercise triggers the body to release chemicals called endorphins. These increase feelings of wellbeing. You can tap into the power of endorphins when communicating with someone in flight mode. For example, their mood will probably improve if you go for a walk with them. You may even find it is easier to discuss touchy issues walking side-by-side than when sitting around a table with someone whose energy is low or negative.

Another physical tactic you can use to influence state is offering a 'difficult person' a lolly. Sucking on a hard sweet can help relax tense muscles. Eating sweets can also bring back happy memories that help reduce upset and anxious states.

Respond with the right words

Every word and action you use when dealing with someone in flight mode matters. If you want them to change, you need to role model the skills of state management, problem solving and action planning. Always aim to build a SAFE environment when talking to someone in flight mode. Until they feel psychologically okay, they won't be able to contribute to the discussion from anything near an alright position. Here are some general principles to keep in mind when handling people who are operating in flight mode.

1. Interrupt their negative thinking patterns

Many people who spend their lives in flight position live in constant states of fear and anxiety. They avoid doing new things or going to new places because of that fear. They believe they're incapable of taking positive action. The more they believe this, the worse their fear becomes. They develop self-reinforcing patterns of beliefs. If you act as though those belief patterns are true, you help the other person maintain them. If you interrupt the negative thinking, you help them find new ways to approach life. Here's a classic example.

I was teaching a six-week course on how to use positive thinking techniques to boost motivation and confidence. One of the exercises involved students recalling and analysing a time they'd felt confident in the past. A young woman came over to me before starting the exercise and announced, 'But I've never felt confident.' I asked a few spotlight questions in an attempt to draw out a positive memory. But she was adamant. She'd never felt confident. 'Are you sure?' I asked. 'Yes,' she replied firmly. 'Well, congratulations,' I said. She gave me an unsure, puzzled look. 'You've just solved that problem,' I said, 'because right now you're 100 per cent confident that you've never been confident.' A startled look crossed her face and then she started laughing. By refusing to go along with her belief, I'd influenced her to change her own mind.

The point of this story is that you can reinforce others' negative beliefs or you can choose to interrupt them. If you want to break a pattern, use gentle humor or spotlight questions to do so. Aim to place the passive thinker in a position in which they can actively change their own perspective. Don't try to force the issue, but simply provide food for thought.

You can also make it easier for others to be successful by giving them safe, comfortable opportunities to learn new skills. Encourage them to sort out their own issues. Praise them when they make effective decisions. Point out their successes. Teach them problem-solving skills and give them feedback regularly. Remember that anyone can change, learn and grow. Don't ignore someone just because they spend a lot of time in flight mode at the moment.

2. Support risk taking

The fact that many flight-based communicators are scared of making mistakes means that their fears cause them to avoid taking on new tasks or making decisions. It creates a vicious cycle – the more they avoid risky situations, the timider they become. They live their lives in flight mode. Until they learn to break through their anxiety, their need to stay 'safe' restricts everything they do.

Libby is a friend who told me a poignant story about learning to take risks. As a child and young woman, she was plagued by depression and anxiety. At last her misery became too much to bear. She decided to end her life. But she wanted to visit Egypt before doing so. Egypt had been her lifelong passion. So for eighteen months she saved every cent she earned. This was going to be the trip of a lifetime.

Finally, Libby arrived in Egypt. Because she believed she was going to take her own life at the end of the trip, she totally let go of her fear. She did things she would never have dared to do at any other time of her life. She visited new places, she spoke to strangers and she ate foods she'd never tasted before. By the end of the month, she'd done hundreds of things she'd been too scared to do before. She learned the joy of living without her old mindset. She didn't end her life at the close of the trip, because she'd realized how much fun life could be when you try new things. Libby went home, set up her own business and started a healthy new relationship.

Libby had learned the art of taking risks. Everyone can do this, no matter how long they've spent in a passive mode. That's where you can be of assistance. Encourage people who spend time in flight mode to try new things. Act as though mistakes are a normal, acceptable part of life. Support them by teaching them solution-focussed, problem-solving skills. Praise them when they successfully take the initiative. And when they make mistakes, help them to learn from the experience. Be supportive in helping passive people become more assertive.

3. Sit through silence

A pause is powerful. When someone is silent, don't rush in to fill the gap. Instead, sit quietly with them. Match their body language so they sense that you're in rapport with them. Remember that not everyone processes their thoughts, feelings and emotions swiftly.

Many people need time to think before they contribute. So give the other person space. Ask a question and then sit quietly until they answer. You'll be amazed at the quality of an introvert's response if you give them time to formulate it.

4. Beware the procrastination trap

Many non-assertive people use procrastination as a way of easing their anxiety about taking on new tasks. This can be frustrating when their inaction impacts on you. Here's an example. Steven is concerned that he hasn't yet seen the draft report that Mary has been working on. When he asked her about it last week, she assured him that the report was progressing well. However, Steven knows that Mary has a habit of taking on more work than she can handle and that she doesn't say 'no' when other people ask her to help.

On the day the report is due, Mary comes into Steven's office ready with an apology. She's not even close to finishing the report. Steven is annoyed that the deadline hasn't been met and angry that Mary didn't let him know about her problems earlier. He decides to not let his annoyance show but instead encourages Mary to find her own way out of the situation. He uses spotlight questions to help Mary redesign her workload so she can make the report a priority. Then he coaches her to work out how to announce the delay to senior management.

By making Mary responsible for managing the consequences of her procrastination, Steven breaks out of rescuer mode. Additionally, he teaches Mary how to analyse and solve a problem. You can use a similar approach when dealing with fearful people who procrastinate. Guide them through the process of developing an action plan with clearly identifiable steps. Then follow up by meeting with them regularly and making them accountable for implementing that plan.

Setting firm review points after action planning helps tackle procrastination problem. Someone coming from a flight position needs support in taking on new tasks. They will put off starting a job if it seems overwhelming. Breaking a big project down into smaller pieces helps overcome this problem. Once the passive person has started the task, keep them on track by regularly reviewing progress.

5. Speak suggestively

People in flight mode are highly suggestible. Without being aware of it, they absorb the subtext of what you say. So be careful what you say to someone in flight mode. If you say, 'This change is going to involve a lot of hard work', they will interpret your message as being, 'This change will be overwhelming and too hard-to-handle.'

Here's a more positive way to say the same thing.

'The effort we put into making this change successful will be amply rewarded.' When using this type of statement, the person will hear a more positive message.

Here are some sentences you could use to help settle someone who is upset or overwhelmed.

- 🗩 Every time you think about this problem, you may begin to find ways to solve it.
- 🗩 As we talk, you may start feeling more relaxed about this situation.
- 🗩 I wonder how many ways you will find to deal with this.
- 🗩 You can choose which parts of the situation you pay attention to.
- 🗩 Yes, that was a problem in the past, wasn't it?
- 🗩 Of all the options available to you right now, I wonder which is most attractive to you?
- 🗩 When you look back on this situation and see it from a new perspective, I wonder what will make you feel happiest?
- 🗩 I'm just wondering what you can do right now to feel better?

6. Scale things into perspective

To help other people reframe worries and concerns, you can use a type of question called a 'scaling question'. As the name suggests, these questions ask people to measure their problems, feelings or reactions using a scale of one to ten. Scaling questions prompt people to reassess their interpretations of events and situations. For example, Sandi, a supervisor, is talking to an anxious team member, Tom. Tom is upset about a minor change to work procedures. Sandi uses a scaling question to put his fears in perspective.

Tom: I just can't cope with another change. I've got too much already.

Sandi: You're feeling stressed because of the change?

Tom: Yes.

Sandi: On a scale of one to ten, with one being no stress and ten being as stressed as you could be, where's your stress level right now?

Tom: About an eight.

Sandi: About an eight?

Tom: Yes.

Sandi: If you think back to the restructure you went through last year, where was your stress level then?

Tom: (laughing) Eleven.

Sandi: The scale only goes to ten.

Tom: Yeah, I see what I'm doing …

Sandi: So now you see things differently? Where do you put these changes now?

Tom: About a two.

Sandi: So how do you feel now?

Tom: Much better.

Once you become skilled at asking scaling questions, you can use them in many ways. For example, you can use them to challenge and reframe someone's worries by asking, 'On a scale of one to ten, where one shows something is not likely to happen and ten means it's highly likely to occur, how likely is it that … will really happen?'

You can also use scaling questions to prompt someone in flight mode to calibrate their own emotional state. Here are some more examples.

- On a scale of one to ten, where one is the worst that things could be at work and ten is the best, where are things for you today?
- On a scale of one, which stands for not worried at all, to ten, which stands for as worried as you can get, where would you rate your concern right now?

This type of questioning often prompts anxious or distressed people to acknowledge their fear so they can choose to do something about it.

Managing common flight-based behaviors

In this section you'll see how to manage different types of flight reactions. You'll learn how to handle situations such as working with people who over-think things, helping shy people to contribute more in meetings and dealing with people who cry or play victim.

Working with people who over-think situations

When someone spends a lot of time in flight mode, they may find it hard to solve their own problems. They may *think* about those problems a lot, but not in a constructive or solution-focussed way. Instead, they ruminate. They recall past situations in which they've felt bad. They focus all their attention on feelings of distress. They try to find reasons for things to go wrong. They beat themselves up emotionally and think of all the things they *could* have done. And as they do this, they become trapped in a negative state.

Someone may be ruminating if you notice that they're often engaging in the following behaviors.

▸ Telling the same story over and over again.
▸ Refusing to 'let go' of feelings of hurt or anger about something that happened a long time ago.
▸ Apologizing frequently and unnecessarily.
▸ Worrying about things that have already happened and which cannot be changed.
▸ Fixating on details of past negative experiences.

People who do this can be very draining. My friend Ralph was someone who ruminated a lot. We used to catch up over dinner once a month. Our conversations were lively, engaging and inspiring. Both of us really enjoyed our dinners together. I always thought we'd had great fun. But Ralph was a ruminator. He'd go home and find something to worry about. He'd replay our conversations in his head, word-for-word. Eventually, he'd find something he *shouldn't* have said or done. And then he'd fixate on it. Two days later, he'd ring to apologize. None of the events he apologized for had ever made an impression on me. Usually, I couldn't even remember them happening. But for Ralph, they'd become huge problems.

Ralph would spend hours telling me about the *insights* he'd gained into his personality through revisiting what he'd done wrong. But he never turned insight into action. He never dropped the habit of beating himself up. The point about rumination is that it expends great energy on situations that can't be changed. Ralph needed to learn how to let go of past perceived *mistakes* and focus on getting the results he wanted in future.

I decided to have an honest and appropriate conversation with Ralph. My aim was to give him feedback on the way he was undermining his own confidence. I also wanted to let him know I valued his friendship and didn't even notice the 'terrible' things he said. During the conversation, I used all the steps of STAIR. I also used two additional techniques, which you'll also find useful when dealing with people who over-think issues.

1. Reframe mistakes as miss-takes

In order to shift Ralph's thinking, I needed to influence (or reframe) the way he thought about making mistakes. I started the conversation by telling him how much I enjoyed our time together. Then I reminded him that he'd called me two days after our last dinner to apologize for challenging something I'd said. I told Ralph that I valued feedback and didn't see his comment as offensive at all.

I then told Ralph of an example I often use in training. A film director doesn't react as though a bad 'take' during a shoot is the end of the world. They treat it as a 'miss-take' and shoot the scene again. The most successful people and businesses in the world approach life this way. They don't see mistakes as disasters or events for which people should be punished. They view them as learning opportunities. Ralph laughed when he heard this story. I knew my reframe had worked.

2. Prompt them to think forward, not backwards

Ruminators focus on the past. This makes them feel powerless because there is nothing they can do to change the past. I pointed this out to Ralph. I asked him what benefit he gained from reviewing past 'errors'. He told me he wanted to make sure he didn't hurt anyone else because of his mistakes. Thinking backwards meant he could apologize if he needed to.

I pointed out that his apologies might be doing more harm than good. I talked him through our last post-dinner phone call, pointing out that he had apologized for actions I hadn't even noticed. Essentially, he'd planted the idea that I should be offended in my head.

Once again, Ralph laughed. I knew the conversation still felt SAFE to him. So then I challenged him gently, suggesting that instead of thinking back over mistakes he might want to plan ahead. For example, he could ask himself how to make the next dinner conversation even better. Or he could brainstorm topics to talk about and topics to avoid. In other words, he could take a solution-focussed approach to improve his social skills.

Again, I told Ralph a story. This focussed on a short conversation I'd had with my own therapist many years before. At the time, I wanted to set up my own business. But I was convinced I wouldn't succeed. I spent ten minutes listing all the things that might go wrong. My therapist looked at me for a moment. Then he asked, 'Has it ever occurred to you that everything just might be alright?' No, it hadn't. But from that moment on, I was able to challenge my own self-defeating ruminations.

Two days after our meeting, Ralph called me. Of course, I was expecting him to apologize for something. But he didn't. Instead, he thanked me. He said he'd learned a lot from our conversation. And from now on he was going to assume that everything just might be alright.

If you're dealing with someone who over-thinks things the way Ralph did, make sure you hold a STAIR conversation with them. And use those two extra techniques to help them put things in perspective.

1. Reframe mistakes as miss-takes.
2. Prompt them to think forward, not backwards.

Here are some words you can use during your conversation, too.
- That could be a good thing because …
- You must have learned a lot from that experience.
- What have you learned from that?
- Okay. So you've learned … How can you use that learning in the future?
- What will you do differently as a result of this experience?
- Let's imagine a similar situation happens tomorrow. Walk me through how you'll handle it.

Drawing out people who don't speak up in meetings

Many people with low self-esteem dread speaking up in groups or meetings. Their behavior therefore becomes flight-based. They find excuses not to attend. Even when they're physically present, they make no contribution. They sit silent and fearful, never mentioning the great ideas they've bottled up inside. Here are some behaviors to monitor if you are concerned someone is scared to speak up in meetings.

- Pulling out of work or social events at the last minute.
- Staying silent during meetings.
- Blushing or getting flustered when you ask for their input.
- Fixing their attention on a phone or other device during meetings.
- Taking sick leave on days meetings are scheduled.
- Refusing to make presentations even though their role requires it.
- Arranging for an 'emergency call' to take them out of a meeting just before they're due to give a presentation.

If you work with someone who is anxious about talking in meetings, there are ways to make it easier for them to contribute. Remember to set up a SAFE environment in your meetings. And try these additional steps to put them at ease.

1. Give advance notice

Start by giving ample warning about the topics to be discussed at meetings. For example, before a formal meeting you can have a one-to-one discussion with them. Go through the agenda and ask them to think about each issue. This 'primes' them, so they can work from an alright mode during the meeting.

2. Manage group dynamics

Act to prevent the more assertive people dominating discussion. Ask for a contribution from everyone. Without putting the non-assertive person on the spot, ask for feedback or comments. A useful way to do this is to pose a question and ask everyone to jot down their thoughts about it. Then go around the table, asking each person to read what they've written. Having a written response ready makes it much easier for a passive person to talk from the alright position.

3. Show you value their contributions

Demonstrate that you value their contributions. Foster trust. Build rapport and work to establish positive work relationships over time. This often encourages quieter types to open up. You can use carefully worded questions to draw your co-workers into conversations. Instead of saying, 'Do you agree?', which encourages a brief answer, say, 'What do you think about this?' Follow up with probing questions to help draw out their thoughts.

4. Acknowledge their successes

When someone who operates in flight mode *does* speak up, acknowledge their contribution. Of course, it's not your job to shore up a passive co-worker's self-confidence. But you can help by letting them know they're appreciated. Express thanks for their contribution. When it's time for you to part, smile and let them know that you enjoyed talking with them.

These techniques are really just steps for making all meetings productive. But they're particularly useful when you want to draw passive communicators into conversation.

1. Give advance notice.
2. Manage group dynamics.
3. Show you value their contributions.
4. Acknowledge their successes.

You can also use the following starter phrases to encourage quieter people to contribute during your meetings.

- I'm looking forward to hearing your thoughts at tomorrow's meeting. In particular, I'd like you to comment on …
- Tomorrow's meeting will focus … Please bring two or three ideas about how we can handle this.
- I'd like to go round the table and get everyone's input on this.
- [name] I'd like to ask you to answer a question in a moment. What do you think about …? (Leave them time to think, then call on them again.)
- Let's each write down our ideas and then I'll read them out.

Responding to nagging

Nagging involves repetitive reminding, fault finding or instructing. Some people who nag are outright aggressive. But believe it or not, nagging is usually a flight-based behavior. It is underpinned by a fear that something will go wrong, or that the speaker will not have their needs met. Many flight-based communicators use nagging rather than dealing with conflict openly and assertively. They hope that by repeating their requests, they will gradually wear you down.

Here are some of the signs that someone is nagging you.

▸ Constantly giving you the same instruction.
▸ Insisting that you do something their way even though you have your own perfectly good way of doing it.
▸ Reminding you again and again about small details.
▸ Going over and over the same event from the past.
▸ Refusing to let you rest until a task is completed.
▸ Bringing up the same issue or topic of conversation repeatedly.

Nagging can be irritating, particularly when the other person takes a 'poor me' stance as they do it.

Belinda was someone like this. She was driving her co-worker Adam to distraction. She was constantly worrying about something. She worried that customer orders wouldn't be processed on time, that a critical deadline would be forgotten or that mistakes would be made when sending out goods to customers. To deal with her worry, she issued '1001 reminders a day'. Adam perceived Belinda as a nag. She perceived Adam as a risk.

Adam needed to help Belinda feel safe and secure. He also wanted to request that she stop checking up on him and reminding him about things he had under control.

After attending a workshop on dealing with 'difficult people', Adam filled me in on how he had assertively managed the situation with Belinda. Essentially, he used the STAIR model. During their conversation, he also used the following strategies for dealing with nagging.

1. Look for their positive intent

Adam was feeling pretty annoyed about Belinda's behavior. So he knew he'd need to calm down before approaching her. He decided to use reframing to do this. He tried to find a positive way to view Belinda's actions. He asked himself why she was resorting to nagging behavior. As he thought this through, he realized something important. Belinda didn't *mistrust* him. She was trying to *help* him.

Thinking this way was a smart move on Adam's part. He'd shifted his attention away from *what* Belinda was doing to *why* she was doing it. He remembered that behind any annoying behavior there is a positive intent. For example, he knew Belinda had unusually high standards. Her positive intent was to pass those standards on to Adam.

2. Deal with the presenting issue first

Adam realized that the next time Belinda 'nagged' him, he had two issues to deal with. First, he needed to address whatever point she had raised. Then he needed to request that the repetitive reminders cease. He decided to respond to Belinda from the alright position the next time she repeated a request. He'd start by acknowledging her positive intent. He'd let her know that he'd understood her message.

Next, Adam decided he'd outline what he was going to do about the issue Belinda had raised. For example, if Belinda had repeated a request that he process all the orders by 4.00, Adam would say, 'Thanks for your feedback, Belinda. I know you want me to process the orders today. And I agree that it is important to get them finished on time. Our deadline for this task is Thursday, so I have put aside time to complete the orders on Wednesday afternoon. You can count on me to finish on time.'

3. Deal with the nagging behavior

Once he'd closed off the presenting issue, Adam was determined to request a change in Belinda's behavior. He knew it would be important to use flameproof language when he did this. After all, using the word 'nag' would spark a defensive reaction. Instead, he decided to say, 'Belinda, you've mentioned the deadline for packing three times today.'

This statement was clear, concise and verifiable. Belinda agreed that she had, indeed, issued multiple reminders about the deadline for orders. She explained that she wanted to make sure all customers received their goods within the promised 48-hour turnaround time advertised on the company's website.

Adam acknowledged Belinda's positive intent by saying, 'I know you're committed to maintaining high standards of service. And so am I.' He saw her shoulders relax as soon as he said this. It seemed he'd got through to her at last. Now she was less likely to resist his feedback message. So he went on to request a change in her behavior.

He gently said, 'I notice a similar pattern every day. Yesterday you asked me about the orders four times. On Monday you did the same thing. So I'd like to explain how I'm managing my time. I have scheduled time to package orders every afternoon between 1.00 and 4.00. This leaves me an extra hour to handle any unexpected problems. So you can be confident all packages will be processed within our promised 48-hour timeframe. If you like, I'll let you know when they're finished each day. And I'd like to request that you don't follow up on this task before I update you each day.'

Belinda was surprized to hear that Adam was actively managing his workload. She'd been worried that he was leaving the processing to the last minute. Now she knew that she could trust him to get the job done. She agreed that receiving an update each day would help her stop worrying. From that day on, she gradually stopped reminding Adam to do things. It took a while – after all, a habit can be hard to break – but eventually she stopped 'nagging'.

If you work with someone like Belinda, remember to focus on their positive intent. Use the STAIR process to keep your conversation on track as well as trying out the extra steps Adam used.

1. Look for their positive intent.
2. Deal with the presenting issue first.
3. Deal with the nagging behavior.

You'll also find the following statements useful when dealing with nagging behavior.

- You brought this up yesterday, this morning and again now. Let me talk you through what I'm doing about it.

- You've raised this issue several times. I think we need to discuss it.
- You've asked me to do this five times now. I will complete it by tomorrow. How about I tell you when it is finished so you don't need to worry about it?
- Thanks for that suggestion. I'll think about it and let you know what I decide to do.

Handling someone who cries

Do you find it tough to handle situations when someone cries? If so, you're normal. Many people feel distressed or unsure of what to do when they encounter another person's tears. One of the reasons for this is that seeing someone crying triggers a mirror neuron response in you – you begin to 'catch' the upset feelings of the other person. A second reason you may feel uncomfortable handling others' tears is that you've been socialized to do so. Many of us view the public expression of negative emotions or distress as something that breaches a social norm.

Nevertheless, you will come across people who cry at some stage in your career. So it pays to learn how to deal with them. You don't need to play the role of a psychiatrist or counselor. But you do need to know how to apply emotional first aid. The earlier you do this the better. Stay on the alert for early signs that someone is about to start crying. Here are some triggers to look out for.

- Flushing or going pale.
- Eyes going red or watering.
- Rubbing eyes.
- Rummaging in a pocket or bag as the person looks for tissues.
- Cracking or choking voice.
- Going silent.
- Looking around the room for tissues.

Here's a process for handling tears with empathy while keeping the appropriate boundaries in place.

1. Stabilize your own feelings
Before doing anything to deal with the other person's distress, manage your own state. Do a quick physical scan to check your reaction to the

tears. Are your own eyes welling up too? Is there a lump in your throat? Has your heartbeat accelerated? If any of these things are happening, use your state management skills. Adjust your posture so that you are holding yourself in a calm, open way. Take a couple of deep breaths. Wait a moment to allow your heartbeat to slow down. Then sit beside the person who is crying.

Next, manage your own thoughts and feelings. Often, seeing someone in tears triggers a desire to sooth them or solve their problem. Hold this reaction in check. Resist the urge to say, 'Don't cry' or, 'It will be okay.' These words stem from your own need to escape a distressing situation – they are not genuine words of comfort.

Remind yourself that you are more able to deal with someone in distress when you keep your own emotions in check. Even if you'd like to relieve the other person's pain, you can't. You probably have no control over the problem or pain they're facing. All you can do is sit through the tears with them.

▸ If you find it hard to keep your feelings in check when someone else cries, download a copy of my audio session, *Manage your emotions*. It's available on my shop page at http://difficultpeoplemadeeasy.com

---

2. Spell out what you're going to do

If someone is very distressed, they are probably experiencing a state of psychological shock. The adrenaline and cortisone running through their system will make it hard for them to think clearly or understand anything you say. So you need to take charge of what happens next.

Briefly and clearly explain what you're going to do for the next few minutes, making sure that your actions will enable the other person to cry without feeling judged. For example, you might say, 'I am just going to sit with you for a moment' or, 'Let's sit quietly for five minutes.'

3. Follow their lead

Allow the upset person time to work through the intensity of their feelings. Some people want to talk at this stage. Others just want to sit and cry. Whatever they do, your job is to follow their lead. If they start talking about whatever has triggered their tears, use 'you frame' statements and your deep level listening skills. Focus on expressing empathy and showing that you're present. If the other person remains quiet, just sit still. Make sure you keep your body language relaxed and open, so you don't send the meta-message, 'Please stop crying.'

Resist the temptation to directly hand the distressed person a tissue. Doing this can be interpreted as a plea for them to cease their tears. Instead, put a box of tissues within easy reach, so they can help themselves when they need to. Also, avoid making statements such as, 'Everything will be okay'. After all, it might not be. And even if it is, the person who is crying doesn't believe that right now.

4. Turn the hug into words

When someone is crying, you may want to hug or console them. But this isn't a wise choice. Hugging can make some people feel uncomfortable or awkward. It can also violate physical boundaries. So you need to follow the advice I was given in a counseling course and 'turn the hug into words'. This means expressing empathy. The best way to do this is to use a 'you frame' statement such as, 'You're feeling very upset because ...' or, 'You have strong feelings about what has happened.'

Never, ever, say something along the lines of, 'I know exactly how you're feeling. Exactly the same thing happened to me last year.' While the intention behind such words is positive, their impact can be negative. The distressed person might hear your message as, 'I've got a better story than yours' or, 'Don't make such a big fuss. Everyone has gone through this sort of thing.'

5. Monitor state changes

As you know, it takes at least ten minutes for the stress reaction to subside. Allow the other person time to express their feelings. Meanwhile, look and listen out for signs that their state is changing in a positive way. Here are some cues to watch out for.

- Shifts in skin color (for example, a pale face beginning to flush).
- Postural changes.
- Decreased flow of tears.
- Calmer voice.
- Shifts from emotive to rational language.
- Slowing and deepening of breathing patterns.

Don't move on to discussing what needs to happen next until you've observed signs that the other person is ready to do so. They will need to be closer to an alright stance before being able to think of or absorb options for action.

6. Ask what they want to do next

Once the other person has settled, gradually shift their focus to what needs to happen next. Don't talk about long-term plans. Simply work with them to develop a plan for the next few hours or days. Try using a spotlight question such as, 'What do you want to do now?' or, 'What is it you need right now?'

If they can't come up with an action plan alone, you can offer a few suggestions. For example, they may want to take some quiet time to consider their position. It may be helpful for you to call a family member or friend. Or they may agree to you setting up an appointment with a professional counselor so they can discuss more serious issues.

In summary, there are six steps you can take to deal with someone who is crying.

1. Stabilize your own feelings.
2. Spell out what you're going to do.
3. Follow their lead.
4. Turn the hug into words.
5. Monitor state changes.
6. Ask what they want to do next.

The following phrases are also useful to keep in mind when you're faced with a situation involving tears.

- I'm just going to sit with you a moment.
- We'll sit here for a while together.
- I'm going to close the door and then come back to sit beside you.
- Take all the time you need. I will stay with you.
- You seem very upset.
- You're distressed because …
- You feel … because…
- You're feeling really sad about what's happened.
- This is really painful for you.

Managing people who play victim

Have you ever had to work with someone who acted like a victim even though they weren't? Perhaps you've been driven to distraction by a co-worker who constantly moans about how badly their partner treats them. Maybe you've been bailed up by a teammate who complains and whinges about everyone else in your department. Or perhaps you've had to deal with customers who bring up problem after problem in an effort to gain attention. All of these people are taking on a 'victim mindset'.

Someone adopting a victim mentality blames other people or fate when they are unhappy. They genuinely believe they have no control over what happens to them. They attribute both their problems and their successes to circumstances or to other people. Theirs can be a problematic mindset because it makes them feel powerless in situations in which they really do have choices and power. The victim mentality is a way of playing out a flight reaction.

Victim mentalities develop over time. They are usually formed when someone goes through a series of negative or disempowering events. These events train the person to expect the worst in life. Unfortunately, such pessimistic mindsets tend to be self-sustaining. The more negative events the person encounters, the more they take on a victim mentality. Their emotional intelligence plummets and they believe that they are being picked on and subjected to harsh treatment. Eventually these people begin to react to everything in a negative way. Negativity becomes a normal state for them and they adjust to having a dour outlook on life. Sadly, being stuck in a victim mindset can lead to depression over time.

Some people with a victim mentality begin to take pride in having lots of problems. They will tell their tales of woe and revel in the attention you give them. But living in a victim state is not healthy. The victim mindset undermines someone's ability to succeed in life. It makes people retreat into cocoons in which they desperately try to protect themselves from the world. If you're dealing with someone who is acting like a victim, you may notice some of the following behaviors.

▸ Giving up quickly on difficult tasks rather than attempting to learn how to do them.
▸ Constantly talking about their problems or about being mistreated by other people.

- Avoiding situations in which they have to take action for themselves.
- Passing the buck when problems occur.
- Complaining about being disrespected.
- Refusing to stand up for themselves.
- Telling lots of 'poor me' stories.
- Repetitively going over situations in which they felt hard done by.

Having a victim mindset can lead to stress and anxiety. For example, imagine what happens to someone with a victim stance when their car breaks down during a long trip. Instead of thinking rationally and figuring out how to get help, they dwell on their own bad luck. They blame their mechanic, their partner or fate. But while they're doing this, they're no closer to finding a way to get home safely. Their negative reaction makes the whole experience more stressful.

People with victim mindsets frequently play the 'blame game'. They suggest that others are responsible for how they feel. Then they try to win sympathy, support or even financial compensation for their situation. So how should you deal with them? Here is a process I saw a training consultant called Peter using with great results.

Peter was a superb facilitator. He had a quiet, calm energy about him. No matter what happened in the training room, he was able to deal with it. One day I was sitting in on a stress management workshop run by Peter. Lucia was a participant in the course. She had a reputation in the business for being hard-to-handle because she became very worked up over small matters. She was adept at playing the victim role. So I was curious to see what she'd make of the course content.

As soon as Lucia sat down, she began complaining. Her back hurt. The chairs were badly designed. She didn't think she could sit in them all day without standing up. Peter calmly pointed out that she could stand up any time she needed to.

Around 11.00, Peter gave the group an exercise that involved drawing a personal timeline. He suggested that each person highlight their best and worst jobs on their timeline. Lucia began sniffing as she drew her timeline. At first I thought she had a cold. Then I realized she was crying. Peter approached her and asked how she was feeling.

Lucia replied, 'Awful.' Then she burst into loud, resonant sobs. The rest of the group stopped drawing and began shuffling uncomfortably. Peter handled the situation calmly and SAFEly, in four steps.

1. Access a calm state

First, Peter sat next to Lucia. He didn't hand her a tissue or try to calm her down. He just sat there. His body language was open and relaxed.

He seemed to have all the time in the world. His attention was focussed solely on Lucia. Because Peter seemed so calm, Lucia's sobs began to subside. Peter simply sat there until she was quiet.

Peter's response really highlighted the importance of managing your own state when dealing with someone who is playing the victim. It was obvious Peter was not taking on Lucia's distress. He wasn't becoming upset himself and he wasn't trying to soothe her. I talked to him later about how he did this. He said he simply reminded himself that Lucia needed time to calm down. His job was to give her that time.

This is something to keep in mind if you're ever dealing with someone who is playing the victim role. Dealing with people in flight mode requires time and patience. Remind yourself that rushing to find a solution or sort out the other person's feelings won't help. It may even aggravate the situation if the other person perceives that their attention-seeking behavior is reaping results. Just wait until they calm down.

2. Express empathy

Once Lucia's tears had abated, Peter used a 'you frame' message to show he understood her distress. He said, 'You're feeling overwhelmed by what your timeline brought up.' Lucia seized on this opportunity to continue playing the part of helpless victim. She also tried to switch into the blame game by saying, 'I can't believe you did such a confronting exercise. All I could think about was how awful my first boss was. She was a bully. She humiliated me over and over again. And then I remembered how badly the team in my first job treated me. I've never had a job I enjoyed in my life.'

Peter didn't try to defend himself. Nor did he attempt to challenge Lucia's perspective that her misery was always caused by other people. Instead, he said, 'You believe that no-one has treated you well at work so far. You're feeling hurt and angry about that.'

This statement was very clever. It expressed empathy. It was non-judgemental (after all, judgemental language makes people in flight mode go deeper into their victim positions). But it also subtly avoided showing agreement with Lucia's suggestion that other people were always to blame for her misery. Peter knew that agreeing with such a mindset would simply reinforce Lucia's victim stance.

If you find yourself dealing with someone similar to Lucia, remember to keep your language flameproof. Don't use words that suggest you're judging their feelings or perspectives. And never agree with their assumptions that they are powerless.

3. Refuse to play rescuer

Lucia responded to Peter's empathic statement by saying, 'That's right. I've never worked in a good team. Everyone always treats me badly. I don't know what to do.'

Lucia's last sentence was a classic baiting tactic. She was attempting to hook Peter into giving her sympathy and advice. But Peter didn't. He just asked, 'How does that make you feel?' Lucia wailed, 'Awful.' There was a pause. Then Peter asked, 'Is that how you want to feel?'

At this stage, he was asserting his boundaries by refusing to take Lucia's bait. Instead of being hooked into giving advice or solace, he was passing Lucia's problem back to her. Of course, Lucia didn't really want to accept responsibility for sorting herself out. So she replied, 'No.'

4. Help them learn

Peter now moved to the fourth step of shifting someone out of victim stance: making them responsible for finding their own solutions.

'Well,' he said, 'how about you write down what you want to feel instead? During the lunch break we can talk about what you want to do next. Here's some paper.'

He then moved Lucia to the back of the room and focussed his attention back on the rest of the group. By focussing Lucia on a solution state (feeling happy at work) rather than a problem state (feeling victimized at work), Peter managed the situation with respect and assertiveness. It wasn't his job to give Lucia one-to-one counseling. But it was his job to manage her behavior so that the rest of the group could continue learning.

During the lunch break, Peter gave Lucia the details of her Employee Assistance Service. He talked her through the benefits of counseling and she agreed to try it out. This was as far as Peter needed to go. He'd provided support by finding someone who could help her. But he hadn't engaged in rescuing behavior.

You should keep the distinction between helping and rescuing in mind if you come across someone who plays the victim role. Remember that role-playing victims usually have very poor problem-solving skills. They get through life by depending on other people to sort out their issues. Don't let them trap you into taking on the wise advisor role. You'll end up spending hours trying to sort out their messes only to find they never take action for themselves.

Encourage them to attend training or to work with a coach or counselor. The more they learn, the more independent they will become. Use the steps of STAIR to keep your boundaries intact as you talk to them.

And if necessary, use Peter's steps for handling their attempts to bait you into solving their problems.
1. Access a calm state.
2. Express empathy.
3. Refuse to play rescuer.
4. Help them learn.

You'll also find the following statements useful when dealing with role-playing victims.
- I understand you are going through a tough time right now.
- You feel really bad right now.
- You're upset today because …
- You feel powerless at the moment because …
- It seems like nothing is going right for you at the moment.
- I can't tell you what to do. What options do you have?
- That's up to you to decide. Let's talk about what you think you could do.
- That sounds like a big problem for you. I can't really do anything about it. But I am sure you can find a way through the situation. What have you thought of so far?
- That's a great question. What do you think you can do?
- I'm not sure I have the answer. But I am sure you can find one. What could you do?

Protecting yourself from chronic negativity

Being exposed to constant negativity can be exhausting and disheartening. If you've ever worked around someone who had a negative attitude, you'll know just how contagious their dark moods can be. Even when things are going well, they'll find something to complain about. Their mindset is expressed through bitter remarks, pessimistic comments, morbid jokes and depressing statements. Walking into a room, these people instantly notice what's wrong. They screen out positives and focus all their attention on the negative aspects of their environment.

Everyone has the occasional bad day. But some people become stuck in an ongoing state of gloom and pessimism. These are the people who gain reputations as team members with 'bad attitudes' or 'negative personalities'. Although they are hard to cope with, you need to keep in mind that their thinking patterns are not normal. Chronic negativity is often a warning sign that a difficult person suffers from depression or anxiety. Someone whose negativity has become ingrained and problematic often behaves in the following ways.

▸ Makes more negative comments than positive comments during conversation.
▸ Picks out small details to criticize, even when things are going well.
▸ Rarely or never expresses happiness or contentment.
▸ Responds to positive statements with 'yes, but...'
▸ Is sullen in meetings.
▸ Fails to take preventative action when it's obvious a problem is developing.
▸ Refuses to take on anything that is not listed in their job description.
▸ Constantly says, 'that won't work because' or, 'we tried it before and it didn't work.'
▸ Raises problems without suggesting ways to solve them.
▸ Makes jokes about illness, death or misfortune.
▸ Takes pleasure in others' problems or unhappiness.

Sadly, you can't really do anything to change a 'difficult person's' mindset. But you can manage the impact their behavior has on you. Miranda realized this after working with her chronically negative co-worker, Julian, for six months. When she first met Julian, he seemed nice enough. But it wasn't long before Miranda was desperate to get away from him.

The problem was that Julian was constantly negative. Miranda sat in the cubicle next to his. This meant she was constantly overhearing his negative commentary. No matter the topic of conversation, Julian would find something to complain about. He filled every interaction with negative statements and depressing observations. Even his jokes were focussed on dark topics, such as death and disease. Miranda compared her experience to that of a non-smoker sitting next to a smoker. She was in a toxic environment of 'passive listening'.

At first, Miranda had tried to cheer Julian up. She baked cakes for the team and gave Julian first pick. When he complained about having a headache, Miranda pulled headache tablets from her bag. When he said he didn't like his chair, Miranda swapped it for hers. But none of this made any difference. Julian was still negative and out-of-sorts.

Miranda came to me for coaching because Julian's behavior was bringing her down. She was thinking about leaving her job – which she loved – because she couldn't face sitting beside Julian day after day. She was also distressed because she hadn't been able to 'help' Julian. When I asked why she thought this was her responsibility, she said, 'Because I don't want to see anyone suffer.'

1. Be realistic

Stage one of Miranda's coaching program involved shifting her belief that helping Julian was her responsibility. It took a while, but gradually Miranda realized that Julian *was getting something out of being negative*. In fact, he seemed to be enjoying it. This insight helped Miranda mentally detach. She accepted reality. Even if she was a master influencer, she might never be able to change Julian's attitude.

2. Know which part of the problem you 'own'

Miranda now had a problem to solve. How would she minimize the impact Julian's attitude was having on *her*? She and I discussed the fact that Julian's attitude was his own business. His thoughts existed within his 'personal space'. Miranda had no right to change what happened within that space.

However, Julian's *behavior* existed within the 'shared space' of the team. It impacted directly on Miranda. Therefore, Miranda 'owned' the problem of how to reduce the impact of Julian's behavior on her. She decided to speak to Julian from the alright position and request that he cut down on the number of negative remarks he made in their shared workspace.

3. Be clear about your BATNA

Miranda wasn't convinced that speaking to Julian would do any good. So I suggested she develop a BATNA. In negotiation, a BATNA is your 'best alternative to a negotiated agreement'. It's your back-up plan because it represents the action you'll take if you have to walk away from the negotiation. By thinking dispassionately about her BATNA, Miranda was able to decide what she'd do if her conversation with Julian went nowhere.

I asked her to brainstorm all the options available to her if Julian's chronic negativity continued. She came up with the following ideas.

- Refuse to work with Julian.
- Complain to her supervisor or HR.
- Request that she be moved to another cubicle.
- Quit her job rather than put up with more negativity.
- Find a new job in another business.
- Request a transfer within the same business.

Once Miranda had completed her list, we reviewed it together. I asked her to identify the best of her options – her BATNA. Miranda decided this was moving to another cubicle. If she minimized her exposure to 'passive listening', she would suffer less harm. As we developed a plan for putting her BATNA into action, Miranda became more relaxed. Knowing she could do something about her situation had made her feel much better.

Her plan now had three stages. First, she'd talk to Julian and request he change his behavior. If that didn't work, she'd speak to her manager and request a new work station. As a final resort, she'd start looking for a new position in the same business or somewhere else.

4. Give them a chance to change

Now Miranda needed to work out what to say to Julian. She and I reviewed the key principles of effective feedback. Then Miranda developed a WISH statement she could use to approach Julian. We role-played various scenarios that might play out after she delivered this statement. This meant Miranda would feel confident in having a SAFE conversation no matter how Julian reacted.

The next week, Miranda reported that she'd spoken to Julian. He'd responded defensively and told her he had the right to say whatever he wanted. Miranda kept her cool and used a series of 'you frame' messages to show she was listening. Then she told Julian she was disappointed by his response.

Miranda calmly explained that she would be requesting a move to a new work station if she continued to be exposed to negative comments over the next week. This left Julian with a choice. He could change his behavior, or have it drawn to his supervisor's attention when Miranda approached her supervisor regarding the move.

5. Implement your BATNA

Sadly, Julian's negativity continued. So Miranda arranged a meeting with her supervisor, Ron, to discuss relocating to a new cubicle. The supervisor tended to operate in flight mode and had avoided addressing Julian's behavior all this time. Ron tried to convince Miranda to stay in the same seat. Miranda calmly explained that this was not acceptable to her because Julian's comments were impacting on her sense of wellbeing.

Speaking from the alright position, Miranda summarized the benefits to Ron of allowing her to move. These included keeping Miranda on the team and honoring Ron's responsibility to keep all members of the team safe at work. Finally, Ron agreed that the move was a good idea. Miranda was shifted to a new cubicle, where she was no longer exposed to the 'passive listening' environment.

A month later, Ron had been inundated with requests from other members of the team, all of whom wanted to distance themselves from Julian's workspace. There weren't enough desks to accommodate all of these requests. So Ron finally had to take responsibility for managing the impact of Julian's comments on team dynamics. Ron enrolled in a management coaching program and eventually worked with his human resources team to manage Julian's inappropriate workplace behavior.

As Miranda's story demonstrates, dealing with chronic negativity isn't always about getting someone else to change. It involves taking responsibility for your own wellbeing and working from the alright position to assert your boundaries. In addition to using WISH feedback statements, you can use five additional strategies to get productive

outcomes when working with people who seem very negative.
1. Be realistic.
2. Know which part of the problem you 'own'.
3. Be clear about your BATNA.
4. Give the person a chance to change.
5. Implement your BATNA.

Here are some ways to get your point across in situations like Miranda's.

- I prefer to find ways around problems rather than going over them again and again. What are you willing to do to sort this out?
- I agree it would be nice to have a perfect plan. Given that we don't, how about we focus on improving this one? What can we do to solve that problem?
- When you said .... I felt ... I'd like to request that you hold back on making comments like that in future.
- I'm finding it hard to concentrate when I hear you saying things like ... and ... To me those comments aren't helpful because they focus on situations we can't change. How about we talk about solutions rather than problems?
- You commented just now that ... was a problem. I thought that comment took us off track because you weren't prepared to talk through solutions to that problem. How about we focus on what we can do rather than on what we can't.
- When the conversation focuses on things you don't like, it causes us to get bogged down. I'd like us to focus on the big picture instead of arguing about small things we can't change.

Planning how to handle YOUR situation

1. What behavior does this person use when they are stressed?

_____

_____

_____

_____

2. What triggers this person's difficult behavior?

_____

_____

_____

_____

3. How can you reduce or eliminate those triggers?

_____

_____

_____

_____

4. Rate the level of risk the behavior poses to your physical and mental wellbeing on a scale of one (low risk) to ten (high risk).

_____

_____

_____

_____

5. If necessary, create an action plan for ensuring your personal safety.

_____

_____

_____

_____

6. List four or five statements you can use to help calm the person down when they are stressed.

_____

_____

_____

_____

_____

_____

7. Write down the steps you will take to respond to their behavior the next time it happens.

_____

_____

_____

_____

_____

CHAPTER NINE

USING FAIR WITH PEOPLE IN SPITE MODE

▶ This chapter explains how you can keep your cool when dealing with the passive-aggressive tactics people use when they're in spite mode. Yes, it takes a lot of energy to challenge the devious games played by spite-based thinkers. But it is worth taking the effort because it puts a stop to their antics. When you challenge a spite-based person's actions, you prevent them from getting their own way at your expense. You let them know you're in control. You block their attempts to harm relationships. You also put in place the boundaries you need in order to be healthy. Handling spite-based behavior from the alright position lets you expose their hidden agendas. It also builds your reputation as a successful communicator who can handle 'difficult people' with flair.

Key points to remember about spite mode

People in spite power mode use their body language and voice tones to express their negative feelings indirectly. Often, they resort to spite-based behaviors when they experience feelings of powerlessness. There's one universal truth about people operating in spite mode: **if you ignore their behavior, it will get worse.**

Many people avoid tackling passive-aggressive behavior because they don't know what to do about it. But this only makes it worse. Time and time again I've been called in to deal with the long-term impact that ignoring spite-based behaviors has had on a team. Believe me when I say that running a one-day team building session isn't going to undo the damage that people in spite mode can do.

Many years ago, I witnessed an example of a spite-based communicator 'gone feral'. Sandra was an administrator in the business faculty of a large university. She had been the unofficial boss of that faculty for fifteen years. Her behavior had driven away countless team members (whom she considered competition).

Rumor had it Sandra had also driven several Deans to transfer out of the faculty. But no-one had done anything about her destructive behavior. In fact, she'd received many 'excellent' ratings on her annual performance review papers because her bosses had been too scared to provide honest feedback.

Finally, a very assertive man was appointed to the Dean's role. He refused to turn a blind eye to Sandra's behavior. When Sandra tried to sabotage team dynamics during a strategic planning meeting, the Dean stopped the meeting and called her out on her behavior. Sandra replied that she didn't know what he was talking about. The Dean looked her in the eye and said, 'You know very well what I am talking about. I'm talking about your sarcastic tone of voice. I'm talking about the way you roll your eyes when I speak. I'm talking about the counter-productive jokes you make. All of this needs to stop.'

The next time Sandra rolled her eyes, the Dean followed up. He told Sandra he considered her body language contemptuous and would be documenting her behavior if it didn't change. For the first time in her career, Sandra had been held accountable for her actions. I'm sure it was no coincidence that she suddenly decided to look for another job. By setting firm boundaries on unacceptable behavior, the Dean had ended Sandra's tyrannical rule.

This story illustrates a very important point. The best way to handle people who operate from spite mode is to set and reinforce extremely firm boundaries. Be ready to repeat your boundary statements. You need to call out passive-aggressive behavior and firmly communicate that it is unacceptable.

When passive-aggressive tactics are countered with an assertive response, your situation changes. Spite-based communicators don't like having their tactics exposed. When you challenge them, they will either move somewhere they can continue being obnoxious (like Sandra did) or they will stop aiming their behavior at you. The message is clear. The sooner you hold the mirror up to their behavior, the sooner a passive-aggressive communicator will back off.

FAIR process

It can be very tempting to react to spite-based behavior in kind. But if you do this, you will add fuel to the fire of conflict. Sulking and sarcasm are childish behaviors. They express the hard-to-handle person's need to feel safe. As you know, attacking someone who needs to feel safe reinforces the fight, flight or spite reaction. It certainly doesn't encourage someone who is operating from spite mode to calm down and step into the alright position.

Like it or not, you need to help spite-based communicators feel safe. One way you can create a sense of safety is to respond in 'grown up' mode rather than matching their childish behavior. Always aim to respond from a more mature position than that taken by a passive-aggressive person. Even if you're inflamed by their sniping, keep your cool and respond in a measured way.

Unfortunately, passive-aggressive behavior is all too common, it happens everywhere. You'll see it in the workplace, at home, in shops, in schools and in your family. But you don't have to put up with it. Instead, add one step to the AIR process and use the FAIR process to confront spite-based behavior.

FOCUS ON META-MESSAGE

ASSESS

INSTALL CALM

RESPOND

The acronym FAIR is also a good reminder to make sure you fight fair even when a 'difficult person' doesn't. Here are some tips on how to get great results from the FAIR model.

Focus on the meta-message

The first step of this process is to focus on meta-messages. This is your key to exposing passive-aggressive behavior. Meta-messages are the 'true' messages expressed through tone of voice and body language. They are extremely important when dealing with spite-based behavior. In fact, without meta-messages, passive-aggressive tactics wouldn't work. A spite-based communicator actively manipulates meta-messages in order to get their point across.

Take sarcasm for instance. It only works when the listener understands that the speaker's words are not congruent with their tone of voice. If someone says, 'Good work, Einstein', it is their tonality that expresses the meta-message, 'I think you're stupid'.

Offensive meta-messages can be expressed through gestures, postures, eye positions, facial expressions and voice tones. In order to challenge passive-aggression, you need to carefully track all of these elements of body language. This is because challenging passive-aggression means exposing a speaker's behaviors in concrete and specific terms. Here are some common nonverbal cues to note when dealing with a spite-based communicator.

▶ Rolling eyes.
▶ Raised eyebrows.
▶ Exaggerated or tight-lipped smile.
▶ Pouting.
▶ Glaring.
▶ Refusal to make eye contact.
▶ Turning away instead of responding to a greeting or question.
▶ Exaggerated slouch.
▶ Crossed arms.
▶ Slumping in their seat.
▶ Sarcastic voice tone.
▶ Exaggeratedly 'nice' voice tone.
▶ Condescending voice tone.
▶ Short, clipped speech patterns.
▶ Exaggeratedly slow rate of speech.
▶ Ambiguous language.
▶ Offensive gestures made behind your back or just within your peripheral vision.

If you see or hear these nonverbal indicators, make a mental note of them. They are the behaviors you need to expose when challenging passive-aggressive meta-messages. Think of them as being evidence of the other person's hostile intent.

To call out passive-aggressive tactics, use a variation of the basic WISH statement formula. I've named it the WIDE pattern. That's because it's designed to help you communicate with your eyes wide open to the other person's behavior.

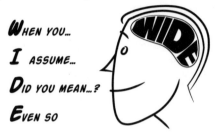

WHEN YOU...

I ASSUME...

DID YOU MEAN...?

EVEN SO

Here's an example of how to use the WIDE formula. One day I was delivering a program on Appropriate Workplace Behavior. Usually, participants in this program don't want to be there. They've been 'sent by the boss'. They often express their anger through spite and fight behaviors. This session was no different. I'd already spotted the man with the strongest negative reaction to being there. He was putting minimal effort into completing the training activities and maximum effort into making smart remarks.

Halfway through the program this man made a passive-aggressive attempt to shame me in front of fifty other participants. I asked a question about the company's dress code. In reply, he loudly announced, 'Women who wear red are all whores.' Guess what color my jacket was? Red, of course. I calmly responded, 'When you say women who wear red are all whores, I assume you mean I'm a whore. Did you mean that?'

The man glared at me and said sarcastically, 'Of course not.' I replied, 'Even so, I'm sure that's what everyone in the room thought you meant. If you continue to disrupt this session, I will ask you to leave. You can explain to your manager why you didn't complete this compulsory session.' Then I calmly went on with the session. The man behaved himself from that moment on. He backed down for two reasons. I had brought his game playing into the open and I had made him responsible for the consequences of his own actions.

Here are some more examples of WIDE statements in action.

▸ When you roll your eyes while I'm talking, I assume you're trying to say you think my ideas are stupid. Did you mean to say that? [Pause to allow the person to respond.] Even so, that's how it looked to me when you rolled your eyes just now.

▸ When you don't answer my 'hello', I assume you are refusing to talk to me. Did you mean to do that? [Pause to allow the person to respond.] Even so, that's how it looked to me when you walked past me this morning.

▸ When you answer 'nothing's wrong at all' in that tone, I assume you're saying you're not willing to tell me about something that is bothering you. Did you mean to imply that? [Pause to allow the person to respond.] Even so, that's how you sounded when you responded to my question.

▸ When you say 'great outfit' in that sarcastic tone, I assume you're implying you don't like my outfit. Did you mean me to think that? [Pause to allow the person to respond.] Even so, that's how you sounded.

Assess the level of risk posed by the spite behavior

Many of the tactics used by people in spite mode are designed to impact on group dynamics as well as to hit you personally. For this reason, you need to take both context and group impact into account when assessing the behaviors of passive-aggressive people. In particular, use the results of your assessment to answer the question, 'Do I deal with this in public or in private?'

This question always comes up when I run training sessions on dealing with spite mode communication. In order to answer it wisely, you need to consider a number of factors. First, think about the group consequences of allowing the behavior to continue unchecked. Second, consider the history and frequency of the behavior. Third, take into account the impact the behavior is likely to have on your reputation.

The following may be reasons to challenge passive-aggressive attacks in *private*.

- The behavior is a one-off occurrence. The person usually communicates from an alright position.
- No important relationships will be significantly damaged by the attack.
- Calling out the behavior in the group setting will negatively impact on the effectiveness of the group.
- It would be politically inappropriate for you to deal with behavior problems (e.g. the matter should be dealt with by the person's line manager, not you).

The following may be reasons to challenge spite-based attacks *in public*.

- The behavior has happened repeatedly. You have already talked to the 'difficult person' in private and let them know you will challenge them in public the next time they use passive-aggressive tactics.
- A continuation of the behavior will damage an important relationship (e.g. the relationship with a key customer).
- The behavior has been occurring over an extended period and is escalating.
- Failing to set a boundary immediately will enable toxic dynamics to emerge in the group.
- Ignoring the behavior will seriously undermine your credibility (e.g. failing to deal with passive-aggressive attacks in assertiveness training would mean the trainer was a poor role model).

Install calm

Of all the communication styles, the spite-based style is the most grating. That's because this style of behavior is designed to bait you into reacting and fighting back. Giving in to the urge to make a clever remark or match sarcasm for sarcasm is unwise. Matching the spite style prompts the 'difficult person' to up the ante. So you need to focus on remaining 'adult' and respond from your alright state.

Keep in mind the fact that the other person's behavior probably has its origins in deep psychological pain. Their childish actions and words are ways of coping. You can't resolve their pain, but you can protect yourself by putting a firm boundary between their emotions and yours.

When you're up against someone who is in spite mode, stay calm and composed at all times. This energy will impact on the other person. Your aim is to respond from a 'grounded' position. This will help the other person realize that their obnoxious tactics will not work on you. Being grounded involves keeping your physical and mental boundaries in place by focussing your energy and attention. One person's grounded state can impact on the physical and psychological states of others in a room.

For example, I once saw the Dalai Lama present at a huge conference. There were thousands of people in the audience. When the Dalai Lama walked in, I could physically feel the energy in the room shift. His centred, calm state had impacted on the entire audience within seconds. When you're dealing with a passive-aggressive person, you're aiming to have a similar impact on them.

Start the process of grounding yourself by focussing on your breathing. Take three or four long, steady breaths. Feel the air going deep into your lungs. Notice the sensation of your belly rising as the air flows through you. Pause for a count of three. Then exhale slowly and steadily. Breathing in this way triggers a relaxation response in your body, which helps counteract any stress hormones that might be in your system.

Next, focus on the sensation of your muscles. If you can feel tightness in your shoulders, neck or face, deliberately relax those muscles. Some people find it useful to picture a tight muscle as a tightly coiled piece of string, then to imagine the coil unwinding and releasing. Move into the alright body posture. Keep your spine straight and your shoulders back and down. Keep your head level and relax your neck muscles. Open your hands if they're clenched, then let them drop by your side. Distribute your weight evenly across both feet, or in your chair if you're sitting down.

Once your physical state has shifted, briefly focus on your thoughts. If you're trying to come up with a smart retort, stop. If you're internally labeling or criticizing the 'difficult person', stop. Use your mantra for calm if you have one. Or run one of the following sentences through your mind.

🗩 Focus on the issue, not the person.

🗩 I am calm.

🗩 I will respond in adult mode.

- My response is my choice.
- Choose to respond, not react.
- As I breathe, I relax.
- This is my chance to respond professionally

Remind yourself to refuse to enter into verbal arguments or power struggles. Then attempt to help the 'difficult' person calm down and move into alright mode.

Respond with the right words

Spite-based behavior can be hard to manage because it is so oblique and difficult to pin down. For example, imagine an employee who is pretending to have misunderstood their supervisor's instructions regarding the prioritisation of tasks. It may be hard for the supervisor to identify how the fake misunderstanding differs from genuine confusion.

To overcome this problem, the supervisor needs to develop their perceptual awareness. Passive-aggressive people leak their hostile motives through body language and voice tones. The employee who fakes making a mistake, for example, is likely to use incongruent voice tones and exaggerated movements while professing their innocence. Here is a step-by-step process for responding to spite-driven people from the alright position.

1. Call out the behavior
When you respond to spite-based communication, you need to give direct feedback on the meta-messages being sent through the other person's nonverbal behavior. Calmly point out that you have noticed.

If necessary, explain the consequences the other person will face if they continue their negative behaviors. Use a WIDE statement to start your message. Then set a boundary, using an ACE statement. Here's an example that shows how the supervisor could handle the employee who is 'accidently' misunderstanding the order in which they should complete tasks.

Supervisor: When you say you didn't understand my instruction, your voice rises in pitch and you use very large hand gestures. That makes me assume you actually did understand my instructions, but chose to misinterpret them. Did you mean to give that impression?

Employee: Oh no! What you said was confusing. I didn't understand you.

Supervisor: Even so, I am concerned by this situation. The instruction I gave you was to set up the room café style yesterday afternoon so it would be ready for the conference today. I know you were busy working on the budget papers yesterday. And the budget deadline is next week, so the conference set up was your top priority. In future, if you're confused about your priorities, I would like you to check with me before deciding which task to do first.

During these types of conversations, it helps to repeatedly use statements that begin with 'I get the impression'. In this way you can address difficult behavior without sounding aggressive. Your aim, of course, is to always speak from the alright position when dealing with spite-based behavior.

2. Follow up sarcasm and jokes immediately

Don't be surprized if someone operating from spite mode pushes back when you set a boundary. In fact, expect that they will. Challenging boundaries is what people taking a spite stance excel in. Never allow an attack on your boundaries to go without comment. When you ignore a boundary violation, you implicitly support it. If someone responds to your ACE statement by making a sarcastic comment, respond straight away. If they say, 'I was only joking, anyway', respond by delivering a second ACE statement. Here are some phrases you can use to do this.

- I am concerned by your tone right now.
- Even though you say it's a joke, I take this very seriously.
- I don't find jokes like that funny.
- I believe that joke was intended as an attack.
- Your tone when you delivered that joke was hostile.
- Let me repeat what I just said …

When you respond to attempts to challenge your boundary statements, make sure you are using assertive language, postures and voice tones. It is all too easy to fall into the trap of sounding defensive or angry when you're reinforcing a boundary. Remember to ground yourself so your energy impacts on the 'difficult person' and sends the message, 'you can't throw me'. Focus on clearly outlining what is acceptable. It can be effective to ask the passive-aggressive person to clarify what they mean or how their comment is relevant to the discussion at hand.

3. Find out what's motivating the problem behavior

As you already know, spite-based behavior is usually driven by anger, frustration or resentment. So sometimes it helps to sort out the issue that has sparked those feelings. Encourage the individual to open up about what the problem is by asking what they're concerned about. Here are some ways of phrasing your question.

- You sound quite angry. What's on your mind?
- I get the sense you're concerned about something. What is it?
- Your behavior gives me the impression you're annoyed about something. What is it?
- It seems there's something bothering you. What is it?
- What's behind that comment?
- You've just said _____. That gives me the impression you're unhappy about _____. Is that right?

Once you've asked the other person to explain their concerns, stop talking. You may need to sit through a pause before they react. But when they do speak, make sure you shift into deep level listening mode. Use lots of 'you frame' statements to communicate that you're paying attention. It may also be useful to use spotlight questions to draw out their perspective. Once you are clear on what is upsetting them, use collaborative problem-solving techniques to work out options for action. Remember that you are acting as a role model for assertive communication.

4. Develop an action plan

Many people use the 'there's a big problem' strategy as a means of sabotaging change. They love telling you what's wrong, but they hate being made accountable for doing something about it. So they generate long lists of problems. Then they harp on and on about those problems. Do not be drawn into this stalling game. Instead, firmly direct the conversation towards a solutions focus.

Sabotaging statements	Alright responses
There's a problem with that.	How can you solve that problem?
That won't work because ...	What will work then?
We tried that before and it didn't work.	How can you use what you learned last time to make it work this time?
They won't let us do that.	How will you make the case that we are going to do it?
We don't have time.	How will we make the time?
We're understaffed, so we can't take that on.	What tasks can you drop in order to free resources to do this?
This will never work.	Please create a list of potential barriers and ways of overcoming them.

Always end this stage of the discussion by setting a concrete step-by-step action plan. Make sure you spell out exactly what the other person is expected to do, as well as deadlines for each task.

5. Put it in writing

Another one of the games people frequently use when in spite mode is the 'I forgot' game. They use this tactic to avoid following through on agreements. They say, 'Yes, I'll do that.' Then they head off to do something else. When you check up on their progress they say, 'Oh sorry. It totally slipped my mind.' Or they claim they never agreed to do the task in the first place.

This is such a common tactic of spite-based communicators that it is best to guard against it right from the start. At the end of any action-planning meeting, quickly jot down a timeline for action. You don't need to use a formal minute-taking format, just scribble down key tasks and dates. Copy the notes and give one set to the other person at the end of your conversation. Keep your own copy on file, so you can refer to it the next time you meet with them. Then schedule regular follow up meetings to keep these 'problem people' on track.

6. Deal with behind-the-scenes bad-mouthing

Spite-based tactics are often covert. This means the other person will not attack you directly. Instead, you may find out from a third party that a spite style communicator has been gossiping or complaining about you. If you are confident your source is legitimate, immediately meet with the 'problem person' to discuss what you've heard. Use a WISH statement to start the conversation.

- When I heard you'd said _____it caused me to realize you're unhappy about _____. So I'd like to hear what prompted your comment. How did it come about?
- When I met with Dee today, she said you'd told her _____ yesterday. It causes us to look unprofessional if we drag other team members into our issues. So I'd like us to sort out this issue between us. How can we do this?
- When I was at the team meeting, I found out you've been complaining about _____. It causes team dynamics to turn sour when we don't communicate with each other directly. So I want you to raise your concerns with me personally in future. How can we deal with the issue of _____?

After making your WISH statement, don't get baited into talking about how you came to hear about the problem behavior. Non-assertive people will often attempt to side-track the conversation by asking this. Simply say, 'The issue isn't who I heard this from. The issue is that I have heard it. I want to focus on solving the problem.' After sorting out the issue, explain that in future you expect the other person to address future complaints to you directly. End by setting clear boundaries on how you want them to behave in future.

Managing common spite-based behaviors

Responding to sarcasm

Your co-worker says, 'You look nice today.' But their tone of voice implies this is not a compliment – it is a sarcastic way of saying you look terrible. If you confront them, you know they will repeat their message in a reasonable tone of voice. Then they will say, 'You're so sensitive. I was only giving you a compliment. What's wrong with you?'

This is a classic example of the way passive-aggressive people use sarcasm to make you feel bad while refusing to take accountability for their own poor behavior.

Or do you know someone who compliments you while rolling their eyes at the same time? Then you know an expert in sarcasm. Sarcasm is designed to hurt your feelings and violate your boundaries. It is most certainly a spite-based behavior. Many people resort to sarcasm because they don't dare say what they really think. But they want to have a go at you, anyway.

People who feel stuck in spite power mode often use sarcasm to express negative feelings. They are denying their feelings rather than being frank, assertive and honest. Some of these people like being sarcastic because it boosts their self-confidence. As children, they learned that being sarcastic made them feel powerful. As adults, they still get a buzz out of putting you down. Just think about how bad these 'difficult people' must feel – they have to attack you to feel okay about themselves. This is damaged thinking. It is a coping strategy that powerless people use to feel strong.

Ultimately then, sarcasm is a tactic born of low self-esteem. It occurs when people are not brave enough to express their feelings openly. They hide behind the norms of polite conversation by using 'reasonable' words to express attacking sentiments.

If you say that you are offended by their sarcastic tactics, many people in spite mode will retaliate by saying, 'Can't you even take a joke?' The aim of this retort is to make you look bad while they look innocent. Spite-based communicators will accuse you of being crazy or unreasonable rather than taking responsibility for their own actions. They will also refuse to take responsibility for the impact of their biting comments. They are masters at making excuses, justifying and rationalizing their own emotionally abusive behavior.

If you fail to challenge sarcastic remarks, however, spite-based communicators will escalate their attacks. This means you need to act promptly and assertively when sarcastic comments are thrown your way. Genevieve's story shows you how.

Genevieve was a quiet, unassuming accounts officer. She worked hard and had a reputation for being efficient, knowledgeable and courteous. Unfortunately for Genevieve, her colleague Ryan was jealous of her reputation. He began undermining her whenever the opportunity arose. His main weapon was sarcasm. At first Genevieve believed something was wrong with her. Maybe she'd misheard Ryan's remark? Or perhaps she really was 'too sensitive'? Wanting to be polite, she stayed silent.

Of course, this tactic didn't work. Ryan's sniping attacks became more and more frequent. Genevieve dreaded the days she had to work closely with him. In desperation, she came to me for communication skills coaching.

As we talked, it became apparent that Genevieve tended to take a flight-based approach to conflict. So she wasn't keen on speaking up the next time Ryan made a sarcastic comment. I explained that his sniping statements were designed to test her boundaries. Each time she turned a blind eye to his sarcasm, she allowed him to step further over the line of civil conversation.

I asked how Genevieve would feel if the current situation continued over the next twelve months. This question put things in perspective. She decided to take action. But she was still unsure of how to do this.

I taught Genevieve a simple three-step process for handling sarcasm. I call this the 'pose, expose, close' technique.

We role-played using these steps until Genevieve was confident she could apply them in real life. The next day, Genevieve wore a new outfit to work. Ryan greeted her with the words, 'You look nice today.' Although his words were civil, his tone was sarcastic. Genevieve grounded herself and put the three-step process into action.

1. Pose a question

The first thing Genevieve did was challenge Ryan's double-message. She used a spotlight question to do this by asking, 'What are you really trying to say, Ryan?'

Of course, Ryan backed off immediately, replying, 'Nothing. All I said was you looked nice today.' I'd warned Genevieve to be ready for such a reaction. It's typical of spite-based behavior. After all, Ryan didn't want to be held accountable for his nasty comments.

2. Expose their real message

When sarcastic people like Ryan deny that their remarks have a double meaning, they need to be challenged. Genevieve didn't enter into negotiation about what Ryan really meant. Instead, she looked him straight in the eye and said, 'Whether you intended it or not, your message had two meanings. When you said I looked nice in that tone of voice, I assumed you meant you didn't like my outfit.'

This statement was a modified form of the WIDE statement formula. Genevieve was using it to expose the incongruity between Ryan's words and voice-tone.

3. Close

Genevieve had learned not to beat around the bush with sarcastic people. She was ready to let Ryan know his game playing had to stop. She was now going to set a firm boundary. This meant giving him feedback on his behavior. She wasn't going to argue with his denials or attempts to shift blame onto her. She was going to be clear about what needed to change.

She used a series of 'I frame' messages to end the conversation with Ryan. First, she let him know she didn't want to hear any more remarks about her outfits. Then she challenged his statement that she was 'too sensitive'. Finally, she redirected the conversation. Here's how their conversation went.

Ryan: That's not what I meant at all. You're just too sensitive.

Genevieve: I'm glad to hear you didn't mean to criticize what I'm wearing. Because that would be inappropriate at work. I'd prefer not to hear any more comments on my clothes from now on.

Ryan: Gosh ... I can't even give you a compliment without having my head bitten off. You're too sensitive.

Genevieve: Whether I'm sensitive or not isn't really relevant. I don't want to hear any comments on my clothes from now on. What I would like is to focus on getting this report finished now. Have you completed the statistics?

Genevieve reported that Ryan's behavior didn't change immediately. Like many spite-based communicators, he tried pushing her boundaries several times that week. However, as she persisted in responding from the alright position, he gradually backed off. Although he continued to sulk and look unhappy during their meetings, his sarcasm stopped.

Like Genevieve, you will find that persistence is important when dealing with spite-based speakers. Don't let a sniping attack pass. Instead, respond with Genevieve's three-step process.

1. Pose a question.
2. Expose their real message.
3. Close.

▸ To help you handle sarcasm from the alright position, I've created a mind programming audio session. Download your copy of *Handle sarcasm* through my shop at http://difficultpeoplemadeeasy.com

---

Here are some phrases you can use when addressing sarcastic behavior.

- When you speak in that tone of voice, I get the impression you're saying you're not happy.
- What are you really trying to say?
- Although you said …, your tone suggested you meant …
- I'd prefer not to hear comments like that in future.
- Please speak to me in a normal conversational tone. At the moment your voice sounds sarcastic.

Handling people who lie to you

You may not like it, but some lies are okay. These are the lies that are told to maintain social order. For example, many people would consider it okay to lie to prevent hurting someone else's feelings. If your friend says, 'Do you think I've put on too much weight?', you may instinctively reply, 'No, you look great' even if they *have* gained a lot. The purpose of this lie would be to avoid upsetting your friend.

Sometimes lies that are told to save face are considered okay. For example, in many cultures it is expected that people tell lies to avoid directly contradicting an authority figure. These lies are intended to maintain respectful communication. Telling a white lie in this situation is considered to be not only acceptable but advisable. White lies are a form of 'social glue'; they help hold relationships together.

A variation on the 'saving face' lie is the self-protective lie. This is a fib someone tells to protect their own self-esteem. For example, someone might downplay their own part in a relationship breakdown. This helps them save face while going through a highly emotional event. This type of lie is not aimed at hurting anyone, but instead aims to help the liar boost their image – both internally (self-image) and externally (reputation).

Damaging lies, however, are a different matter. These are the sorts of lies that passive-aggressive people tell. A damaging lie is a statement that distorts the truth and is made to deceive someone. Some hostile people manufacture stories just to score points. They use lies to gain personal benefit, perhaps at your expense.

Taken one step further, manipulative lies become anti-social lies. These are lies that are told specifically to create harm. An example of this sort of lie would be telling a senior manager a story designed to undermine a colleague's reputation or to stir up workplace conflict. Don't let damaging lies like this go unchallenged. As soon as you become aware that a damaging lie has been told, calmly confront the other person.

The person who tells a damaging lie intends to manipulate you in some way. You need to speak up when you're exposed to this type of lying. Specifically, you need to speak up when a mistruth has one or more of the following effects.

- Poses a high risk to safety.
- Creates an ethically unacceptable situation.
- Severely damages the reputation of the business.
- Results in claims of corruption or misconduct.
- Damages team dynamics or customer relationships.
- Jeopardizes your ability to work with the other person.

In less serious situations, you may decide to let a lie go unchallenged. For example, you might let a lie pass in the following situations.

- It is more important to let the other person save face than it is to clarify the situation.
- The mistruth will not cause any damage or risk.
- Everyone knows the speaker is distorting the truth.
- Addressing the issue will make you look defensive, hostile or unprofessional.
- The issue doesn't have any significant impact.
- The 'lie' might really be an innocent mistake, which does not need correction.

As you can see, it is important to think carefully before challenging a distorting statement. Sometimes it's wiser to let a lie pass rather than wasting time and energy on addressing it. However, it's still important to know how to speak up when you need to.

Glenys found herself in this position at work. She had an important job interview coming up. She'd asked a friend, Andre, whether he knew anything about the people on the interview panel. He said he didn't. Then he offered to help Glenys review her LinkedIn profile. Glenys gladly took Andre up on this offer. She was relieved when he said that her profile was 'perfect' and didn't need any revisions.

Later Glenys found out that Andre had applied for exactly the same job. He hadn't known about the vacancy until she told him about her application. He formatted his LinkedIn profile in exactly the same way as Glenys had done hers. He had even copied many of her exact words and included them in his profile. How would you feel if you were Glenys? Dumbfounded? Betrayed? Angry? These are all perfectly natural reactions to exposing a lie. Glenys experienced them all. She felt like screaming at Andre in front of the entire team.

Recognising that she was in fight mode, Glenys made a sensible move. She came to me for coaching. We spent an entire session assessing her situation. After thinking things through rationally, Glenys decided that she did want to address Andre's behavior. She wanted to set a firm limit on the boundaries of their relationship, which she no longer considered a trusting friendship. She developed a plan for talking to Andre from the alright position. Here's the six-point plan Glenys used.

1. Explain your perception

Glenys invited Andre for coffee and opened the conversation with a WISH statement. She was direct and to the point, saying, 'When I heard you had applied for the HR team leader position, I was shocked. And I was even more surprised to see you'd copied sections of my LinkedIn profile into your own. So I want to talk to you about this situation. How did this come about?'

Andre replied, 'You never asked me whether I'd be applying for the job.'

2. Repeat back their story

Although Glenys felt angry, she kept to her plan. Instead of biting back or making a smart comment, she used deep level listening skills. Doing this serves two purposes when dealing with lies. First, it ensures that you've accurately understood what the other person has said. This can save you time and energy if there's been a misunderstanding. Second, it helps you pin the suspected liar down to a single version of events. This makes it easier to challenge their misrepresentations.

Glenys used a 'you frame' message to show she'd heard Andre's position. She calmly said, 'So you're saying that because I didn't ask, it was okay to hold back the information that you were applying. And to copy sections of my professional profile into your own LinkedIn profile?'

Andre said, 'I haven't copied anything.'

3. Express surprize

Glenys confronted Andre's statement gently. Instead of attacking him, she expressed surprize using an 'I frame' message. She said, 'I'm surprized to hear you say that.' This was a way of challenging Andre's story without painting him into a corner. It minimized the risk that he would experience a stress reaction and resort to even more toxic behavior. Glenys was allowing him to save face. This would make the next step of her process easier.

4. Contrast their truth with yours

Now Glenys was ready to challenge the lie. Her aim was to show up the disparity between what Andre had done and what he had said. She used a 'contrast frame' to do this. A 'contrast frame' is a verbal pattern that highlights differences between what has been said and what has been done. It helps you challenge lies without seeming to be judgemental. This reduces the risk that you'll elicit fight reactions from 'difficult people' when you challenge their distortions.

To create a 'contrast frame', Glenys first summarized what Andre had said. Then she outlined the facts that contradicted his version of events. She did this very simply, saying, 'So you're saying you haven't copied anything. But I've seen three paragraphs on your profile that are identical to mine.'

5. Invite investigation

Now Glenys called Andre's bluff. She told Andre she believed the situation needed to be resolved immediately. She invited him to work through the situation with her, by comparing their LinkedIn profiles. Doing this was a way of gathering evidence about each person's position. She didn't argue with Andre's statement. Instead, she suggested they use evidence to clarify the situation.

6. Summarize the evidence

Glenys then took Andre through the two LinkedIn profiles, highlighting the areas she was concerned about. Andre admitted that there were a lot of phrases from Glenys' profile appearing in his own. He claimed that this must have been a 'mistake'. Glenys knew there was no point challenging this statement. Instead, she allowed him to save face by redirecting the conversation.

From the alright position she asked, 'What can we do to resolve this difference?' She and Andre then negotiated an action plan. Glenys made sure she treated the situation as a problem-solving session, rather than as an investigation of fraudulent statements. Her aim at this stage was to rectify the problem without backing Andre into a corner. She ended the conversation by recapping their action plan and thanking Andre for working with her.

Glenys told me later that she was pleased she'd been able to handle the situation assertively. By speaking from the alright position, she'd been able to address her concerns without inflaming the situation. Although she was still annoyed that the situation had happened, she knew she'd handled it professionally.

You too can challenge mistruths assertively. Just remember to apply the six-step process.
1. Explain your perception.
2. Repeat back their story.
3. Express surprize.
4. Contrast their truth with yours.
5. Invite investigation.
6. Summarize the evidence.

Here are some phrases to help keep the process on track when challenging lies.
- I'm surprized to hear that …
- That seems strange to me …
- I feel unsure about that statement.
- Let's investigate this right now.
- We'd better sort this out immediately.
- Let's check why there's a discrepancy between your records and ours.
- I'd like to check what really happened here.
- Let's find out what has led us both to have different views of what has happened.
- I'll confirm our agreement by email so everyone has a clear record of what we discussed.
- I'm pleased this matter has been resolved and that we can leave it here.

Dealing with someone who gossips about you

In many ways, gossiping is similar to lying. After all, it usually involves tall tales that are less-than-true or exaggerated. Gossip happens in every workplace. It's all about sharing unsubstantiated information. Usually, that information is dramatic or intriguing, which is why gossip can be so alluring. Being involved in gossip is a perfectly normal behavior – gossiping is a way of sharing news or stories.

For example, you might find yourself being drawn into conversation when someone says, 'I've heard the boss has called Jon into her office. Do you know what that is about?' That's gossip. Most gossip is innocent and helps connect people and build workplace relationships. But when gossip becomes malicious and nasty, it is a toxic behavior and can seriously damage team dynamics or individual reputations. You can tell that a conversation has moved beyond harmless chit chat into toxic gossip if any of the following are true.

▸ What has been said casts negative aspersions.
▸ Rifts are created and people take sides against each other.
▸ There is a negative, emotionally abusive tone to the conversation.
▸ A conflict is being created or perpetuated as a result of 'innocent talk'.
▸ Something hurtful or damaging is being said about someone who is not there.

This type of conversation harms people. It creates conflict and fuels disputes. Gossiping in this way is not acceptable behavior. However, it's a favorite pastime of spite-based communicators. If you're the target of malicious gossip, you'll feel singled out and vulnerable. You may also start to feel like an outsider. You will quickly lose trust in the people who make you the target of their nasty comments, as well as the people who take their tales seriously. This can cause you to feel alienated, depressed or anxious. So damaging gossip is not 'harmless'.

The reasons people in spite mode enjoy gossiping are varied. Some enjoy the attention they gain by engaging in gossip. They smile and laugh as they tell their stories. But remember that these people are never as happy as they seem. On the surface they might seem interesting and in control. That's what draws their 'audience' to them. However, beneath the gossip's glossy façade lie dark, powerful emotions. These are feelings such as jealousy, frustration, weakness or anger.

▸ Accelerate your success. Download my mind programming audio
session, *Be a gossip buster* at http://difficultpeoplemadeeasy.com

Gossip is often triggered by low self-esteem. Workplace bullies can resort to gossip to undermine their targets. But you don't have to put up with toxic, bullying behavior such as workplace gossip. To challenge a tale spread through gossip, use the same process you would use to challenge lies. Additionally, keep these points in mind, too.

1. Manage your hurt before you speak up

It can be very hurtful to hear that a colleague is spreading tales about you. But reacting from fight, flight or spite position won't help you deal with the situation. Make sure you manage your feelings *before* you approach the person who has been gossiping. Keep things in perspective by remembering that gossip is a natural, bonding behavior. All groups do it. Don't think about how unfair or mean the gossip is. Simply accept that it has happened.

If you're tempted to ruminate, don't. Replaying the gossip in your mind will trigger a stress reaction. The more you think about the story that has been spread – even if you're mentally searching for evidence to counter it – the more likely you are to go into fight, flight or spite mode. Remember that you need to speak from the alright position. And to do that, you need to take action rather than dwell on negatives.

Also avoid telling 'poor me' stories to other people. As you tell others about the unfair way you've been treated, you'll work yourself into an unproductive state. Don't justify speaking to others to seek moral support. You're more likely to spread the rumor further or to start breaking people into factions. Besides, you don't need moral support. You're perfectly capable of challenging the other person yourself.

2. Spell out the consequences of continuing to gossip

You have used the six-step process for confronting lies. Still the gossip refuses to take responsibility for their actions. What do you do next? If the matter is serious, use a consequence statement. These statements simply and assertively outline what you will do next, and they give other people a choice about whether or not you do it.

For example, you could say, 'If you talk to the team yourself, you'll be in control of the explanation you give for your own behavior. If you don't speak to them, I will tell them that you have been spreading malicious rumors.' Or you could say, 'You have a choice here. Either you clear up this matter yourself, or I will approach management and explain how I feel about your misleading comments.'

When you combine these two steps with the process for handling lies, you have a complete strategy for managing gossip.

1. Manage your hurt.
2. Explain your perception.
3. Repeat back their story.
4. Express surprize.
5. Contrast their truth with yours.
6. Invite investigation.
7. Summarize the evidence.
8. Spell out the consequences of continuing to gossip.

Here are some useful phrases to use when handling gossip.

- I don't like being the target of gossip.
- I am happy to discuss any problems directly with you. But I'd prefer not to hear about them from anyone else.
- Perhaps you didn't realize how offensive the stories you've been spreading about me are. So I'd like you to know they're inappropriate.
- Please consider the consequences of your gossip. This isn't just about me. What you're saying is also impacting on our team dynamics.
- I'm concerned that what you said has colored others' perceptions of me. So I'd like you to let them know the real facts.
- I'm unhappy about what you've told … I'd like you to let them know that information was incorrect.
- I'd like you to let other people know the information you gave them was inaccurate.
- I'm unhappy that you gave the wrong information to … I'd like you to tell them what really happened.

Reacting to sulking

Doesn't sulking seem like a venomous behavior? It's a characteristic spite mode tactic, which is designed to punish you for the user's anger. Spite-driven people sulk because they don't like talking openly about problems or conflicts. Instead, they spend hours trying to make your life difficult. For example, you may have a problem co-worker who refuses to talk to you when you've hurt his feelings. Or your partner may give you the cold shoulder when you stay out too late. Both of these situations are very common examples of sulking.

Although sulking is grating, and at times infuriating, it is actually a sign that someone is in emotional pain. It's a coping strategy, which is usually learned in childhood. Children are dependent on adults for care and survival. They lack the skills and freedom required to defend themselves assertively against boundary violations. So they use sulking behaviors to express the message, 'stay away from me'.

Some adults never learn more constructive ways to stand up for themselves. They continue to rely on sulking to protect their fragile sense of self. Sulking is generally a cry for attention. Really, your sulking co-worker wants to say, 'I am hurt and upset but I don't know how to fix the situation. I want you to notice something is wrong with me and come to my rescue.' But they feel incapable of sending this message assertively.

Sometimes, however, sulking becomes more malevolent. Emotionally abusive people, for example, sulk in order to force you to comply with their desires. They sulk when they don't get what they want, using the subtle nuances of body language to convey their anger. They don't communicate their needs and wishes directly, but instead slouch into an exaggerated posture of despair.

Mia was someone who used behaviors like these to gain power at work. Her colleagues tiptoed around her because her body language conveyed hostility and contempt. No-one enjoyed working with her. Rumor had it that the team's last manager had quit her job rather than having to confront Mia's toxic behavior. Now Mia had a new boss, Jed.

It didn't take long for Jed to work out what was going on. He noticed the way Mia ignored her colleagues' greetings and 'accidently' slammed the door when leaving the office. During their weekly catch-up meeting, Jed tried to discuss these behaviors with Mia. She denied that anything was wrong. Then she told Jed she had an important client meeting to attend. She slammed the door as she left the room.

The next morning, Mia walked past Jed without saying 'hello'. She turned her back whenever he approached her work station. It was clear to Jed that Mia was giving him the cold shoulder. He decided to challenge her straight away. But the conversation didn't go well. Here's what happened.

Jed: What are you angry about?

Mia: I'm not angry.

Jed: Well, you're sulking about something.

Mia: No I'm not.

Jed: You've ignored me all morning. You're sulking.

Mia: No. I'm just really busy.

Jed's mistake was that he started the conversation by making a generalization about Mia's actions. This allowed Mia to play games by challenging his language. It's a very predictable move on a passive-aggressive person's part. Jed needed to open the conversation in a different way. Here's what he could have done instead.

1. Spotlight the evidence

Jed needed to spotlight Mia's *actions* rather than the meta-messages they conveyed. He could do this by using the third part of the ACE process: the evidence-based challenge statement. These statements are clear, factual and concrete. They make it harder for someone in spite mode to deny what they've done. For example, Jed could have tackled Mia's offensive body language by saying, 'When I said good morning, you walked straight past and didn't answer me.' This statement would communicate his intention to stick to facts rather than debate whether or not Mia felt angry.

2. Articulate the meta-message

As you know, spite-based communication is all about sending unspoken, attacking messages. These meta-messages are expressed through voice tones, contemptuous body language patterns and hostile facial expressions. Often, the words spoken by someone in spite mode are perfectly reasonable. It is the meta-message that is offensive or hurtful.

In the case of sulking, the meta-message is generally something along the lines of, 'I'm upset', 'I feel hurt by something you've done' or, 'I'm angry about something you've done.' These are all legitimate ways to feel. But the sulker is using unfair tactics to express their feelings. You need to make the conversation FAIR as quickly as possible.

As with all spite-based communication, when focusing on the meta-message with someone who is sulking, you make their covert message explicit. For example, Jed could say, 'Your behavior makes me assume that you're angry about something.'

Of course, it is likely that Jed will need to add an 'even so' segment to his message later. People who sulk rarely admit that they are doing so. Nor are they easily persuaded to honestly express their disturbing feelings from an alright position. So the conversation with Mia is likely to sound like this.

Jed: When I said good morning, you walked straight past and didn't answer me. Later, I asked for your opinion during our meeting. You said, 'I don't care what you do' in a hostile tone of voice. Your behavior makes me assume that you're angry about something.

Mia: I'm not angry about anything.

Jed: Even so, the way you're behaving makes me uncomfortable. It's hard for me to work with someone who ignores me when I speak. I'd like us to sort out any problems so we can both focus on getting the Bliss package finished today.

During this exchange Jed is using WIDE statements and 'I frame' messages to lead into setting limits and boundaries with Mia. This is the next step of the process for dealing with sulking behavior.

3. Set clear boundaries

You may have noticed that in the previous dialogue, Jed gave a *business* reason (head-based reason) for Mia to change her behavior. Logical language is more likely to get through to Mia than starting a conversation about feelings. This is because most people who use passive-aggressive tactics are highly uncomfortable talking about feelings. Their discomfort is the reason they're using spite style communication in the first place.

When you're setting boundaries with someone who sulks, don't be lured into the trap of arguing about whether your interpretation of their actions is correct. This is where many people will try to take the conversation. You can use your 'even so' statement to redirect the conversation, just as Jed did in the example above.

Overall, this three-step process sends a clear message about sulking. it's unacceptable in professional contexts.

If you need to address similar behavior to Mia's, remember to use all three steps.
1. Spotlight the evidence.
2. Articulate the meta-message.
3. Set clear boundaries.

If necessary, repeat the process until the sulking stops. By holding a spite-based communicator accountable for their actions, you are setting the scene for improved team dynamics. Here are some phrases you can use to set boundaries and limits when dealing with people who sulk at work.

- 🗩 As you know, we have a code of conduct here. It says that everyone must be treated with respect. In the future, I'd like you to respond to my questions when I ask them.
- 🗩 I know both of us want to do a great job on the Bliss package. So I'd like us to work together collaboratively and talk through any problems as they come up.
- 🗩 When someone doesn't contribute to meetings, it makes the job of solving problems much harder. In future, I'd ask that you give your opinion when I ask for it in meetings.
- 🗩 I know you care deeply about this project and want to move it forward. It's important that the team works together on this. We'll get a better outcome if disagreements are sorted out respectfully.

Addressing go-slow tactics

Some 'problem people' use go-slow tactics in order to express their bitter or angry feelings. They drag out simple tasks and pretend to misunderstand simple directions. Or they 'forget' to follow important instructions. Here are some of the signs that show you're dealing with go-slow tactics.

- ▸ Easy tasks are being made to look complex.
- ▸ The 'difficult person' refuses to do jobs that are 'not in my duty statement'.
- ▸ The person's productivity levels are way below those of other

members of the team.

- They speak for hours to a customer, in the guise of giving great service, rather than completing their paperwork.
- The person focuses on irrelevant details rather than getting their work completed in a timely manner.
- They put off vital tasks to complete less important ones.
- They make a huge fuss about taking on additional tasks.
- The person's low rates of productivity are impacting on team dynamics and causing conflict.

JON 'ACCIDENTLY' WRECKS MEL'S BIG PRESENTATION.

A combination of three or more of these cues shows that you are probably dealing with someone who is procrastinating deliberately. Julie was someone who seemed to use *all* of these behaviors. She could drag a simple task out for hours. She made a huge fuss whenever she was given extra tasks. The words 'not on my duty statement' seemed to be programmed into her voice-box.

If you've ever had to work with someone like Julie, you'll know how infuriating they can be. They're really hard to pin down because it is hard to define the point at which work pace becomes an expression of bad attitude. Julie claimed she was doing the best she could. When Roberto, her supervisor, raised the issue of her productivity, Julie retorted that he had unreasonable expectations. Roberto came to my course on *Dealing with Difficult People*. There he worked out an action plan for handling Julie's go-slow tactics.

1. Raise the issue using WIDE

Roberto had already learned that letting Julie's go-slow tactics pass without comment was a bad idea. As with all spite-based behavior, the longer it was tolerated, the worse it got. Roberto decided to raise his concerns using the WIDE statement structure. He thought about some recent examples of situations in which Julie had dragged out a task. Then he workshopped some WIDE statements to address these situations. Here are a couple of examples he came up with.

- When it takes three days to complete the accounts check, I assume you're dragging the task out because it usually takes half a day to complete. Did you mean to take so long on this job? ... Even so, I am concerned about the time it took.

- When I delegated the task of developing the induction process, I anticipated it would take a month to complete. I assume that you have been over-working the task since it's now taken three and a half months and is still unfinished. Do you want me to think you're not interested in this task? ... Even so, I'd like the process finished within two weeks.

Another course participant role-played the part of Julie so that Roberto could practise managing any hostile responses he might encounter in real life. He discovered that keeping his posture upright and open was important when delivering his WIDE statements. Once he felt confident raising each problem behavior, Roberto developed the next step of his management plan.

2. Limit their options

The second step of Roberto's action plan took a bit of thinking through. On one hand, he knew that allowing Julie control over how she did her tasks resulted in procrastination. On the other hand, Roberto was concerned that giving her no choice at all would prompt her to slow down in retaliation. So he decided to be strategic. He'd force Julie's hand by giving her three options from which to choose. This would allow sufficient freedom of choice to motivate her, but set firm enough parameters to prevent procrastination.

Roberto brainstormed different ways of laying out Julie's choices. He came up with a simple sentence for doing this. 'You have three options: _____, _____ and _____. Which will work best for you?'

After trying this sentence out in role-play, Roberto felt it would work in real life. He also discovered that once he'd offered Julie the options, it would be wise to ask which option she was choosing. This ensured that Julie committed verbally to a specific course of action rather than making vague promises to act.

3. Break deadlines into smaller target dates

Roberto then discussed the fact that Julie tended to cover up the fact she wasn't meeting appropriate timelines. If he asked her how she was going with a long-term goal, she'd say, 'fine'. Then, at the last minute, she'd reveal that absolutely no work had been done. Roberto suspected that Julie was doing this deliberately in order to sabotage tasks. He wanted to prevent this from happening again.

His role-playing partner suggested that Roberto break larger tasks into smaller pieces. Doing this would mean he could set specific deadlines for completing each sub-task. He could also schedule catch-up meetings on the date each sub-task was due to be delivered. This would make it harder for Julie to cover up any delays or barriers to completing her tasks.

4. Set clear standards and performance indicators

As he talked about holding catch-up meetings with Julie, Roberto realized something important. He slapped his head as he said, 'No wonder she's got away with this for so long. She has no performance indicators.' It quickly became obvious that setting Key Performance Indicators would help Roberto manage not just Julie's performance, but that of his entire team.

After all, if performance expectations are not formally documented, there is no standard for good performance. Roberto needed to get his team together and develop a set of clear performance indicators for the entire group. Then he needed to make each member of the team accountable for tracking their own performance. He decided to have people report on performance at both individual and team levels – so that it would harder for anyone to claim a co-worker's output as their own.

5. Explain that you won't take on their tasks

Finally, Roberto acknowledged that he had been making it easy for Julie. He'd compensated for her underperformance by handing some of Julie's tasks to other team members. While this got the job done in the short term, it had eroded team morale. It had also resulted in Roberto himself being overloaded because he'd been taking up the slack caused by Julie's poor work habits. He decided to prevent this from happening again by setting clear and unambiguous boundaries around his own workload. He was going to make it clear he wouldn't pick up the work Julie was avoiding.

Roberto left the training course with a clear plan for handling Julie's go-slow tactics. You too can use this process for dealing with staff or colleagues who drag out tasks. If you're dealing with a peer's underperformance, involve your manager in your discussions, too. You may teach them a few tricks for dealing with 'difficult people' in the process.

In summary, use this process to handle go slow tactics.

1. Raise the issue using WIDE.
2. Limit their options.
3. Break deadlines into smaller target dates.
4. Set clear standards and performance indicators.
5. Explain that you won't take on their tasks.

The following starter sentences can be used to get your conversation about work pace or productivity off to a good start.

- I've noticed there have been delays with ... recently. I'd like to discuss this with you.
- When we agreed that the project tasks would be finished by today, I understood this deadline was firm. So I am surprized to hear you thought it was tentative. We need to clarify our expectations on deadlines.
- I'm concerned that the timeline for our Priority One project hasn't been maintained. So I'd like to review your progress on this.
- When I asked you to complete the report by this week, I expected that this was a reasonable timeline. Now you're saying it wasn't. I'm disappointed that you didn't bring this to my attention earlier. I am also concerned about the time this task is taking. We need to talk about this today.

Managing emotional blackmail and manipulation

My chiropractor once proudly announced that he'd been awarded the title 'Manipulator of the Year'. I'm sure most professionals wouldn't think this was an honor! After all, the word 'manipulation' usually carries negative connotations. Common manipulative tactics used by 'difficult people' include crying, blaming, playing victim, pretending to be super-rational, lying and shaming.

These can all be difficult actions to deal with because most of them are designed to make you feel negative emotions such as shame or guilt. Once these feelings kick in, many people find it hard to maintain their boundaries. Thus manipulative people get their own way because others feel bad about standing up to them.

The good news is that you *can* avoid being pushed around in this way. But first you have to recognize their behavior for what it is. Here are some common signs that someone is trying to use emotional blackmail or manipulation to get their own way.

▸ The use of extremely passive statements like, 'Poor me. No-one understands me.' People who want to manipulate tend to present themselves as victims. This is to get your attention. It may also be intended to spark your fear that something will go wrong for the 'difficult person' and then you'll feel guilt about it.

▸ They aim to trigger guilt. This is the easiest way for manipulative people to get their needs met. They use guilt-inducing words in an attempt to make you feel bad. They sulk or cry. They look hurt. They express disappointment nonverbally rather than speaking up about their feelings with assertiveness.

▸ They are too charming, admiring or supportive. You know their charm is fake. You get the sense that they are trying too hard to connect with you. The aim of this strategy is to lower your defences so you'll do what they want.

▸ You feel bad, selfish, naive or foolish after speaking to them. Some 'difficult people' use emotional abuse to con you into doing what they want. This behavior also makes toxic people feel good – it relieves their own negative feelings.

▸ You constantly feel you are wrong. This strategy taps into your fear of failure. The manipulative person uses statements like, 'I've talked to all my friends and none of them do this' or, 'I spoke to her and she agrees with me.' This simply makes you feel guilty and you end up giving in to all the demands made by this type of 'difficult person'.

Manipulative behavior is designed to satisfy the 'difficult person's' needs. When you've been taken in by it, you're likely to feel ripped off. For example, have you ever been the target of a less-than-ethical sales pitch? Perhaps you bought a suit because it looked okay in the changing room (no doubt because of the soft lighting and slimming mirrors). The sales staff assured you that it looked wonderful on you. And this was the last suit in your size.

Of course, once you got it home, you realized it was uncomfortable and unflattering. You'd been manipulated. What's worse, you knew at the time what was happening. But you didn't know how to handle the situation assertively. Well, this need never happen to you again. Remember to use all the steps of FAIR. And you'll find these extra tips help, too.

1. Pinpoint their objective

Remember that if you feel manipulated, it's because the other person has a hidden agenda. So you need to work out what that agenda is. Start by assessing what the other person has said or done. Then ask yourself, 'What does this tell me about their intent?' Once you have identified their real objective, work out whether or not you want to help them achieve it. If not, get ready to say 'no'.

2. Say 'no'

Many people find it hard to say 'no'. And people who use manipulative tactics often count on this. So you need to send a clear and unambiguous 'no' message. You can use an 'I frame' message to do this. Here's an example.

Salesperson 1: Wow! You look great in that suit!
You: I think it is too tight around the chest.
Salesperson 1: It's designed to be left unbuttoned … see, it looks fine when you leave the jacket open … Liz, what do you think?
Salesperson 2: Wow. It looks fabulous. I have the same suit at home. And all of my friends compliment me when I leave it unbuttoned.
You: I prefer a looser fit.
Salesperson 1: Is there a larger size out the back, Liz?
Salesperson 2: No. That's the last one in that color. And they're selling so fast. If you don't buy it today, you'll miss out. Shall I wrap it for you?
You: No thanks.

3. Don't get locked in by closed questions

In the scene above, Salesperson 2 used a classic manipulative tactic. The question, 'Shall I wrap it for you?' was designed to lead you into a forced sale.

Always be on the alert for this tactic. It's used because it works on a sizeable proportion of the population. Many people feel rude when they answer 'no' to a question that is phrased as an invitation. Don't be one of these people. Just respond with a simple 'no'. Or simply refuse to answer the question. Here are two examples of how to do this.

Telesales person: Would you like to reduce your power bills by 15%?
You: I'm not interested in talking about my power bills right now.

A second way to deal with forced choice questions is to add another option to the list they are offering you.
Salesperson: Do you want to order the manual or the automatic model?
You: I will be looking at other brands before ordering anything.

4. Refuse to play their games

Manipulative behavior is really classic psychological game playing. The person using it is setting out to bait you. Typically, they'll use crying, emotional blackmail or guilt trips to do this. Once you take their bait, they will insist that you do what they want. This can lead you to taking action you don't want to take. So you need to resist joining the game in the first place. How?

The trick is to politely expose the game. For example, imagine you ask a graphic design company for a quote on creating a logo. Their sales representative visits you to assess your needs. Without sending you that quote, the company immediately designs a logo. It's accompanied by a large bill. This manipulative tactic is designed to shame you into paying for work you haven't authorized. Don't play along. Instead say, 'I'm surprized to receive this design and this bill. My email clearly explained that I wanted a quote only. And I have not been given a quote. I won't be paying this bill.'

5. Close the conversation down

Sometimes, people using manipulative tactics will try to drag discussions on. They're usually hoping to wear you down, so you'll say 'yes' to their requests. Deal with this tactic from an alright power position by using a simple 'I frame' message. This message needs to communicate that the conversation is now closed. Be careful not to be led back into discussing the issue once you've delivered your statement.

For example, I once saw a woman handling a man's request for money this way. The man approached her at the bus stop and said, 'Can you give me five dollars for some cigarettes?' The woman said 'no' politely but firmly, staying in the alright position.

The man then said, 'How about two dollars, then?' The woman replied, 'I'm saying "no" to this conversation, not a price.' The woman was still polite and respectful, so the man stopped haggling and left. Two minutes later I saw him using exactly the same tactic on a second woman, who was taken aback and donated two dollars. This second woman didn't know how to close a conversation.

Once you've mastered the skill of creating 'I frame' messages, you'll find it much easier to deal with manipulative tactics from the alright position. **Remember to keep the conversation FAIR and to use five additional tactics when dealing with situations involving manipulation.**

1. Pinpoint their objective.
2. Say 'no'.
3. Don't get locked in by closed questions.
4. Refuse to play their games.
5. Close the conversation down.

▶ Program yourself to use this process with my audio session *Handle guilt mongers*. Visit my shop at http://difficultpeoplemadeeasy.com

---

You'll also find these sentences useful when responding to manipulative behavior.

- 🖛 I prefer not to …
- 🖛 No. I have other priorities right now. Those priorities are …
- 🖛 It sounds like you're in a tight spot. I'm afraid I can't take that on, so you'll need to find another way to get this done.
- 🖛 No. I'm not willing to …
- 🖛 It's a pity you don't like my decision. However, I am still going to …
- 🖛 Even so, I prefer to …
- 🖛 I'd prefer to stop this conversation now.

- I've told you my decision is to ... Now I'd like to talk about something else.
- I prefer to stick to my original plan/decision. Let's close the matter here.
- I'm going to finish this conversation now, as I have clearly explained my position already.

Dealing with attention-seeking behavior

Do you know someone who always directs the conversation towards their own problems or achievements? Then you know someone who is resorting to attention-seeking behavior. This is a form of passive-aggressive behavior that unassertive people use to alleviate their own feelings of pain or low self-worth.

Others' attention-seeking tactics are annoying because they violate your boundaries. You end up with truck-loads of information being dumped into your personal space – information you didn't want to hear. Or your needs are totally ignored because the attention seeker wants all the airtime.

People who use lots of attention-seeking behavior often have no awareness of their own boundaries. Additionally, they don't respect the fact that *you* have boundaries. Their actions become problematic when they infringe your sense of personal space or impact on group dynamics. Here are some examples of attention-seeking behavior that can cause problems at work.

- Your co-worker dresses very provocatively.
- Your manager takes credit for all of the team's ideas so they can look good at the senior management meeting.
- Your melodramatic teammate talks loudly on the phone all the time.
- A customer shares intimate, personal information with you.
- Your co-worker constantly seeks sympathy and tells the team they've been neglected or overlooked for promotion.

Of course, everyone craves some attention. But looking for validation becomes problematic when conversations become unbalanced and egocentric. Some individuals who use attention-seeking behavior believe they are superior to you. They can become angry, aggressive or frustrated when things don't go their way. They create dramas out of nothing. Sometimes they create team conflict simply to get attention. Without attention, they feel worthless and depressed.

In this situation, some individuals will become disruptive and try to get attention by misbehaving. For example, imagine you are Rochelle's supervisor. Rochelle wears very revealing clothing, such as short skirts and low-cut tops. When male customers are in your office, Rochelle giggles, flicks her long hair and makes inappropriately suggestive comments. This behavior gains her a lot of attention, which Rochelle obviously revels in.

How should you deal with acting-out strategies like these? Start by applying the four steps of FAIR. If necessary, you can also use these three additional tips.

1. Speak up when others are silent

Because they tend to dominate conversations, many attention-seekers never receive corrective feedback. So make it your priority to give them fair and honest information about how they are impacting on others.

Design an honest and appropriate feedback statement. Use the WISH formula to do this. When you deliver that statement, start by acknowledging that the feedback might be unexpected.

For example, if you were talking to Rochelle, you might say, 'Rochelle, you may not have received any feedback on your personal presentation in your previous roles. Now that you are client facing, it's important to be aware of the company's dress code.'

Next, move on to deliver your WISH statement. Remember that there is no need for you to apologize. Explain the impact of the person's words or actions. Then calmly request that they change what they're doing. Give them a reason to change by pointing out that this will make others more receptive to them. For example, you might say to Rochelle, 'I know you are keen to make a great impression.'

2. Reward positive behavior

People repeat behaviors that are rewarded. You can 'program' attention seekers to behave constructively by engaging with them when they behave well. For example, if Rochelle wore a more appropriate outfit the day after you gave her feedback, you'd need to give positive feedback immediately.

3. Withdraw attention when they resort to attention-seeking tactics
Obviously, the flip side of reinforcing positive behavior is failing to reward annoying behavior. In Rochelle's case, for example, you might remove her from the client service space if she wore inappropriate clothing to work. You'd also explain to her why you were taking this action, in order to reinforce your message that change was required.

Handling attention-seekers can take some persistence. But it is easier when you keep these three points in mind.
1. Speak up when others are silent.
2. Reward positive behavior.
3. Withdraw attention when they resort to attention-seeking tactics.

You'll also find the following phrases useful when dealing with attention-seekers.
- Thanks for your input. We need to hear others' opinions now.
- I know you feel strongly about this. Please write an action proposal and send it to me.
- I'd like to remind you of the five-minute time limit we've set on contributions.
- We need to move on.
- I'm not sure how that story relates to the agenda item we're discussing. Has anyone else got something to say?

Responding to people who say 'yes' when they mean 'no'

Many spite-based communicators will say one thing and then do something else. This is usually because they feel incapable of expressing themselves assertively. They say 'yes' because they don't know how to say 'no' from the alright position. They prefer to grumble and complain instead of directly sending a 'no' message. They avoid overt conflict. Instead they use indirect methods to discourage you from asking them do anything.

For example, your teammate is asked to finish a task within a specific time frame. They don't want to do this task. But they agree to take it on. Rather than working on the task, they spend huge amounts of time talking about how complex it is. The task is not completed by the deadline and you end up having to do the work.

This is a typical example of how some people procrastinate in order to avoid responsibility. Their behavior destroys team dynamics because nobody trusts them.

When someone says 'yes' but really means 'no', they are using tactics of passive resistance. They are being submissively rebellious. They do this because they have low self-esteem and poor state management skills. Someone in spite mode is not confident to speak up about what they feel. So they express their position covertly. They use 'forgetting' as an excuse for not delivering on their promises. They pretend to forget deadlines, special events and anniversaries. They claim not to remember agreements you have made with them. And then they subversively go about doing exactly what *they* want to do.

If people let you down occasionally, that behavior is normal. But when they do it frequently, their unreliability becomes problematic. Here are some signs that you need to take action to manage the impact of someone's unreliability.

▸ You are reluctant to ask them to do anything because you know they won't deliver.
▸ The person's behavior has led to a serious problem, such as losing business or upsetting a major client.
▸ You are frequently being called in to take over tasks that were initially assigned to the other person.
▸ The other person has failed to show up to appointments three times or more recently.
▸ Other people are making jokes about the passive-aggressive person's unreliability.
▸ Team members refuse to work with the person because they're known to be 'difficult'.
▸ You know to 'pencil in' meetings with this person because they usually cancel at the last minute.
▸ The person breaks their bad news by text or email rather than speaking to you.

If you work with someone whose unreliability is posing problems, it's time to speak up. Here's how to deal with people who let you down or say 'yes' instead of 'no'.

1. Don't dwell on 'why'

Avoid wasting time analysing this behavior. It doesn't really matter why they continually let you down. What matters is that you stop tolerating their actions. Commit to changing what you do so you are not impacted by their actions. If a particular person consistently lets you down, stop expecting anything from them. Limit their ability to impact on you. Don't involve them in your projects. Prepare back-up plans. Report their sabotaging tactics to someone more senior. Take an assertive stance so you can focus on getting on with your own life and work.

2. Put agreements and deadlines in writing

Confirm all your verbal agreements with unreliable people in writing. For example, after meeting with your teammate to discuss the distribution of work for a project, send a follow up email. Your messages don't need to be long or complex. Simply use dot points to summarize what has been agreed. Make a list of who is responsible for each action item, as well as specific completion dates. If necessary, copy in your manager or supervisor so they can stay in the loop.

3. Pass accountability back to them

As you've heard many times, ignoring poor behavior simply reinforces it. Don't remain silent when someone lets you down. Instead, use an 'I frame' message to give them feedback on the impact of their behavior. Then make them accountable for solving any problems they've created.

For example, Bec was angry because Angela had promised to deliver a presentation at an important client meeting. The day before the meeting, Angela announced that she'd 'forgotten' a prior arrangement and would not be attending the meeting. Bec responded by saying, 'I am disappointed that you won't be attending, since your presentation is an important part of the meeting. Who have you organized to replace you?'

Be prepared for a defensive reaction when making a spite-based communicator accountable. For example, Angela's response to Bec's assertive statement would probably be something along the lines of, 'I had no choice. I really have to go to the other appointment.' In this case, Bec could respond assertively by reinforcing the impact of

Angela's behavior. For example, she could say, 'That may be the case. However, I am still disappointed and I still need someone to present your session.'

4. Spell out consequences of future unreliability

Some people will only change when they realize that continuing their current behavior will have consequences. Make sure you get your point across at the end of conversation with anybody who has let you down. Use a consequence statement to do this, remembering the difference between consequences and threats. By using the right words, let the other person know they have a choice about what happens next. For example, you might say, 'In future, if you fail to deliver on a deadline, I will need to let the team leader know I've finished my tasks and that we're still waiting for your input.'

As you can see, dealing with others' unreliability is simply a matter of having a SAFE conversation. Aim to raise their awareness of the impact of their actions. Then set clear limits and boundaries. **Use the four-step process for handling unreliability.**

1. Don't dwell on 'why'.
2. Put agreements and deadlines in writing.
3. Pass accountability back to them.
4. Spell out consequences of future unreliability.

Here are some examples of assertive statements you can use when dealing with unreliable behavior.

- When you failed to deliver the data on time, our project schedule was thrown by a week. In future, I need the data by the agreed date. How can you get it to me on time?
- When key team members pull out of client meetings at the last minute, we all look unprofessional. If you pull out of another meeting at the last minute, I will cancel the meeting and let the client know you were responsible.
- When your tasks weren't finished on time, we all had to work back late. The next time we agree on task allocations, I'll send a copy to you and the team leader, so we're all clear on our workloads.

Planning how to handle YOUR situation

Think of someone who operates from spite mode when under stress. Use the questions below to plan how to deal with them assertively in future.

1. What behavior does this person use when they are stressed?

_____

_____

2. What triggers this person's difficult behavior?

_____

_____

3. How can you reduce or eliminate those triggers?

_____

_____

4. Rate the level of risk the behavior poses to your physical and mental wellbeing on a scale of one (low risk) to ten (high risk).

_____

_____

5. If necessary, create an action plan for ensuring your personal safety.

_____

_____

6. List four or five statements you can use to help calm the person down when they are stressed.

_____

_____

7. Write down the steps you will take to respond to their behavior the next time it happens.

_____

_____

WHAT TO DO WHEN THE PROBLEM KEEPS HAPPENING▸

CHAPTER TEN

DEALING WITH CHRONICALLY PROBLEMATIC BEHAVIOR

▶ If someone has gained a reputation as a 'difficult person', it's likely they're displaying an ongoing *pattern* of challenging behavior. They don't just use toxic communication patterns occasionally. They use them a lot. Their behavior is chronic. In these cases, it's likely that something more serious than a one-off fight, flight or spite reaction is driving the person's behavior.

Perhaps the person is 'stuck' in fight, flight or spite mode. A 'stuck' state can be triggered by factors such as pain, physical health problems, chronically stressful personal situations or emotional distress.

Or perhaps the person is experiencing distorted perceptual or thinking patterns. A number of factors might be at play in such a situation. These can include shock, a medical condition, side effects of prescribed medications, use of non-prescription drugs, alcohol consumption and some mental health conditions.

This chapter explains how to recognize the difference between reactive and chronic behavior. Then it shows you how to manage the impact of others' chronic behavior patterns on your wellbeing.

THE TEAM FINALLY GETS HELP
DEALING WITH THE ELEPHANT
IN THE ROOM.

How to tell the difference between chronic and reactive behaviors

Chronic behaviors occur over and over again. They form a pattern and are often habitual. People with repeated patterns of difficult behavior may have ongoing physical or emotional psychological problems. Or they may have lacked role models and learning opportunities growing up. Some of these people need professional assistance. Others just need to learn some new skills.

Reactive behavior happens on a one-off basis. People using reactive behavior are easy to spot. They are okay most of the time, but will occasionally slip into fight, flight or spite mode. These people have a short-term, fleeting style of behavior. They will quickly return to an 'okay' state once the trigger for their stress reaction subsides. This style of behavior is perfectly normal – we all revert to defensive behavior when we're stressed, in pain or tired.

Assessment tool: identifying chronic patterns of behavior

Chronic behavioral problems can be challenging to deal with. They are long-term, fixed and ongoing. The emotional or psychological problems experienced by many people with chronic difficult behavior can be deep-rooted and may require professional intervention. It's not your job to diagnose or 'fix' these people, but you do have to work out how to survive around them. This checklist will help you work out whether you're facing a chronic pattern of problematic behavior.

Think of someone you find difficult to deal with. Then tick any of the characteristics they exhibit.

☐ The person has a reputation for being a 'difficult person'.
☐ Co-workers, family or friends tiptoe around them, desperately trying not to 'set them off'.
☐ The person often cuts themselves off from social interaction, community engagement and work relationships.
☐ There is always a conflict happening in the person's life.
☐ When the person talks, they are most often negative or bitter.
☐ Their communication is sometimes – or frequently – erratic or irrational.
☐ They fixate on small issues and make a big deal out of them.

If you have ticked two or more items, it is likely that you're dealing with someone who has a chronic pattern of difficult behavior. Here are some tips for handling the impact this person's communication style is likely to have on *you*.

Handling chronic behaviors

Handling chronic behavioral difficulties involves acting to minimize their impact on you. You may not be able to stop or prevent the problematic behavior. Instead, you need to learn how to limit your exposure to it. You may also benefit from learning how to set clear, unambiguous boundaries with people who display ongoing patterns of difficult behavior.

For example, Trish's 20-year-old daughter, Naomi, has an addiction to alcohol. When she's drunk, Naomi is verbally abusive and aggressive. This behavior is impacting on Trish, who is feeling guilty and depressed. Trish desperately wants to help Naomi. However, giving in to Naomi's demands and emotional blackmail only makes the situation worse.

Accepting that Naomi has a chronic pattern of fight-based behavior helps Trish detach emotionally. She is then able to set limits on the behavior she will tolerate when Naomi is in the family home. At first, Trish finds that enforcing these limits feels cruel and unnatural. As she works on her boundaries, however, she finds herself able to limit the impact of Naomi's behavior on her own life.

Responding to reactive behaviors

Managing reactive behavior is a lot easier. That's because you know it will be short lasting. When dealing with reactive behavior, you need to focus on minimizing the other person's stress and then finding ways to sort out the source of that stress.

For example, Brad's 35-year-old son, Ian, is normally even-tempered and polite. Lately, however, he has been abrupt and snappy when talking to Brad. Instead of snapping back, Brad asks Ian whether anything stressful is happening for him right now. Ian opens up and admits that he is having problems dealing with a new boss at work. Father and son talk through the situation and Ian comes up with an action plan for dealing with it. He is soon back to his normal state and speaking from an alright power mode.

Steps for addressing chronic behavioral problems

Being exposed to chronically difficult behavior can cause stress and discomfort. So it's important that you learn to manage your situation. Remember that you won't necessarily be able to put a stop to the other person's actions. But you can choose not to be negatively impacted by them. Here are some steps you can use to do this.

1. Know it's not about you

Step one is to accept that you can't change anyone else's psychology; you may not even be able to stop what they're doing. Taking this on board is easier to do if you remember that someone with chronic behavioral problems is treating everyone else the same way they treat you. Their actions are not targeting you – they are this person's way of coping with some form of distress. Remember that you are responsible for your own boundaries and that you can choose what you internalize (take personally) and what you don't.

To help cut yourself off from a 'difficult person's' behavior, answer three questions. First, ask yourself, 'What does this behavior tell me about this person's mental state?' Then pose the question, 'What percentage of this is really about me or aimed at me personally?' Finally, ask yourself, 'How much of this is about the other person and their state of mind or feelings?'

2. Clarify your boundaries

As you know, a boundary is a limit on what you will tolerate. Ask yourself some spotlight questions to work out what your boundaries are when dealing with repeating difficult behavior. For example, think about which of the other person's behaviors, specifically, make you feel uncomfortable or unhappy? Then ask yourself whether you need to take action to be psychologically safe or physically safe. Finally, ask yourself whether you should remove yourself from the situation at any point. After all, safety always comes first.

3. Assert your boundaries

Asserting a boundary means acting to maintain it. There are many ways you can assert your boundaries. You can use an 'I frame' message or a WISH statement to communicate the boundary. You can also keep yourself psychologically safe by reminding yourself that what other people say is not necessarily true. Their words are just a reflection of their mental state. You can also give the other person a choice about what happens next – for example, stop the problem behavior or the discussion will end. If all else fails, you can walk away from the situation.

4. Opt out of games

Problem behavior often aims to bait you into game playing. For example, a 'difficult' customer who hurls personal insults at you is trying to bait you into fighting back. Why? Because once you fight back, they can complain about your behavior and have power over you. If you refuse to play their game, you take their power source away.

Games can be designed to trigger a fight, make you feel guilty, shame you or stress you into making mistakes. Avoid being hooked into games by listening for verbal warning signs. Insults such as, 'You're totally useless' are a common sign that game playing is happening. When someone insults you, they want you to play a game involving a long-winded exchange of demeaning statements.

Wild generalizations are also a signal that someone is trying to hook you into playing psychological games. For example, the statement, 'No-one ever does anything properly around here' is meant to hook you into defending your team. If you give the desired response, you'll find yourself listening to a long-winded explanation of how awful the team is.

Another cue to listen out for is the person who answers every suggestion with the words, 'Yes, but ...' or, 'I can't, because ...' This person is baiting you into playing the 'rescuer' game. In this game, you wear yourself out trying to come up with ideas or stay positive. Meanwhile, the other person takes pleasure in discarding everything you suggest. This makes them feel more powerful – and it's a total waste of your time.

Also be on the lookout for people who play the game of 'poor me'. These people make lots of statements such as, 'You wouldn't believe what they've done to me now' or, 'They're really mean to me.' They want your attention. If you give it to them, you'll be trapped. They'll whinge and complain for hours unless you find a way to escape.

So what should you do if you suspect someone is playing psychological games? You need to make a conscious decision to manage your own feelings and deal with their problem behavior assertively. Make sure you give them an unexpected reaction. This will mess up their game. For example, my associate, David, was running a workshop for a team of consultants. One of the workshop participants, Brett, arrived forty-five minutes late. Brett's colleagues made sarcastic remarks as he drew up a chair. Brett responded by saying, 'F___ off.' Then Brett turned to David and said, 'And you can f___ off too.'

David could have responded defensively, which would have been playing Brett's antagonistic game. Instead, he said, 'Wow. I'm surprised to hear you saying that. Usually it's at least lunchtime before anyone tells me to f___ off.' Brett dropped the game playing from that moment.

5. Build your support system

If someone's trying behavior is chronic, other people will be aware of the situation. Seek support from them while making sure you don't engage in gossip. For example, team members might agree to take it in turns dealing with a particularly difficult customer. Or they might agree that when a transaction with that customer has ended, the person who managed it can have a ten-minute state management break. Or they might formally debrief and support each other after tough interactions.

6. Manage your stress levels

Living or working with chronically difficult behavior can be taxing. If you're constantly exposed to someone who has ongoing behavioral problems, make sure you take time to recharge your batteries. If necessary, work with a coach or counselor to develop your resilience to difficult behavior.

7. Stay safe

In some situations, difficult behavior may constitute a health and safety risk. For example, at home sustained patterns of aggression can escalate into physical violence. Or in the workplace, fight-based behavior can escalate into workplace bullying. You might become anxious or depressed as a result of being exposed to the conflict generated by a very abusive co-worker or family member. In these situations, consider what you can do to keep yourself safe.

Your options will include physically removing yourself from the situation or asking someone else to intervene. You may also consider getting assistance from a counselor (if the 'difficult person' is someone at work, try your organization's Employee Assistance Program). And you can also try talking to your manager or someone in the Human Resources team.

What to do when someone is irrational

Irrational behavior can be a sign of shock, stress, some medical conditions, perceptual disturbances, cognitive problems or some mental health problems. It's important to understand that someone who is irrational is *incapable* of thinking rationally. This leads to them displaying irrational behavior.

Behaving irrationally means doing things that are less useful than more well considered alternatives. Irrational behavior stems from irrational thinking. It can include behaviors such as taking offence or becoming angry about minor or non-existent issues, expressing emotions exaggeratedly (such as crying hysterically), holding unrealistic expectations, engaging in irresponsible or dangerous actions, being very disorganized, spending extravagantly or being overly optimistic or pessimistic.

Dealing with someone who is irrational is challenging. You may feel frightened by their inability to think coherently. Or you may be frustrated and angry about the things they are doing. What's important to remember is that their actions are not designed to threaten you. They are the result of distorted thinking.

Obviously, there is no value in arguing with an irrational person because they really can't think straight. Instead, you need to focus on limiting the impact of their distorted thinking. Here are some tips to keep in mind when dealing with irrational behavior.

1. Acknowledge that the behavior is irrational

Irrational behavior can catch you off guard initially and you may question yourself. For example, you may ask yourself whether something is wrong with the other person or with you. For example, Anna was a team leader. Jocelyn was one of her direct reports. Over a period of six months, Jocelyn changed from being the team's star performer to being disruptive and a problem to manage. She started a number of arguments with her colleagues, during which she seemed irrationally fixated upon proving she was 'right'.

Jocelyn also became highly reactive to feedback, at one point screaming at Anna when she'd requested a minor change to a report. To Anna's surprize, Jocelyn came to work the following day and acted as though nothing had happened between them. This type of thing happened several times. Anna didn't know how to handle Jocelyn's inconsistent behavior.

At first, Anna was concerned that she was causing Jocelyn's behavior. She stayed awake at night, analysing their conversations and trying to work out how to improve her relationship with Jocelyn. Eventually, Anna decided she needed help managing what had now become a very difficult staffing situation. She spoke to her Human Resources business partner, Mel, who recognized warning signs in Anna's description of Jocelyn's behavior.

Mel organized a meeting with Jocelyn, during which Jocelyn disclosed that she was being treated for a mental health problem. Over the following month, a plan for managing Jocelyn's condition in the workplace was developed in consultation with her psychiatrist. Over the next year, Jocelyn returned to being the team's star performer.

Anna's decision to consult an expert was a wise one. You, too, should be willing to seek assistance if you believe someone else's behavior is highly irrational. People who can help at work include your supervisor, Human Resources team or a mental health professional.

2. Don't engage in arguments

Fighting the irrational ideas of someone with distorted thinking will lead you nowhere. It will only leave you feeling exhausted and demoralized. Don't try to make sense out of the irrational. A genuinely irrational person may not be in a position to think logically. Focus on finding out their perspective rather than challenging it. Sometimes spotlight questions can help you do this.

3. React calmly

Consider how you currently react to irrational people. What do you think, feel and do in response to their behavior? Is the way you react making things worse or better? Note whether you are being reactive or defensive. You may not be able to control the irrational behavior of the other person, but you can control how you react to it. Take a moment to manage your own state. Then make a cool decision about what to do next.

4. Find a support system

If you have to deal with an irrational person on a regular basis, consider who you can rely on to act as your support system. This can include mental health professionals, colleagues, friends or family members.

5. Call for help in critical situations

As with serious physical illnesses, there are occasions when an expert is needed to help someone with distorted thinking. If you're worried about someone's wellbeing, check for the following behavioral cues.

Think of a specific 'difficult person' who you need to deal with. Tick any of the characteristics this person displays regularly (on a daily basis) or in an extreme form.

☐ Expresses a lot of negative feelings or thoughts.
☐ Heightened sensitivity to sensory data (e.g. sounds or light).
☐ Fixation on irrelevant details or others' behaviors.
☐ Poor concentration or inability to focus.
☐ Speaks from a grandiose perspective.
☐ Has great difficulty interacting with others.
☐ Incoherent speech.
☐ Highly emotional reactions to feedback.
☐ Extreme adherence to and reliance on routines (often perceived as rigidity or inflexibility).
☐ Distorted or confused processing of information.
☐ Chronic complaining.
☐ Constantly talks about 'threats'.

□ Unexplained absences from work.

□ Has very rigid boundaries (e.g. refusing to interact with others at work; refusing to share anything about themselves).

□ Refusal to follow the norms and boundaries of polite conversation.

□ Extreme restlessness, agitation and irritability.

□ Threatens to harm themselves.

If you have ticked four items or more, or one behavior is being demonstrated in an extreme way, seek professional advice quickly. Here's a list of people and services who can help.

▸ Your manager.

▸ Human Resources team.

▸ Security.

▸ Police.

▸ Medical practitioner.

▸ Counselor.

▸ Employee assistance hotline.

What to do if you're concerned about someone's mental health

Sometimes you might be worried that a person's behavior is caused by a mental health problem, such as anxiety or depression. For example, perhaps a colleague seems quite down and you're not sure whether they need help. In this situation, it helps to keep these key steps in mind.

1. Ask how they're feeling

Remember that it is not your job to label or 'diagnose' someone. But you can show that you care about their wellbeing and are willing to offer support. Let them know you've noticed a change in their behavior and are concerned about them.

Find a private space where you won't be interrupted. Start the conversation by pointing out that you've noticed a change in the person's behavior. Give them some examples of the behaviors you've noticed. Explain that these behaviors give you a sense that the other person is distressed. Tell them that they are a valued colleague or friend and that you care about them. Also let them know that your conversation will be confidential and that they can choose what they talk about.

Carl Rogers was a highly regarded psychologist who based his counseling techniques on the idea of 'unconditional positive regard'. He saw this as a form of complete support and acceptance. If you operate from a mindset of extending unconditional positive regard, you can keep other people psychologically safe.

Let the other person know you are not judging their behavior or their feelings. Make it clear that you are willing to listen without breaching their boundaries or expecting anything back from them. Let them know that you don't expect them to change, but you are willing to listen to them.

Ask whether anything is bothering them. If they share any concerns with you, follow up with gentle questions about how they are coping. Use 'you frame' messages to respond empathically to what they say. Remember not to rush the conversation. It can take a while for someone to feel comfortable talking about how they feel.

2. Listen without judging or advising

Simply listening can be one of the most helpful things you can do. This means taking the other person's worldview as valid for them. Effective listening is not just about hearing the words being said to you, but also showing empathy and respect. You can demonstrate that you really hear where the other person is coming from by reflecting back what they are saying to you. Use 'you frame' statements to do this.

Turn off your inner advice-giver. You may want to help the other person by offering your suggestions and opinions, or even help to solve the problem for them. Or you may not understand why the issue is so important and feel tempted to tell them to get a sense of perspective. Resist the urge to take over the conversation or pass judgement. The other person may not have the headspace to process what you're saying. They may well be only managing to cope with their own confused thoughts and feelings. Keep the focus of the conversation on them and enable them to talk openly by showing you are prepared to listen.

3. Be prepared for denial

You may not get a warm response to you raising your concerns. The other person may be embarrassed or angry about their behavior being under the spotlight. At first, they may not be ready for any conversation. Ultimately, though, they will have to acknowledge the problem before they can deal with it. Remember to keep the door open if the other person responds aggressively or passively to your feedback. They may come back to you when they're ready to do something about their situation. So it's important that you let them know you're willing to listen at any stage.

4. Manage your own reaction

If someone is behaving very irrationally or aggressively, you may feel stressed. That's because their actions have triggered a fight or flight reaction. It's natural to feel defensive in this situation. However, expressing these feelings won't help. Aim to manage your own state before responding to the other person. The other person will be finding it hard enough to deal with their own feelings. So don't make them face your fight, flight or spite reaction. They're probably unaware of the impact their behavior has on you.

You need to stay calm and assertive so you can manage the situation. Focus on staying in an alright power mode, no matter what the other person says. Although it may be difficult, try not to feel upset or take the other person's behavior personally. Avoid getting drawn into unnecessary arguments or conflict. Keep your requests and instructions simple. Don't complicate your message with long explanations or by being indirect about what you mean.

5. Let them know help is available

Ask what they've done to handle their situation. Then gently suggest that they may benefit from professional help. Be ready to give them information about counseling or employee assistance services they can contact. The first step may be as simple as visiting their GP. You could offer to drive them to a doctor or counselor and wait outside for them if that is appropriate.

▸ Find more tips on dealing with mental health issues on the tips page of my website: http://difficultpeoplemadeeasy.com

What to do when someone threatens violence

Luckily, threats of physical violence rarely escalate into actual violence. But it is always wise to know what to do if you find yourself at risk of being the target of violence. There are three important things to do in order to protect yourself.

1. Set up a safe haven

Don't wait until threats of violence become reality. Know where you can go in order to remain physically safe. Memorize the phone numbers of people who can help. These might be security personnel, your Human Resources team, your manager or the police.

2. Build safety in numbers

Avoid being alone with anyone who might turn violent. Don't put yourself at risk by staying alone in the room with a potentially violent co-worker, customer, relative or friend. If you must be with an aggressive person, make sure there are other people in the room.

3. Avoid aggressive responses

Never use violence yourself. This will escalate the situation and may lead to extreme violence. Try to keep the aggressor as calm as possible. Never threaten a violent person, either with a weapon or with words. If possible, get them to sit down. This will reduce the risk that they will erupt into sudden acts of violence. It may also help them to calm down.

Planning how to handle YOUR situation

What is the specific behavior that is causing you concern?

_____

_____

_____

How much of this situation is about the other person and their state of mind or feelings?

_____

_____

_____

What percentage of their behavior is _really_ about/aimed at you personally?

_____

_____

_____

What (if any) is the point at which you will need to take action in order to be psychologically/physically safe?

_____

_____

_____

What (if any) is the point at which you need to remove yourself from the situation in order to remain safe?

_____

_____

_____

What limits do you need to set with the other person? (Think in terms of behaviors you are unwilling to tolerate.)

_____

_____

_____

_____

If they refuse to change their behavior, what can you do? (e.g. walk away, ask someone else for assistance, tell them you'll finish the conversation once they change what they're doing/saying, end the relationship.)

_____

_____

Is the person using any of these language patterns, which may indicate game playing is happening?
☐ Insults.
☐ Wild generalizations.
☐ Yes, but ...
☐ Poor me.

If the person is game playing, how can you give an unexpected response?

_____

_____

On a scale of 1 to 10 (with 1 indicating no stress), how much stress is this person's behavior causing you?

_____

What are three things you can do to minimize that stress, starting right now?

_____

_____

Do you need support from anyone else to manage the impact of this person's behavior on you over the long term? If so, who will you talk to?
▸ Your supervisor or manager.
▸ Your Human Resources team.
▸ A coach.
▸ A counselor or psychologist.
▸ Your medical practitioner.
▸ Your legal advisor.

SUMMING UP

▶ Congratulations. You've covered a lot of ground as you've worked your way through *Difficult People Made Easy*. You have learned to identify the different modes of behavior that can come across as 'difficult'. And you know what to do when faced with people who are communicating in fight, flight and spite mode. Before you finish reading, let's quickly recap the main points you've covered in this book.

The most important thing to remember about difficult behavior is that it's triggered by the stress reaction. When someone is stressed, they're likely to resort to fight, flight or spite mode behaviors. Their behavior is not caused by you. Nor are you 'to blame' for how the other person feels.

By reading patterns of body language and language use, you can work out which mode a 'difficult person' is operating from. Then you can choose appropriate ways to respond. Always start by establishing a SAFE dynamic for the conversation. Resist the temptation to argue, defend yourself or fight back. Focus your attention on sorting out the issue rather than judging the other person's behavior.

Next, assess the verbal patterns the other person is using. In difficult conversations, it's likely they'll be using one of the six toxic communication patterns.

▸ Verbal intrusions on your personal zone.
▸ Head/heart mismatch.
▸ Baiting.
▸ Perceiving problems as personal attacks.
▸ Interpreting difference as threat.
▸ Perceptual distortion.

Respond to the difficult behavior by using a verbal antidote pattern.

Toxic communication pattern	Verbal antidotes
Verbal intrusion on your personal zone.	'I frames'.
Heart/head mismatch.	'you frames'.
Baiting.	WISH statement.

Personalisation of issues.	Flameproof language.
Perceiving difference as a threat.	Accord statements.
Perceptual distortion.	Spotlight questions.

Because one-line responses rarely create change, you will need to use your verbal antidote patterns to structure an entire conversation. This is where the AIR model – and its three variations – comes in. AIR gives you a step-by-step process for keeping tough conversations on track. As long as you know where you are in the process, you'll know what you need to do next.

To deal with people in fight mode, you add one stage to AIR. You start the conversation by acting to **prevent** escalation of the other person's fight reaction. This turns AIR into PAIR. Techniques you can use to prevent escalations include removing potential triggers for anxiety, modifying your own behavior and using flameproof language patterns.

When you're dealing with flight-based behavior, you add *two* steps to the basic AIR process. First, you mentally **separate** yourself from the other person. This prevents you stepping into 'rescuer' position and creating an unhealthy, imbalanced relationship dynamic. Then you consciously manage the pace of the conversation – **taking things slowly** in order to match the potentially defensive reactions the other person might experience. This transforms the AIR process into the STAIR process.

In situations in which you're handling spite-based behavior, you turn AIR into FAIR. Start by **focussing** on the meta-message sent by the other person's behavior. Remember that spite-based behavior always involves the 'difficult person' sending a double message. Usually, their body language mismatches their verbal message. Focussing on this incongruence sets you up to challenge their offensive behavior from the 'alright' position.

Finally, you may come across people who have long-term behavioral problems. Some of these people may need help from a trained professional – so don't beat yourself up if YOU can't shift their behavior. Instead, focus your attention on keeping yourself safe physically and mentally. Create an action plan and be prepared to put it to use.

You'll notice there was no chapter eleven in this book. That's because chapter eleven is the next chapter of your life. It's the chapter in which you put your new skills into action. It's the phase of your life in which you handle difficult behavior more resourcefully. Who are you going to start with? Where and when will you try out the ideas you've covered in this book?

To help you get started, here are things to think about.

▸ Which skills do you need to get better at using?
▸ What steps can you take to develop those skills?
▸ Who can you ask to help you or give you feedback?
▸ Where can you try out your new skills in a psychologically safe context?
▸ Which types of difficult behavior do you want to tackle first?
▸ How will you do things differently when handling those behaviors?
▸ What questions do YOU still have? If you'd like your question covered in the next edition of Difficult People Made Easy, send it to me through my website: http://difficultpeoplemadeeasy.com.

I hope you've found *Difficult People Made Easy* useful. Dealing with difficult behavior presents many challenges. If you're interested in receiving more free tips on how to succeed, subscribe to my newsletter at http://difficultpeoplemadeeasy.com. Each month you'll receive two tip sheets and two videos. Plus a few cartoons to help keep you in alright mode, no matter who you're dealing with!

UK £14.99
US $19.99